GW00838843

# Eucharistic Services for Sundays & Feast Days

Octavio Hidalgo C.Ss.R.

a redemptorist publication

(Year A)

# Redemptorist
## P U B L I C A T I O N S

Published by Redemptorist Publications
Alphonsus House
Chawton
Hampshire
GU34 3HQ
England

Text: Octavio Hildago C.Ss.R.
Editor: Rosemary Gallagher

Design: Orchid Design

Copyright © Redemptorist Publications
First Printing: February 2002

This book is sold subject to the condition that it shall
not be lent, re-sold, hired out or otherwise circulated
in any form other than that it in which it is published
without the publishers prior consent.

No part of this book may be reproduced or copied
in any way whether electronically or otherwise
without the prior written permission of the
copyright owner. All rights are reserved.

ISBN: 0 85231 256 3

Printed by: Polar Group Ltd.

**Eucharistic Services for Sundays & Feast Days**

# Contents

# Introduction

It has been an obvious reality, for some decades, that there is a scarcity of priests, diocesan as well as religious. The fact that a large number of seminaries are practically empty has escaped nobody's attention. The statistics reflect a certain stabilisation of the figures in recent years, but the numbers show a disturbing reduction. In the short term, one cannot envisage Christian communities that will be as well ministered as in the past. Neither has the figure of the permanent deacon become more widespread, for whatever reason. Could it be a sign of the times, by which God wishes to tell us something?

It is a result both of the breath of fresh air that the Second Vatican Council represented for the Church and of this scarcity of priests, that lay and religious members of the Church have been acquiring a greater responsibility and a growing prominence in evangelisation; their participation is greater and there exists a greater common responsibility, through which has been promoted a new vision of the Church as the people of God. In many laypeople, a new ministerial vocation is emerging, as a fruit of catechumenal processes and as a response to the aspirations and needs of the different Churches. Many of them are exercising ministries that previously were covered by priests, with the result that lay and religious members are becoming associated with the pastoral ministry. Can we consider this situation to be merely transitory? Does it represent a remedy for getting over this period of transition, or something good and an opportunity for the Church?

What is certain and an urgent matter is that, for one reason or another, there are many parishes and/or small Christian communities without the regular presence of a priest. Neither is it unusual, in some urban centres, to have Sunday service without a priest. In some cases this has led to some communities having Mass only on Sundays, or even only once a month.

This situation has already been dealt with, nearly forty years ago, by Vatican II. In the Constitution on the Sacred Liturgy, it states: "May the sacred celebrations of the Word of God be fostered on the eve of the most solemn festivals, on some holy days in Advent and Lent and on Sundays and festive days, above all in places where there is no priest, in which case a deacon or other delegate of the Bishop should direct the service".[1] In this way, the Council recognised a phenomenon that has been growing since then.

The Code of Canon Law, in canon 517.2, foresaw that, due to the lack of priests, parishes and chaplaincies might be conferred on people who are not ordained, under the authority of a guiding priest.

Later, in 1988, the Congregation for Divine Worship officially published, for the whole Church, a Directory for Sunday and feast day celebrations in the absence of a priest.

In relation to all of this, we believe that the publication we are now presenting has significance. It is aimed at those parishes and communities without the frequent presence of a priest. We haven't concentrated exclusively on the rural world; still less on townships in the process of disappearing. Although holding them in great respect and considering them among the recipients, we have had a wide constituency in mind: from communities where a priest visits, but not every Sunday, to urban or suburban parishes, where the presence of a priest is even more infrequent.

## Need for celebrating the faith

It is clear that the frequent presence of a priest is not necessary for a community to be alive. The vitality of a Christian community depends on the dynamism of its members. But we know that this dynamism needs nourishment and celebration. Priests should not be depended on for either of these. One of their functions is to animate and preside, as long as this is possible for them. But, when it is not possible, they must seek a way for the community to function. It is also up to the community itself to seek a solution, so that its dynamism is not reduced. We have got to get used to the idea, in a positive way, that neither are priests indispensable in communities, nor is it the case that, if there is no priest, nothing or almost nothing is done. The circumstances, and the growth in responsibility of lay people, favour the opportunity of creating a Church in a different form from that of the past.

If a community does not feel the need to celebrate the faith, it is because it is not alive. And if it is not alive, one must diagnose why. Faith is personal, undoubtedly; but it is also communal. And experience proves that what is not expressed, and not celebrated, grows weak and ends up dying.

In a celebration of faith, the community is active, not passive. For this reason, there has to be movement in the celebrations: expression, signs, rites, songs, applause; but there may also be, and should be, silences, listening, prayer, reflection upon Jesus and the Word. The celebration of the faith must be a vibrant and human expression of the life of faith, with symbols, signs and suitable forms.

We are symbolic beings, not only through culture, but also by nature. Having been given our spiritual nature, we need to act and express ourselves in a symbolical and celebratory way. For this reason, it is very important to cultivate sensitivity, imagination, intuition – in short, spirituality. The celebrations of faith must have a taste for the symbolical. We Christians have profound experiences to communicate and celebrate: the call to be and to live like Jesus; our daily living in the presence and the love of God; the recognition of sin, openness to forgiveness and reconciliation; service as a continuous attitude; the mission of furthering the Kingdom of God, and so on.

## Indications and scheme

It is clear that the ideal and objective of the whole Christian community is to be able to celebrate the Eucharist, bringing out, at the same time, the value of Sunday as the day of the Lord. It is equally clear that these celebrations, without a priest, are officially allowed as long as they are in connection with, and subordinate to, the Eucharist, which is the centre and the fulfilment of the community. As a consequence, the celebration having priority will always be the Eucharist.[2] These others are understood by the Directory to be "celebrations of the Word of God that can be opportunely followed by the Holy Communion. In this way, the faithful can be nourished at the same time by the Word of God and the Body of Christ."[3]

The prime movers or guides for these celebrations are the deacons. However, if there are none, it is necessary to select and prepare lay or religious people, men or women, outstanding for their membership of the Church and for their witness, and with basic ability. These co-ordinate, guide or monitor the celebration, but they do not preside over it themselves in a way that competes with the priest or deacon. For this reason, they do not take the place of the priest, but rather a discrete place in the sanctuary within the assembly. It is a matter for the parish or, if it falls to him, for the bishop, to appoint the chosen people for this service, taking into account the needs of the local Church.[4]

And so, in order to develop the initiatives that this book proposes, it will be necessary for any community to go through a process of consideration, co-operation and sharing of responsibility. It will also be necessary, as we have just indicated, to have a suitably prepared person (even better if a group can be arranged). But a special process of preparation is not required. It is enough that they are familiar with the form of the celebration, using as a starting point the experience that they already have of participating in the Eucharist. With the Christian life as indispensable, and with a little practice, suitable people, whatever their background or level of education, may lead the celebrations, making use of the resources that are provided.

In accordance with the official Directory, we first present a summary of the Order of Celebrations. It only applies to the cases where a lay person is co-ordinating. After this, we include in each celebration what we might consider as variable texts. In this way, with this book and the official Lectionary, each celebration can be developed with ease. We also draw attention, for those who want to use it, to the Roman Missal and the document from which we have just quoted: *Sunday and Feast Day celebrations in the absence of a priest.*

In preparing and developing each celebration, one must seek maximum participation and a suitable distribution of functions. We have opted for a general scheme, in line with the Directory, that we recommend as a frame of reference, because there is sometimes room for variations or exclusions.

---

1 SC 35,4.

2 Cf. SECRETARIADO NACIONAL DE LITURGIA (National Secretariat of Liturgy), *Celebraciones dominicales y festivas en ausencia de presbEDtero* (Sunday and feast day celebrations in the absence of a priest), Barcelona 1992, 16.

3 Ibid, 15.

4 Cf. ibid, 17-18.

# Order of Celebrations

## 1. SETTING THE SCENE

It is very important that the arrangement of the Church accords as much as possible with what we are going to celebrate. The position of the people, the placing of the symbols and posters, the preparation of the offerings, of the signs, of the hymns and of the readings, the lighting, the microphones, etc. require care and attention beforehand.

## 2. INTRODUCTORY RITES

The layperson who guides or co-ordinates the celebration may dress in alb. He will occupy a discrete place in the sanctuary, or the nave, from where he can be seen and heard well. He will not use the presiding seat, reserved for the priest or deacon. He will never use the phrase "The Lord be with you" or any other greeting appropriate to the ordained minister himself, nor will he bless the assembly at the end of the celebration, but will use other phrases.

When the community has come together, and after the **introduction and hymn**, the leader says: *In the name of the Father, and of the Son, and of the Holy Spirit.* Everyone makes the sign of the cross and responds: *Amen.* The **greeting** follows, which the minister announces with these or similar words: *Brothers and sisters, let us praise the Lord together;* or instead: *Brothers and sisters, let us bless the Lord, who has called us together for this fraternal gathering.* The assembly responds: *May you be blessed forever, O Lord.*

The Penitential Rite can take place according to different formulas, but also in a spontaneous way, once it has been introduced by the minister, with these or similar words: *Brothers and sisters, the Lord has called us to conversion; let us acknowledge our sins.* The celebrations have their own formulas, or instead, the common one: *I confess* The minister always concludes with a brief prayer: *May almighty God have mercy upon us, forgive us our sins and bring us to life everlasting.* The assembly responds: *Amen.*

When the Penitential Rite is finished, the minister intones the **Gloria.** The Gloria is said in all Sunday and feast day celebrations, except in Advent and Lent.

Afterwards, the minister introduces the **prayer**, saying: *Let us pray.* There is a brief silence for personal prayer followed by the prayer of the day. At the end of the prayer, all respond: *Amen.*

## 3. LITURGY OF THE WORD

After the **introduction**, the reader goes to the lectern and announces the **first reading** of the day. Between the first and the **second reading** is a **psalm**. Between the second reading and the Gospel, there is an **acclamation**, which is generally an *Alleluia.* Whoever proclaims the **Gospel** introduces it with the following words: *Listen, brothers and sisters, to the Holy Gospel, according to Saint X.*

Once the Gospel has been proclaimed, it is fitting to have a **brief silence**, for the first interior reception of the Word. Then, the **Reflection** is read slowly, after which follows a longer period of silent reflection.

Next, the profession of faith (**credo**) takes place, and afterwards, the minister introduces the **prayer of the faithful.**

This part concludes with the **symbolic offerings** and/or with a **sign**, separated by a brief hymn, so that the particular significance of each stage can have its impact.

## 4. RITE OF COMMUNION

After the **introduction**, the minister approaches the tabernacle, opens it, genuflects, takes the ciborium, places it on the altar and genuflects again. Meanwhile, the assembly sings a suitable hymn. Afterwards, everybody together or some individual, representing those gathered together, says the **prayer** and introduces the **Our Father**. Next, the minister invites people to give the **sign of peace** with these or similar words: *May you give the peace in brotherhood;* or instead: *As sons and daughters of God, make a sign of brotherhood.*

Continuing, the minister genuflects, takes a Host and, raising it a little above the chalice, says: *This is the Lamb of God, who takes away the sin of the world. Happy are those who are invited to this Communion.* And the assembly continues: *Lord, I am not worthy to receive you.* The minister communicates first of all, saying in a low voice: *May the Body of Christ preserve me for eternal life.* Afterwards, he gives **Communion**, saying to each person: *The Body of Christ.*

When Communion has been distributed and the ciborium returned to the tabernacle, it is fitting to have a silence for **personal prayer**. Next, the communal **act of thanksgiving** is made, in which spontaneous interventions can be made, a participation that can also figure in the prayer of the faithful.

## 5. CONCLUDING RITE

All communal prayer or celebration of the faith should finish with a **resolution** being made. The minister exhorts the assembly, according to the theme of each celebration.

He continues by invoking the **blessing** of God and crosses himself, saying: *May the Lord bless us, preserve us from all evil and bring us to eternal life;* or instead: *Most merciful Lord, Father, Son and Holy Spirit, bless us and preserve us.* The assembly responds: *Amen.*

The **conclusion** captures the meaning and spirit of what has been celebrated. With the **final hymn** and the **dismissal**, the celebration is finished. For the dismissal, different formulas can be used: *You may go in peace;* or instead: *In the name of the Lord, you may go in peace;* or: *Glorify the Lord with your life. You may go in peace.* The assembly responds: *We give thanks to God.*

# The Season of
# ADVENT

# First Sunday of Advent

## 1. SETTING THE SCENE

### Poster with one of these texts:
"Come, Lord Jesus"
"Let us walk in the light of the Lord"
"Let us conduct ourselves with dignity"
"Open the doors to the Saviour"

### Symbols:
Advent Wreath (or other design) with four candles. Each Sunday, one is lit.
Four large black marks (some 25 cm in diameter) placed in visible sites in the church. Each Sunday, one is taken away: a commitment to eliminate defects or black marks from our lives.
Purple sash, or covering, for the lectern of the Word.

## 2. INTRODUCTORY RITES

### Introduction
Brothers and sisters, today we begin Advent and, with it, a new Liturgical Year. Advent is a meaningful time to commemorate the extraordinary initiative of God, in coming to us and redeeming us.

Christ Jesus is always *he who comes*. We do not await another Saviour. In him is fulfilled all that we seek and desire. For this reason, Advent is *to prepare the way of the Lord*. And, in this sense, it is to make a place within ourselves, so that God and Jesus may enter into us even more.

During the four weeks of Advent, we prepare to celebrate, as is fitting, the Nativity of God.

### Hymn

### Greeting
Brothers and sisters, we praise the Lord together, who calls upon us to celebrate Advent.

### Penitential Rite
■ Because we have preferred our darkness to the light, *Lord, have mercy.*
■ Because we live in forgetfulness of you, *Christ, have mercy.*
■ Because we often do not listen to you, *Lord, have mercy.*

### Prayer
God, bountiful Father, awaken in your faithful ones, at the beginning of Advent, the desire to go to meet Christ, accompanied by works and signs of conversion. May our Church be open in faith to redemption and may this community bear witness to your Kingdom. Through Christ, our Lord. Amen.

## 3. LITURGY OF THE WORD

### Introduction to the Readings
The readings provide us with a path that Christians should tread. Jesus demands active vigilance of us. The prophet Isaiah invites us to walk in the light of the Lord, just as Saint Paul does, for whom Jesus is the greatest light, capable of enlightening our conduct.

### Readings
Is. 2:1-5. *Psalm.* Rom. 13:11-14. *Acclamation.* Mt. 24:37-44. *Brief silence.*

## Reflection

The Word of God invites us to make our way through life, awake and with dignity. The Liturgical Year opens with the warning that a Christian must always be *a child of light,* never *an accomplice of darkness,* that is to say, of evil.

Therefore, reawaken your conscience, refine your sensibilities, be prepared, so that nobody manipulates you, so that nobody snatches anything away that is worthy in your personality. Friends, we propose to act in accordance with the truth and the light, like Jesus, who had nothing to conceal, nor any dark blemish to hide.

The ideal and objective come together, in the expression of the second reading: "let us conduct ourselves with dignity, as though we are in the full light of day". For this reason, no evil desires, nor licentiousness, nor quarrelling, nor making life impossible for ourselves. We propose now, at the beginning of Advent, to take on the mantle of Christ, that is to say, to come as close as possible to his way of being, of feeling, and of acting.

We begin our journey in this new Liturgical Year, encouraged by hope. It is one of the three essential virtues of the Christian; and, because it is theological, it gathers together all the human hope that we bear in our hearts. *(Silence for internal reflection.)*

## Creed

## Prayer of the Faithful

- Lord, we pray to you that your Kingdom may come to us.
- That all peoples may walk in the ways of justice and solidarity.
- That all Christian communities may let your light shine forth within society.
- That we Christians from X., may know how to bring the Gospel closer to our neighbours.
- That we may keep our hope alive, especially those of us who are most weakened and confused.

- We offer up to you, also, our communal and personal intentions.
*We pray to the Lord.*

## Offerings

*Large taper or candle in a bowl with four flowers around it:* Lord, we wish to live in a thoughtful way, so that we may conduct ourselves with dignity.
*Map of the town or the region or area:* Thank you, Lord, because you wish to save this entire town.

## Hymn

## Sign

On a cloth hanging from the altar is placed the letter "H". On the Sundays of Advent, the word HOPE is formed, letter by letter.

## 4. RITE OF COMMUNION

## Introduction

Let us nourish ourselves with the *Bread of Life.* Jesus himself is offered to us, as nourishment. May his presence encourage us to preserve the witness and the strength of true believers.

## Hymn

## Prayer

God, our Father,
from the four corners of our land,
we bless you with the men and women,
the young, children and adults from our town.
We raise our voices in a song of hope,
because we believe in you.
We rejoice that we have known your salvation.
Through your Spirit, you set out to cleanse
our society and the Church.
Guided by Jesus and by his Gospel,
we walk with the encouragement
that the community gives us.
Attracted by the fulfilment of your promises,

and sensing Jesus among us,
as one, we bless you, saying: Our Father…

## Sign of Peace

## Distribution of Communion: Hymn

## Act of Thanksgiving
- ■ We give you thanks, God our Father, because we live the faith in community. Belonging to this parish gives us heart. In it, we can experience the enthusiasm of the Spirit and the warmth of brotherhood.
- ■ We beseech you, that in all parishes, especially in little and simple ones like ours, Christian dynamism and the Gospel mission may grow.
- ■ God our Father, we entrust ourselves to you.

## 5. CONCLUDING RITE

## Resolution
To take away "black marks" from our personality (one of the "black marks" placed in the church is removed). To work for conversion.

## Blessing

## Conclusion
Advent is a time of healthy enthusiasm and definite hope. Today, also, we need salvation. We Christians know that when Jesus is accepted, human history acquires a better meaning and destiny. A proof that Christ the Saviour has already reached us, is that we know how to share and we are capable of increasing our closeness and our generosity.

## Closing Hymn and Dismissal

# Second Sunday of Advent

## 1. SETTING THE SCENE

### Poster with one of these texts:
"May God make us more human"
"The Lord is near"
"Bear the fruits of conversion"

### Symbols:
The signs from the previous Sunday remain for the whole of the Advent season.
A plant with a stem and bud: fresh from the stem of Jesus.
An axe or pruning scissors.

## 2. INTRODUCTORY RITES

### Introduction
Brothers and sisters, Advent is moving on, that time so linked to God's initiative, for us all to come to know the truth and salvation. Advent is a gift and a hope. It is an undertaking, on the part of God, to bring our lives into a state of salvation. Only God can inspire our hope. In the brotherhood of faith, we sing to God who loves us and blesses us, in the person of Jesus.

### Hymn

### Greeting
Brothers and sisters, we bless the Lord, who calls us together to celebrate the faith.

### Penitential Rite
Make us like you: *Lord, have mercy.*
Show us your salvation: *Christ, have mercy.*
Reunite us with you: *Lord, have mercy.*

### Prayer
God, bountiful Father, we bless you for the generous gift of Jesus. He is a model of holiness and a mirror of our wish to be transformed. Do not allow us to be deceived by any temptation, nor to be distracted by the desires of this world. Lead us with your wisdom, in such a way that we journey through life as true Christians. Through Christ our Lord. Amen.

## 3. LITURGY OF THE WORD

### Introduction to the Readings
The first reading presents us with highly graphic images of God's dream to overcome our sin, bestowing on us a new and pure way of life. The second invites us to cultivate hope and solidarity, in order to bless our common Father with one voice. In the Gospel, the outstanding figure of John the Baptist now appears, as a person who, with his physical presence and his word, denounces and makes proclamations, explaining that we can all change for the better. As a precursor of Jesus, he makes the way clear and bears an urgent message for us, if we wish to prepare ourselves fittingly for the way of the Lord.

### Readings
Is. 11:1-10. *Psalm*. Rom. 15:4-9. *Acclamation*. Mt. 3:1-12. *Brief silence*.

### Reflection
How beautiful and shocking is the message of Isaiah! The prophet of messianic hope describes, in expressive language, that we can overcome our impulses of injustice and aggression, and avoid evil influences and poisonous contagion. The way of life that God dreams for us is to live together in solidarity and in harmony.

Isaiah also says that a son, filled with the Spirit and with insight, will spring forth from among the people, full of wisdom and sense, speaking of God's plans, like no one else, he will defend the poor and helpless and bring justice as God intends. What a great message for any society that seeks to live together in peace and unity! We, who live the history of the Church, know that this great sprouting branch, sprung from the people, is Jesus, and that his Gospel contains unlimited justice and encouragement.

Also shocking is the figure of John the Baptist, an austere man, who manages on what is strictly necessary. His clothing and his food are a sign of his personality and his testimony. A prophet in words and deeds, he was for many a great spiritual master. His message was provocative, demanding the signs and fruits of conversion. He baptised if these conditions were present. The people, who approached to listen to him, confessed their sins and John plunged them into the waters of the Jordan. It was a symbol of cleansing, and also of rebirth, of beginning again, leaving behind an evil state.

To transform oneself is a great task for all believers. These words have more impact on those who suffer from remorse of conscience. It implies a change in one's way of thinking and way of acting, returning to the bosom of God and working, according to his standards.

John was an authentic, brave person, but he was also a humble and simple believer. His mission was to prepare the way for the Messiah. He was not the Light, but a witness to the Light, that is to say, to Jesus of Nazareth, the man full of the Spirit of God. John only baptises with water; but Jesus baptises, with the Holy Spirit and with fire. For this reason, it is fitting for Jesus to rise up and for John's role to diminish. (*Silence for internal reflection.*)

## Creed

## Prayer of the Faithful
- For solidarity and hope to grow in the world, *we pray to the Lord.*
- For our Church to work more each day for the Kingdom of God, *we pray to the Lord.*
- For us to be effective in fulfilling the Gospel, understanding it more each day, *we pray to the Lord.*
- For the sick, those who are alone and all those who suffer, *we pray to the Lord.*
- For all of us to go forward, as though baptised, in courage and in commitment, *we pray to the Lord.*

## Offerings
*The parish book of baptisms:* Lord, we have a history of faith. We present it to you.
*Large knot:* Lord, we present to you this knot of union, as a sign of our unity as Christians.

## Hymn

## Sign
*The outline of the previous Sunday continues.*

## 4. RITE OF COMMUNION

## Introduction
Let us share in Jesus together, nurture interest in holiness and dynamism for the good of the community. We need to be strong, in order to bear the fruits of true conversion.

## Hymn

## Prayer

We bless you, God, our Father, for the
Christian experience.
We recognise that Jesus is the most worthy
of human beings,
the first-born of the *new creation,*
with such a great radiance
that it could not be extinguished by the
ravages of history.
His way of life inspires us,
because he truly knows all things,
with a disinterested love,
in chosen poverty, freely and with detachment.
We wish also the values that belong to those
who seek to do your will. We also wish to bear
the fruits of conversion,
leading a life worthy of our baptism
and making use of the riches that are given
us by our redemption.
Receive, Father, the personal and communal
expression of our faith.
We are a simple community,
but capable of enriching this place
with our gifts and with the beauty of the Gospel.
We say to you: Our Father…

## Sign of Peace

## Distribution of Communion: Hymn

## Act of Thanksgiving

- ■ We give you thanks, Father, for the Church,
  because, by means of it, the redemption and
  message of Christ the Saviour have come to us.
- ■ We also give you thanks, because we experience
  that inner virtue which is the main driving force
  for producing a good community.
- ■ The example of John the Baptist helps us to
  understand that we are not happier when we
  have more, but when we need less.

## 5. CONCLUDING RITE

## Resolution

To work for personal conversion with regard to our
families and our neighbours.

## Blessing

## Conclusion

In Advent, we are also impelled to be active. As
sensitive and hope-filled Christians, we continue the
work of improving our lives, filling them with goodness.
In each and every one, may the spirit not falter.

## Concluding Hymn and Dismissal

# Third Sunday of Advent

## 1. SETTING THE SCENE

### Poster with one of these phrases:
"The Saviour is near"
"Come, we are in need of you"

### Symbols:
The signs remain for the whole of Advent.
Broken chains: the *retribution* of God.

## 2. INTRODUCTORY RITES

### Introduction
To contemplate the approach of Christmas means welcoming Jesus within us, opening our doors to him, each one of us. It means recognising his Divine Presence, in signs and symbols, he that is the one who is to come, as the true saviour and guiding force in history.

We celebrate the faith together, sharing our feelings and concerns. And we ask ourselves, in our hearts, how the Gospel of today manifests itself. To ask ourselves questions is good and healthy.

### Hymn

### Greeting
Brothers and sisters, we are gathered together in the faith. Let us bless the Lord who loves us as his children.

### Penitential Rite
Because you are close to us, *Lord, have mercy.*
Because you accompany us on our way,
*Christ, have mercy.*
Because we have need of you, *Lord, have mercy.*

### Prayer
You see, Lord, how your people await the birth of your Son with faith; help us to greet the approaching feast of Christmas, festival of joy and salvation, and to be able to celebrate it with abundant joy. Through Christ our Lord.

## 3. LITURGY OF THE WORD

### Introduction to the Readings
The prophet Isaiah speaks of a better future. He announces an important event. Do you know what it refers to? The apostle Saint James invites us to remain firm and patient in our hope. The Gospel advises us to take the way of John the Baptist, so that, like him, we will be able to recognise Jesus as the Messiah, sent by God.

### Readings
Is. 35:1-6a.10. *Psalm.* Jas 5:7-10. *Acclamation.*
Mt. 11:2-11. *Brief silence.*

### Reflection
The salvation that Jesus Christ brings is a challenge for the restoration of life: "Go and proclaim to John what you see and hear: the blind see and the lame walk; lepers are cleansed and the deaf hear; the dead are raised and the Good News is proclaimed to the poor." The prophet Isaiah was already proclaiming it centuries before: "behold your God who comes with retribution; a person is coming, and he will save you". Therefore, "strengthen your weary hands, steady all trembling knees, say to the faint-hearted: be strong, do not be afraid".

The messianic salvation is always a positive challenge. And within this challenge, the "retribution of God" is even more surprising. "Retribution" is similar to "vengeance". How shocking! Does God desire to take revenge? Yes, but in his way; his vengeance consists in resolving the ills of this world. And, for this reason, there is nothing better than opening the eyes of the blind, opening the ears of the deaf and returning with joyful singing to the first situation, that is to say, to the original state. Then, God saw that all was good. This retribution of God is humanising and instructive. The paradox of his vengeance rests on the awakening of all the senses of human beings, including the moral sense.

These signs of the Messiah are the best proofs to remove John the Baptist's doubts. But we notice in Jesus' praise of the Baptist: "What did you come out to see in the desert? A prophet? Yes, I say to you, and more than a prophet: I assure you that no man has been born of woman greater than John the Baptist." Certainly, Jesus felt a great admiration for John. With the passion of the movement that the Baptist generated, Jesus' vocation certainly matured. For this reason, there is nothing strange in the fact that, upon the death of John, Jesus would take over the exercise of his word and his prophetic dynamism.

There is a great similarity between the lifestyle of John and that of Jesus. They were not active in any religious or political group of their time. They did not marry. Until the end of their lives, they lived and acted in an independent way, as laymen on foot. They were both pacifists. They prophesy a change of life in people and they invite conversion. Both of them are recognised by the people, as prophets of God. And both play their part for the same cause: the Kingdom of God and its justice. They both make a sign of their faith with martyrdom. *(Silence for internal reflection.)*

## Creed

## Prayer of the Faithful

- We pray for the world, that it may rejoice at the surprising *vengeance* of our God.
- We pray for the Church, that it may be an active and constant symbol of abundant salvation in Jesus Christ.
- We pray for the Christians around us, with whom we work, for all those who have the same commitment, to the positive transformation of our society.
- We pray for the poor, the needy, those who live alone, the sick, that they may feel loved and accompanied.
- We pray for each other, so that, opening our hearts to God, we may feel his closeness.
- For these and for all our intentions, *we pray to the Lord.*

## Offerings

*Laurel branch or crown:* Father, you wish to save us through Jesus; we offer you our desire to be redeemed completely.

*A receptacle with some clay in it and a flower fixed in it:* Although we are of clay, we offer you, Lord, our collaboration in making our town become your Kingdom.

*Collecting box (Christmas Campaign):* We offer you, Lord, a sign of common solidarity that we must have with the needy.

## Hymn

## Sign
*The outline of the first Sunday in Advent continues.*

## 4. RITE OF COMMUNION

## Introduction
Jesus, you wish to nourish us with all your being. Let us live our communion intensely with you, with each other and with our town.

## Hymn

## Prayer

Gathered together
Father, we celebrate
that we are a community of salvation.
We join together with the saints of yesterday and today,
to bless you with faithfulness of life.
Thanks to them, our ability
and our commitment to holiness is growing.
Your salvation, Father, is like another way of life:
to open the eyes of the blind,
open the ears of the deaf,
remove obstacles from the lame,
restore the speech of the dumb.
Such is your vital and inspiring example.
You are not a God of the impossible,
but of the Gospel:
a challenge of salvation and joy,
of enthusiasm and of striving for all that is new.
Look at our faith immersed in weakness,
but receive our open hearts.
Bring us your Word and your Christ.
With him, we say to you: Our Father…

## Sign of Peace

## Distribution of Communion: Hymn

## Act of Thanksgiving

- ■ We give you thanks, Father, because you are good and you are involved in our history with surprising dedication.
- ■ We bless you for the fascinating personality of Jesus, a complete and effective person.
- ■ We value and are grateful for the presence of the Spirit: who helps us to get in touch with the nobility within our own selves and enriches us with his gifts.

- ■ And in this time of Advent, we give you thanks for Mary, a woman full of faith and mother of the Church. Her example helps us to follow the way of Christian life.

## 5. CONCLUDING RITE

## Resolution

To proclaim, through word and deed, that Jesus is even now our salvation.

## Blessing

## Conclusion

Our celebration continues now in the streets, at home, with our friends and tomorrow at work. May we reflect, in word and deed, what we are thinking and feeling about the meaning of Christmas. This does not usually correspond to the commercial Christmas, made false by so much deliberate propaganda. Let us compare the two, and may we follow the message that seems the most human.

## Final Hymn and Dismissal

# Fourth Sunday of Advent

## 1. SETTING THE SCENE

### Poster with the phrase:
"The Saviour draws near"

### Symbols:
The signs remain for the whole of Advent.
An empty cradle.
An image of Mary, if possible, looking towards the cradle.

## 2. INTRODUCTORY RITES

### Introduction
We are practically on the threshold of the Christian Nativity. The other Christmas, the commercial and consumer one, has already been with us for weeks. With points of view that are so divergent, at the very time when meaning is given to Christmas, we Christians must be supportive and exponents of unifying values. Without a sharing and generous love, Christmas is poor, almost indecent. If Christmas has something special, it is precisely closeness and deep communication for the happiness of all. May this shared joy be a reality among us.

### Hymn

### Greeting
Brothers and sisters, let us praise the Lord together, who has called upon us to come together as his people.

### Penitential Rite
You, who are the desire of the people: *Lord, have mercy.*

You, who are proclaimed by the prophets: *Christ, have mercy.*
You, who are the blessed fruit of Mary: *Lord, have mercy.*

### Prayer
Father, you have called us to be part of your holy people. You have made us your children by adoption and you want us to be witnesses to the Light. Awaken in us sensitivity towards the Gospel, so that we may grow in conscience and in commitment to redemption. Through Christ our Lord.

## 3. LITURGY OF THE WORD

### Introduction to the Readings
Among the publicity and many advertisements of today, try to open yourself to the word of God, which tells us of the Messiah. God has brought fulfilment, with the coming of Jesus to us. Now, we have to have the conviction that it is possible and necessary to continue his undertaking.

### Readings
Is. 7:10-14. *Psalm.* Rom. 1:1-7. *Acclamation.* Mt. 1:18-24. *Brief silence.*

### Reflection
One of the signs that characterises the way God works is that he counts on people to further the history of salvation. Those of us who have experience of it know that the initiative springs from him. He calls for our collaboration.

It is very clear in the example of Joseph and Mary. They are of the people, simple workers. They live in

Galilee and are part of the social, political and religious situation of the time. God singles them out and chooses them for a very special mission. Their response is that which corresponds to good believers: *yes* to God and to history; but a *yes* that is not exempt from conflict and debate, a *yes* that is not easy to maintain.

It has to be emphasised, in honour of Joseph and Mary's example, that they were both faithful, that they were tireless in collaborating with God's plans and that they did this in a simple and discreet way. This presupposes that they had both given up the whole of themselves to God, remaining available for the mission he might ask of them.

Mary and Joseph are, above all, great believers, who also knew how to tread the path when their faith became clouded. In order to be open to the Spirit, they knew how to interpret the call of God. For this reason, they offered themselves up in willing collaboration.

Through the gift of Jesus, we also have been called to the faith, to form part of a holy people, that has the sacred duty to fulfil the history of salvation, that is to say, the Kingdom of God. *(Silence for internal reflection.)*

## Creed

## Prayer of the Faithful
- For the Church, that it may show the true face of Jesus in all places, *we pray to the Lord.*
- For our parish, that it may become more open to the Messiah, *we pray to the Lord.*
- That we may know, in the example of Mary and Joseph, how to accept and collaborate with God's plans, *we pray to the Lord.*
- That we may celebrate Christmas in unity and without unnecessary waste, *we pray to the Lord.*
- That the hopes of the poor and of those who are less fortunate may not be squandered, *we pray to the Lord.*

- For all of us, that we may be symbols of the presence of God among the people, *we pray to the Lord.*

## Offerings
*Gospels or the New Testament:* We offer to you, Lord, the message of life and the testament of salvation, that you have given to us, as Good News.
*Catechisms (for children, young people or adults) and working clothes:* We offer to you, Lord, these symbols, as an expression of our commitment as believers.

## Hymn

## Sign
*The outline of the first Sunday in Advent continues.*

## 4. RITE OF COMMUNION

## Introduction
Jesus wishes to permeate our whole being. He wants to enlighten us completely. Let us open ourselves to him, even our most intimate selves. That is also communion.

## Hymn

## Prayer
On the eve of Christmas, Father, we unite ourselves in the prayer of Jesus amongst the people and we say to you: "Blessed are you because you have hidden the Gospel from the proud and revealed it to the simple.
Yes, Father, for that is what it pleased you to do."
You have manifested yourself in a thousand ways, so that you can be found by those who seek you.
You wish that all may be saved and may come upon the experience of truth.
You call upon us and invite us insistently to the great banquet of your Kingdom.
You have sent your Son for our salvation.
But there are those who resist the Light,

who reject your invitation
and so are incapable of accepting the Gospel.
We also are sinners.
For this reason, Father, bring your presence even
closer to us
and come to save us.
Inject into society and the Church
a powerful experience of the spirit.
Those of us who want to know you, unite
in saying: Our Father…

## Sign of Peace

## Distribution of Communion: Hymn

## Act of Thanksgiving *(spontaneous)*


## 5. CONCLUDING RITE

### Resolution
A Christmas of discipline, unity and communion
with those near to us and far away.

### Blessing

### Conclusion
Thanks to the collaboration of Mary, it was possible
for the seed of Jesus' salvation to germinate. On the
eve of Christmas, Mary has returned to be, for us, a
model of the sensitive Christian, close at hand and
collaborating with us. Now it falls to us to put other
plans of service and solidarity into practice.
Christmas is a gift.

### Final Hymn and Dismissal

# The Season of
# CHRISTMAS

# Nativity of the Lord
## 25 December

### 1. SETTING THE SCENE

**Poster with one of these texts:**
- "Christmas is love, joy and peace"
- "God is with us"
- "God comes as Man into life"

**Symbol:**
Bethlehem, the birth or mystery of the Nativity (if the symbolic act of the introduction that follows is not performed).

**Carol music for the welcome**

### 2. INTRODUCTORY RITES

**Introduction**
The first Christians saw Jesus as their guiding light. He himself signified the dawn of a new era. Because of this, the Christian Nativity is, above all, a symbol. In it, we behold the loving gesture of God in becoming one like us and saving us from within. Celebrating the Nativity is to welcome Jesus as saviour.

With Jesus Christ, a different type of person is born: a person who is for peace, who fosters human hope, who humanises work, who is freedom and frees us from all slavery, who even loves his enemies, who experiences and reveals God as Father, who is faithful even unto martyrdom. We rejoice in the Lord and begin the celebration with a symbolic representation:

*(Two people appear who symbolise Joseph and Mary. They go to the altar where the cradle of the Child has been prepared beforehand.)*

**Hymn**

**Greeting**
Brothers and sisters, we bless God who has visited and redeemed us in such a human way.

**Penitential Rite**
- You are the Word of God made man:
  *Lord, have mercy.*
- You are the image of the invisible God:
  *Christ, have mercy.*
- You are the holy one of God:
  *Lord, have mercy.*

**Gloria**

**Prayer**
Bountiful Father, we give you thanks for Jesus Christ, the Messenger of peace. Born of Mary, he is the expected one, the Light of the world, the Messiah, the Lord. He offered up his whole life in order to save us from sin and so to prepare a people, according to the plan that you conceived. In awareness of our redemption, we renew our faith before you. You may rely on us to transform society. Amen.

### 3. LITURGY OF THE WORD

**Introduction to the Readings**
Christmas is the highest expression of the union of God with human history. He gives us his divinity and accepts our humanity in order to bring it to a definite state of hope. For this reason, what is most important about Christmas is that it encourages us to live the Gospel.

## Readings

Is. 52:7-10. *Psalm.* Heb. 1:1-6. *Acclamation.* Jn 1:1-18. *Brief silence.*

## Reflection

God has communicated with us on many occasions and in many different ways. How beautiful are the feet of the Messenger on the mountains proclaiming peace, bringing us the good news!

Yes, Christmas is jubilation, applause, a first sign of victory, because God has fulfilled his promises. In Jesus, there is an alternative humanity that can never now be erased from history.

Jesus is the Emmanuel (God-with-us), God's most human association and communication possible. And we, who contemplate the mystery of the Nativity throughout the extensive history of the Church, are able to affirm: Jesus is the Messenger and the Covenant, the Redeemer and Witness, the Light, the Way, the Truth, the Life, the Resurrection, and an infinity of titles and symbols of profound human significance.

Christmas is about welcoming and gratitude, because "God loved the world so much that he gave his only Son, so that all who believe in him may not be lost, but may have eternal life. God did not send his Son into the world in order to condemn it, but to save it" (Jn 3:16). In fact, God wished to descend from the heights and save us from below, from within humanity itself.

For this reason, Christmas is a time when we should not lose ourselves in simple emotions contemplating, for example, a child shivering with cold…, but take in, as a whole, the great gift of Jesus, for the present and future of humanity.

Finally, Christmas is a challenge: it reminds us that redemption follows… and that in order to make it happen, God relies on us. That is when, the true Nativity takes place, when a person opens himself to the light and removes himself from darkness, when there is resolution, not conflict. *(Silence for internal reflection.)*

## Creed

## Prayer of the Faithful

- For the world, that it may welcome the Nativity of God as a light that shines and strengthens hope, *let us pray to the Lord.*
- For the Church, that it may show forth, day by day, the true faith of the Saviour Messiah, *let us pray to the Lord.*
- For the people most in need, that they may go forward in peace, justice and development, *let us pray to the Lord.*
- That, however tired and cast down people may feel, the Nativity of the Lord and the Gospel may give them strength and rekindle their hope, *let us pray to the Lord.*
- For all our families, that at this time they may strengthen their union, *let us pray to the Lord.*
- For our community, that we may appreciate the mystery of Christmas and be faithful to our commitment to serve the Gospel. *Let us pray to the Lord.*

## Offerings

- *Basket with words written on strips of blank card*: Father, you have given us Jesus. We would like to reciprocate with good works and sentiments, such as peace, enthusiasm, courage, union, generosity, love, forgiveness, and other things that we can write on strips of blank card…
- *Castanets, tambourine and drum:* Father, we rejoice because you have visited and redeemed us. Accept our desire to follow your plan of redemption.
- *Lighted candle:* Lord, we wish to be children of light.

## 4. RITE OF COMMUNION

## Introduction

God has come down from heaven to be with us on our daily journey. May Christ's human adventure be shared by everyone. May we receive it, opening our hearts completely to him.

## Hymn

## Prayer

O Lord, our God, you are a Father to us
and we are children to you,
because you have made Jesus into our brother.
We bless you, because today
a great light has shone: we have seen the Redeemer.
The heavens declare your goodness
and the peoples wish to sing your praise.
Thank you, loving God, because you have revealed
yourself and have delivered yourself in your Son, Jesus.
He has come to extend your Kingdom
with unending peace,
with an attitude of overflowing devotion
from the cradle to the cross.
Because you have wished to be so good to us,
pour forth your Spirit upon this community,
so that the gift of Jesus may be a motive for us, an inspiration for peaceful living
and for bold commitment.
Bountiful Father, we thank you
for the best gift that you could give us:
Jesus, your presence and human symbol
for all those who wish to make our history good.
May the Spirit help us to walk
with the courage and hope of the redeemed.
Because of your exceeding kindness towards us,
we say to you with brotherly joy: Our Father…

## Sign of Peace

A placard is shown with the word "Peace" or "Peace in the land". Someone says: On such a significant day as this, may the peace of Jesus flow into our hearts and fill them with love towards others. Let us offer one another the sign of peace with love and affection.

## Distribution of Communion: Hymn

## Act of Thanksgiving

■ We give you thanks, Father, for sending us your Son.
■ We give you thanks for Mary, our mother.
■ We give you thanks for the gift of the faith.
■ We give you thanks for celebrating this Christmas together.

## 5. CONCLUDING RITE

## Resolution

To put into practice the values of Christmas that we have stressed in this celebration.

## Blessing

## Conclusion

Christmas time is a great expression of the nearness of God. He desires to dwell among us and to be our neighbour, in order to share in the journey of our lives. We rejoice in this friendly presence of God with faith and enthusiasm. May we be witnesses of his presence among us.

## Final parting gesture:

*The two people, who symbolise Joseph and Mary, kiss the Child.*

# Sunday within the Octave of Christmas
## The Holy Family

### 1. SETTING THE SCENE

**Posters in the church with texts like:**
- "The family, the first school"
- "The family, the necessary hearth"
- "The family depends on each one of us"

**Symbol:**
A round table covered with a family tablecloth, with chairs around it, is put in the sanctuary.

### 2. INTRODUCTORY RITES

**Entrance**
*Once the assembly is gathered, a family enters (grandparents, their children and grandchildren) bringing:*

- One of them, a large loaf: the communal table.
- Another, a pine-cone: the united family.
- Another, a branch or a vase of varied flowers: the unity and diversity of the family.
- Another, a lighted candle: Jesus, the light of family life.
- Another, a large tray with working implements: knitting needles and balls of wool, a spanner, a duster, text books…

*This family presides over the celebration.*

**Introduction**
Brothers and sisters, to be welcomed has a special significance, when we are gathered together as a family. In the name of the family God, who welcomes us, we greet each other.

The reason and the symbol for today's celebration is the family: the human family and the family of the faith. The family is a necessary and sought-after reality for everyone. It is our roots. The home has always been a special nest for each one of us.

In the midst of celebration, we are united with all the households that live happily together, but also those who suffer the rupture of a broken relationship. May our spirit and understanding go with them.

**Hymn**

**Greeting**
Brothers and sisters, we bless God, who wants to be a member of our family.

**Penitential Rite**
If we are realistic, we certainly have to recognise that our family life is far from the ideal that we find in the family from Nazareth. For this reason, we recognise our personal and communal sins:
- Because we are lacking in love, we do not bear the Christian witness that we should:
  *Lord, have mercy.*
- You who knew how to combine obedience to the Father with family responsibility:
  *Christ, have mercy.*
- You who are the Spirit of unity:
  *Lord, have mercy.*

Bountiful God, have mercy on us, forgive our sins and help us to be witnesses to the Gospel. Amen.

## Gloria

## Prayer

Together, as a family of believers,
we bless you, loving Father.
Because you are love,
you have breathed affection into our family life:
into the relations between parents and children,
the love between man and wife,
the communal life of grandparents,
children and grandchildren.
We praise you, Father, for uniting us with so many households,
who live happily in loving communion.
But we are also united with those who,
suffering and frustrated,
bear the tensions of daily life with difficulty.
We wish that our relationships may be channelled in love and that forgiveness may be far-reaching and generous between us.
Help us in this exciting adventure
of creative and selfless love.
Grant us understanding, so that we may reach agreement when there are legitimate differences between us.
Thank you for the warmth that we experience and for the brotherhood that we extend as your gift.

## 3. LITURGY OF THE WORD

## Introduction to the Readings

The family must have strong ties. Without bonds of closeness and affection, the family does not survive, it breaks up. The author of the letter to the faithful at Colossae widened the scope of the kinship family to include the aspect of the Christian family. In both of these, the crucial elements are understanding, getting on well together and love.

Jesus was clothed and protected from birth by his parents. The example of the Holy Family should serve to encourage us to clothe each other physically and spiritually.

## Readings

Eccl. 3:3-7. 14-17a. *Psalm.* Col. 3:12-21. *Acclamation.* Mt. 2:13-15.19-23. *Brief silence.*

## Reflection

In this Christmas season, we have a day marked out for meditation on family matters. It is also a very appropriate date to bring out in the community the true values that should predominate in Christian families. In a Christian family, as in any other family, what should never be lacking is love. To this end, dialogue is essential at all times, listening to each other and putting oneself in another's shoes.

Sometimes parents wield their authority without understanding sufficiently the stages that their children are going through. Children, too, should listen more and be more reasonable. We all have need of open, peaceful and affectionate dialogue.

The family is the first school in which we learn the fundamental values for making our way through life. These values are not transmitted only with words, but also and principally with actions. No teaching will convince or strike home, if it is not demonstrated in life.

It is important to be concerned for the welfare of everyone in the family. But we must never forget the cultivation of values, such as humility, initiative, service, forgiveness, compromise… precisely the values of Jesus.

We have the mission to create the Kingdom of God on earth, and this task begins in our homes, with the aim that love, respect, mutual service may reign… even as we remain vigilant for those who are most in need.

Finally, we must also be aware that all of us form a Christian family. For Jesus, anyone who fulfils the will of the Father, that same person is his brother, his sister and his mother, that is to say, his true family. We live together in brotherhood, valuing everything to do with Jesus and considering it as our principal concern. (*Silence for internal reflection.*)

## Family Creed

We believe in God the Father, God the Son and God the Holy Spirit, the community and home of kindness and love,

which has permeated the universe with tenderness, pouring down affection on all that exists.

For that reason we believe in the pure and disinterested love that comes from God.

We believe in the affection that unites man and woman on their journey through life.

We believe in the love that is expressed in each child who is born.

We believe in the family, the home of communal life, where the bread of unity, welcome and forgiveness are shared each day.

We give thanks for the many things it has given us and we commit ourselves to look after it like a seed of the original love of God.

## Prayer of the Faithful

- That there may be brotherhood and peaceful community, *let us pray to the Lord.*
- That the Church may resemble a family as much as possible and that we may all feel united in faith, in hope and in love, *let us pray to the Lord.*
- That there may be love in all homes and any difficulties may be overcome with dialogue and respect, *let us pray to the Lord.*
- That orphans and separated people may find help and understanding among us, *let us pray to the Lord.*
- For Christian families, that they may cultivate the Word of God and prayer among the other activities in their home, *let us pray to the Lord.*

- For all our families, that they may be blessed and in this way we may live in unity in our parish, *let us pray to the Lord.*

## Offerings

- *Family book:* We offer you, Lord, this symbol of a fruitful, hard-working and grateful love.
- *Family album:* We offer you, Lord, the history of our family, of which you also are a member.
- *House keys:* We present to you, Lord, these keys of our house, so that you may continue to bless us and that we may know how to persevere in our witness to Christian life.
- *A gift or present:* We also offer, Lord, this gift, as a symbol of mutual recognition, reciprocal giving and of our effort to make our lives pleasing to you.

## 4. RITE OF COMMUNION

### Introduction

Jesus is our food, for personal and community life. To share in Holy Communion, signifies sharing the life, the commitment and the common calling of our Christian mission.

### Hymn

### Prayer

God, source of all fatherhood,
in heaven and on earth;
Father, you who are love and life,
may each human family be transformed,
through your Son, Jesus Christ, born of woman,
into a true sanctuary of life and love,
for the generations still to come.
Lord, may your grace guide married couples
for the good of families,
of all the families of this town.
May the new generations
find strong support in the family
for their human life and progress.

May love show itself to be stronger
than any weakness or any crisis
that families may undergo.
We ask you, Father, through Christ
who is the Way, the Truth and the Life.
United in him, we say to you: Our Father…
*(adapted from a prayer of Pope John Paul II)*

## Sign of Peace

## Distribution of Communion: Hymn

## Act of Thanksgiving

Thank you, Lord, for being part of a family.
Make of our home a house for your love.
Because you unite us,
may there be no distances.
Because you bless us,
may there be no bitterness.
Because you give us understanding
may there be no intolerance.
Because you give us forgiveness
may there be no rancour.
Because you are with us
may there be no abandonment.
Because you give us joy
may there be no sadness.
May each day be an occasion for more giving and
service and each night may we find ourselves in
greater family communion.
May we give of our best to be happy in the family and
may we find in love a reason for loving you more.

## 5. CONCLUDING RITE

### Resolution
Unity as a family and Christian example among our
neighbours.

### Blessing

### Conclusion
The family is a privileged centre of love and liberty;
it is a fundamental part of society and the best
school of life. But the changes that it is going
through at the moment are not always of benefit to
it. Let us help one another, so that each family may
be a seedbed of brotherhood and harmony, in the
spirit of the Kingdom of God.

## Final Hymn and Dismissal

# Mary, Mother of God
## 1 January

## 1. SETTING THE SCENE

### Poster with one of these texts:
- "Mary, an example from the very first day"
- "Each year is a gift"

### Symbols:
- Image of the Virgin.
- Beside it, a cradle with the Child.
- Calendar and diary for the year just begun.
- Bottle of champagne and a glass.
- Flowers in an army boot.

Someone, representing the community, welcomes people at the door of the church, wishing everyone a Happy New Year.

## 2. INTRODUCTORY RITES

### Introduction
Welcome to this celebration in which we are going to give Christian expression and content to what we have already lived through, in the family and with friends. At the start of a new year, we have wished for happiness. If this desire springs from the heart, it should logically impel us to work for its fulfilment. We will have to do a lot so that this year may be a happy one.

Let us pray that our daily efforts may bring about the peace and happiness that we give voice to today.

### Hymn

### Greeting
Brothers and sisters, we bless God the Father, who has sent us his Son, born of Mary.

### Penitential Rite
On taking an overall look at the year gone by, we surely will discover that there are many reasons for being grateful and for asking forgiveness:

- Grateful, because life has taught us many things, smiled on us, warmed us… because we have collaborated with it and we have taken advantage of its favours.
- Forgiveness, because we have not reached the heights that life offers us, we have abused it in other people and in ourselves… (*Brief silence*).

We are accustomed to saying: New year, new life. What must change in each one of us for this desire to be fulfilled? (*Brief silence*).

What can we do, so that none of our neighbours may be in want of the basic necessities throughout the year? (*Brief silence*).

Peace and unity are two great desires that we especially express at this time. What can we do to make them a reality every day of the year?

### Gloria

## Prayer

Lord of all goodness, we thank you
for the new year which we have just begun.
In brotherly union, we recognise your blessings
and the many gifts which we receive from you,
both small and great, material and spiritual.
But we also recognise our failings and idleness,
our distractions and superficiality,
all the bad things that we have done
and good things that we have failed to do.
Because of this, Father, we ask forgiveness:
because we have not played fair in life,
we have not duly returned the gifts that you gave
us, we have nourished the faith but little,
we have fallen short in our witness to you.
Trusting in your mercy,
we ask for your revitalising grace. Through Christ…

## 3. LITURGY OF THE WORD

### Introduction to the Readings

The Word of God stresses today the most important
value: "We are children of God". The Gospel points
out an important characteristic in Mary's
personality: "she kept these things to herself,
meditating on them in her heart". It also records
how Jesus is subject, from the beginning, to the
customs and traditions of his people. That is why he
is circumcised. In his circumcision, he receives the
name that defines the meaning of his life:
Jesus, the Saviour.

### Readings

Num. 6:22-27. *Psalm.* Gal. 4:4-7. *Acclamation.*
Lk. 2:16-21. *Brief silence.*

### Reflection

This day gives us a starting point for highlighting a
number of lessons, according to whether we pay
heed to them for liturgical, or social reasons.

On the threshold of another year, the liturgy
introduces Mary to us as a mother and as one who
has a great gift for internal reflection: she meditated
on events from the perspective of her faith and the
history of salvation. Mary pondered deeply on God's
plan, conscious that obedience, in faith, is a daily
task. This feature of Mary's represents a persuasive
invitation to live life through the year, with a
constant practice of internal reflection. (*Pause*)

Each new year is a gift: be grateful for it! It is not a
matter of filling up your life with years, but of filling
up your years with life. In this sense, each year is a
challenge: it is new and different. Do we value it as
such? Discover the surprise in each day and see it
as a time of grace. (*Pause*)

Institutions nowadays are promoting the value of
peace. Socially, we are encouraged to live the
whole year in the revitalising atmosphere of peace,
calm, living together in harmony. We remember
that beatitude: "blessed are those who work for
peace". And we can expand on it with these others:

- Blessed are those who live in peace with
  themselves and with God.
- Blessed are those who build peace in the family.
- Blessed are those who disseminate peace
  among their neighbours.
- Blessed are those who do not create enemies.
- Blessed are the apostles of non-violence.
- Blessed are those who know how to forgive and
  who accept forgiveness.
- Blessed are those who think that dialogue is
  always possible.
- Blessed are those who know how to understand
  and who hunger for peace.

(*Silence for internal reflection.*)

### Creed

## Prayer of the Faithful

- That peace and human rights may be promoted and respected in the whole world, *let us pray to the Lord.*
- For the Church, that it may bear fervent witness to the value of peace, *let us pray to the Lord.*
- That mutual assistance, peaceful community and quality of life may grow among us throughout the year, *let us pray to the Lord.*
- For those who view this new year with despair, that the assistance of others may bring them encouragement and hope, *let us pray to the Lord.*
- For our community, that it may progress through service in the mission of the Kingdom of God, *let us pray to the Lord.*

## 4. RITE OF COMMUNION

### Introduction

Jesus is the *living bread*, kneaded in Mary's womb. This is how God feeds us, in such a divine and human way.

### Hymn

### Prayer

Kind and loving Father, we bless you
at the beginning of this new year.
To you, more than to us,
time and history belong.
Our journey is like a pilgrimage:
"passing through everything once, once only and lightly, lightly, always lightly"…
In a circle of our brothers and sisters, we celebrate life:
the birth of children
and of adults who are born again.
We also celebrate peace
and the triumph of people,
the rebellion of the oppressed
and the valour of people of genius.
Yes, the Saviour has been born:
he brings a loud cry for the Gospel of justice

and a brotherly embrace.
He bears in himself a liturgy of life,
a power and example that encourages us to follow him.
And in a circle of our brothers and sisters, let us celebrate Mary,
the Virgin Mother, who is both silent and prayerful,
who has planted in the furrow of history
the fruit of her womb: the seedling of peace,
the definitive Word of God
the sacrament of love, justice and salvation.
This, Father, is our prayer,
that we affirm saying: Our Father…

### Sign of Peace

*Someone opens the bottle of champagne and pours it into a glass that another is holding. They both raise the bottle and glass, in the manner of a toast, while a third person says:* A new year has begun. It will bring difficulties and joys, opportunities and setbacks, satisfactions and crises… Relying on our hope and our solidarity, we make bold here, also, to drink a toast, recalling those that were made last night:

- For a year of peace and blessing, as God wills it.
- For Jesus, the great gift with whom God the Father has blessed us.
- For love shared and given, the best medicine for the problems that await us.
- For all of us, that throughout this year, we may preserve a pure mind, a warm heart and a high moral spirit.

Let us express our feelings, by warmly giving each other the sign of peace. *The bottle and the glass are left where they were.*

### Distribution of Communion: Hymn

### Act of Thanksgiving *(spontaneous)*

## 5. CONCLUDING RITE

### Resolution
- The personal intention to lead a Christian life throughout the year.
- A parish intention for the whole year, if one has not already been made.

### Blessing

### Conclusion

*Best wishes* is perhaps the expression most often heard over this Christmas period. Now it remains for us to make it a reality, on each day of the year that we have just begun. We are on the right path, if we try to do this together, genuinely and with constancy.

### Final Hymn and Dismissal

# Second Sunday after Christmas

## 1. SETTING THE SCENE

### Poster with one of these texts:
- "We are children of God"
- "God blesses us in Christ"

## 2. INTRODUCTORY RITES

### Introduction

Although important feasts have passed, the Christmas season continues. The message of this day can be summed up, in that God blesses us by coming down to us as the Word made man, light and love. A caring and gracious attitude on the part of God. Our own attitude is not usually of that nature, we who often prefer the darkness and reject his presence.

Let us allow the Word, now made flesh, to come into our hearts, to bring us great energy and revelation.

We prepare this celebration with the *symbols* that we present:

- *Bible and flowerpot:* The wise Word of God wants to take root in our earth.
- *A candle in a transparent bowl of water:* God chose us to be saints and predestined us to be his children.

### Hymn

### Greeting

Brothers and sisters, we praise the Lord together, who took the step of reaching out towards us.

### Penitential Rite

In gratitude for the love of God who forgives us, we recognise our personal and communal sin. *(Brief silence.) I confess…*

### Gloria

### Prayer

We bless you, loving Father, because you have kept us in your mind since ancient times and called us into existence, to lead a worthy life in your presence. We recognise that your seed is within us. Help us to live up to our vocation, so that we may learn how to communicate your wisdom and your blessing. Through Christ…

## 3. LITURGY OF THE WORD

### Introduction to the Readings

In his desire to come near to us and manifest himself, God has planted his wisdom in the field of history and it has put down roots wherever it has been received. Because of this, as people and as believers, we have many reasons for blessing God. He was the first to bless us. Already, before we were born, he had pronounced our name, had chosen us as his children and had conceived of us in the image of Jesus.

## Reading

Eccl. 24:1-4. 12-16. *Psalm.* Eph. 1:3-6. 15-18. *Acclamation.* Jn 1:1-18. *Brief silence.*

## Reflection

Although we scarcely deserve it, God has revealed himself and has communicated his wisdom to us, above all by means of Jesus. His person (his words and deeds) is the culminating message, the supreme and definitive Word of God, which defines the human condition most convincingly.

Jesus, the wise Messenger of God, will announce and let it be known with clarity, that whosoever listens to his words and puts them into practice, is a sensible person and is building his personality upon a solid foundation… For this reason, we emphasise that Jesus is the ideal and basis for sound living. It is, therefore, pointless to busy our minds looking for anyone else . Upon this foundation, each one of us may see how his or her personality is built up, because a day will come, the day of judgement, when the works of each one of us will be revealed.

That is the way it is. Already now, in accepting Jesus, we are experiencing the blessing of the one who chose us, before the creation of the world, that we might be saints. It is God the Father's ideal that we should come to experience the feeling that we are his adopted children. The Nativity confirms this aim: God invites us to share in the inheritance of the saints.

How great and amazing is this impulse of God! He desired to come into history as a cradle of light. And he has left us his Spirit, in order to extend this Light from generation to generation, in such a way that we may be able to understand the hope to which he calls us and the glorious riches that await us, if we work for our personal and community holiness of life.

For this reason, it is a mistake and a lack of grace to turn one's back on this Word that is Light, Wisdom and Love: he came to his own people and they did not receive him… However, the pure in heart and the simple folk are those who see this Light, understand the Word and profit by the Wisdom that it instils. (*Silence for internal reflection.*)

## Creed

## Prayer of the Faithful

- That the human message of the Word made flesh may reach everyone, *let us pray to the Lord.*
- For our Church, that it may present the human presence of God and the truth of the Gospel in an appealing way, *let us pray to the Lord.*
- For those of us who form part of this community, that our lives may reflect our acceptance of the Word, *let us pray to the Lord.*
- That the experience of feeling that we are children of God may strengthen our brotherhood, *let us pray to the Lord.*
- For the wishes and the needs of each one of us and for those of our people, *let us pray to the Lord.*

## 4. RITE OF COMMUNION

## Introduction

God chose us and blessed us in the person of Christ. Now, he nourishes our Christian vocation. Let us share in this communion with profound gratitude.

## Hymn

## Prayer

Father, you who are with us
spreading your blessing, wisdom and message of
salvation, blessed are you, for the great love that
you have shown us.
History and creation are infused with your presence,
but awareness and sensitivity are needed
in order to perceive you right by our side, deeply
involved with us.
You have sown your wisdom in our little plot
and you call us in freedom to be your children.
Receive our prayers and praise:
your light has shone,
we are born of you,
you have blessed us with all manner of good things,
we have contemplated your glory.
In heartfelt gratitude and in communion
we say to you: Our Father…

## Sign of Peace

## Distribution of Communion: Hymn

## Act of Thanksgiving

- Thank you, Father, because you have hastened
  to bless us in the person of Christ.
- Thank you for raising us to be your adopted
  children.
- Thank you for your Word, so charged with light
  and life.
- Thank you for your Spirit of wisdom and
  revelation.
- Thank you, because we are able to know you
  and to come to understand the hope and
  richness of grace that you have reserved for us.

## 5. CONCLUDING RITE

### Resolution

To communicate the experience of the fatherhood
of God and how he blesses us.

### Blessing

### Conclusion

The time of Christmas is especially expressive of the
nearness of God. As the Gospel has recorded, he
wished to live among us, to be our neighbour and
to share in the journey of our lives. Let us live in this
bond of friendship with our God, with faith and
eagerness. Let us be witnesses of the one who is
already living among us.

### Final Hymn and Dismissal

# Epiphany of the Lord

## 6 January

## 1. SETTING THE SCENE

### Poster with one of these texts:

- "Jesus is for everyone"
- "The name of the truth is Jesus"
- "The truth has no frontiers"
- "Jesus, the great star"

### Symbols:

- Atlas or globe of the world.
- Other symbols of a missionary nature.
- A lighted paschal candle.

Small candles are handed out at the entrance.

## 2. INTRODUCTORY RITES

### Introduction

The liturgical name of the feast that we are celebrating today is *the Epiphany of the Lord*, which means *the manifestation of God*.
As Christians, we have to consider today that Jesus is the supreme gift from God, for all people and for all nations; and that he is the great Star, able to lead us in the right path. So, let us allow ourselves to be guided by the light of God, following Jesus.

### Hymn

### Greeting

Brothers and sisters, let us bless God, who has revealed himself in Jesus.

### Penitential Rite

- You are the Light, that shines in the darkness:
  *Lord, have mercy.*
- You are the Light, that enlightens all people:
  *Christ, have mercy.*
- You are the Light, that gives life to the world:
  *Lord, have mercy.*

### Gloria

### Prayer

God, our Father, you have revealed yourself completely, because you want everyone to be saved and to come to knowledge of the truth. We confess that Jesus Christ is the light and salvation of all people and of all nations. We receive your generosity and renew the commitment to our missionary faith. Rely on us to proclaim and spread the Gospel. Amen.

## 3. LITURGY OF THE WORD

### Introduction to the Readings

The universal character of God's self-revealing is emphasised in the readings that we are going to hear. The author of the letter to the Ephesians confesses that he has reflected deeply upon the originality of the ministry, which has been revealed in Jesus Christ in favour of all people, and, captivated by it, he dedicates his life to proclaiming it.
The Gospel reveals that in Jesus, the Star of God, there shines a bright light, capable of enlightening those who are near and far away.

## Readings

Is. 60:1-6. *Psalm*. Eph. 3:2-3a. 5-6. *Acclamation*. Mt. 2:1-12. *Brief silence*.

## Reflection

Throughout these days, we have been entering more deeply, in different ways, into the great truth of our faith: God has visited and redeemed us. Now, we reflect that this redeeming visit is for every people and culture. Epiphany is the manifestation of God, bringing into relief the universal character of salvation.

It is clear that our God does not allow any kind of privilege that might limit the access to and the enjoyment of the fruits of the Gospel. The gift of Jesus is for everyone and his reach must extend equally to all people. For this reason, today's feast has a missionary perspective and impact: the spreading of the grace of God must reach all corners of the world.

We must also emphasise on this day that Jesus is the great Star, with a light so bright that he focuses and humanises like no other. We, who are children of the darkness, try to avoid his influence, to take a different path… There is a mass of publicity and advertising to attract us to other lesser leaders, who, in many cases, are dubious, if not false: celebrities from the worlds of finance, politics, sport, music, cinema… We do not bend our knee before anyone, except the one Lord: Jesus, exalted by God the Father, because he was faithful unto death and death on the cross.

To sum up, today we must realise the missionary significance of our faith. We who have known Jesus and have experienced the impact of the Gospel, are now charged with making sure that his human influence reaches everyone. At this time, we are the hands, the feet, the lips, that is to say, the human instruments of Jesus the missionary. *(Silence for internal reflection.)*

## Creed

## Prayer of the Faithful

- That the light of God may reach all peoples, *let us pray to the Lord*.
- For the missionaries who strive to bring this light of God to all the corners of the world, *let us pray to the Lord*.
- That our community may have more missionary zeal, *let us pray to the Lord*.
- For those who do not recognise in Christ the great Star of God, *let us pray to the Lord*.
- That children may receive, above all, the gift of a good education, *let us pray to the Lord*.

## Symbolic representation

*Some individuals light their taper in the area reserved for candles and bring the light to the others. Someone says:* We all have the vocation to be witnesses to the light. The Word of God exhorts us to be missionaries.

## 4. RITE OF COMMUNION

## Introduction

Jesus encourages us with his example and enlightens us with his word. Let us receive it in communion in order to become, like him, good communicators of the Gospel.

## Hymn

## Prayer

We bless you, Father, for Jesus of Nazareth,
your great Star and the Star of all times.
We say it with pride:
at no time in history
has it been possible to deprive it of its purpose;
Jesus is the celestial and vigorous seed
planted in our soil,
the light who guides our paths,
the sacrament of human dignity.
Yes, Father, no one has been able to extinguish Jesus.
Our voice finds its resonance and harmony in him.
He is the Master who deserves to be followed,
the Redeemer charged with the Gospel.
We unite in his work and his prayer
and say to you: Our Father…

## Sign of Peace

## Distribution of Communion: Hymn

## Act of Thanksgiving

- We give you thanks, Lord, because in your love you have wished to descend to all men and women. You do not hold with privilege. You want salvation to reach everyone.
- We thank you for Jesus, the true light who enlightens and guides all those who find his Word and his Spirit.
- We give you thanks for our Christian faith, that urges us to bear witness and carry out its mission.

## 5. CONCLUDING RITE

## Resolution

To strengthen our missionary commitment.

## Blessing

## Conclusion

To reclaim the name and the meaning of this feast is a task that still lies before us. One must avoid confusing it with the consumerist fantasy of giving presents, so as not to fall into the commercial trap.

Our world continues to need the bright revelation of God. This is what is really important. We believers are today the light of God. For this reason, may our light shine before the people, so that the world may believe and act according to the values of the Gospel. Jesus, the great eternal Star, accompanies us on our way.

## Final Hymn and Dismissal

# Baptism of the Lord

## 1. SETTING THE SCENE

### Poster with one of these texts:
- "You are my beloved Son"
- "Jesus also was baptised"
- "Baptism is a commitment"

### Symbols of baptism:
A paschal candle and font or receptacle with water.

## 2. INTRODUCTORY RITES

### Introduction
Jesus, who wanted to belong to the people of his time, considered it a gesture of redeeming fellowship that he himself should undergo baptism by John. All of us who are here have also been baptised. Since we, too, have received this sacrament, we want our lives to be guided by Jesus' example. If only we might be recognised by the special character and qualities of those who have been baptised.

### Hymn

### Greeting
Brothers and sisters, let us bless God the Father, who has sent his Son in order to save the world.

### Penitential Rite
- You, who approached baptism as though you were just another sinner: *Lord, have mercy.*
- You, who took on the sins of all: *Christ, have mercy.*
- You, who take away the sins of the world: *Lord, have mercy.*

### Gloria

### Prayer
God, Holy Father, who in the baptism of Christ in the Jordan wished to solemnly reveal that he was your beloved Son, sending your Holy Spirit to him; grant your adopted children, reborn by water and the Holy Spirit, to be continuously steadfast in the fulfilment of your will. Through Christ…

## 3. LITURGY OF THE WORD

### Introduction to the Readings
God, in order to convince, you do not use the argument of force, but of humility and of meekness. That is how it is expressed in the first reading. Jesus adopted a similar attitude when he was baptised. Placed in a position to accept the experience of all human beings, he joins the queue of sinners and receives baptism at the hands of John. God the Father blesses this gesture, fills Jesus with the Spirit and recognises him as his beloved Son.

Our living out of baptism unites us with this experience of Jesus: the Spirit fills us, strengthens us and God the Father receives us as his children.

### Readings
Is. 42:1-4. 6-7. *Psalm* . Acts 10:34-38. *Acclamation.* Mt. 3:13-17. *Brief silence.*

### Reflection
Jesus makes his appearance in society, joining the queue of sinners and approaching like just one more, among so many repentant people, to ask for baptism. He, who had no sin to wash away in the river, took on the sins of history. He took the step of baptism for us, because he had the greatest empathy with the human condition. This he took on, wishing to carry the burden of all our faults.

From this gesture, so full of meaning, the early Church was already forming a conviction: Jesus was identical to us in everything, except with respect to our sins. He came into the world, doing good works, because he allowed himself to be led by the Spirit, and he gave no quarter in his struggle against sin and its influences. Nevertheless, with this gesture, Jesus confirms publicly that he is in favour of conversion and that his plan is to fulfil the will of his Father. Therefore, if Jesus assumed and took on the burden of our sins, if he saves us from within human experience and history, if he committed himself by making a fundamental choice – to go about in this world doing good – what other course of action must we take?

We who are baptised must always be on Jesus' side, we must incarnate the spirituality of the Gospel and it should be clearly seen that we are working for the Kingdom of God. Like him, we will be confronted by a thousand temptations. But the Spirit enlightens us and stiffens our resolve, so that we can maintain the dignity that corresponds to our membership in Christ. And so it is very important for us to maintain our consciousness of being baptised. The adventure of Jesus is also the adventure of everyone who is baptised. (*Silence for internal reflection.*)

## Creed

- The tradition of the Church has brought us close to the experience of a God, a Father close to us, who saves us in Jesus Christ and loves us with amazing affection. Do you believe in this holy and merciful God? – *Yes, I believe.*
- The Christian community recognises in Jesus the Son of God, who is the Light of history, the Redeemer who liberates and encourages us like no other. Do you believe, through experience, that the true meaning of life is embodied in Jesus? – *Yes, I believe.*
- The Bible tells us that we are made in the image and likeness of God. Do you believe that the Spirit of God lives in us, in the community, and inspires us to improve our personal and social life? – *Yes, I believe.*
- The Gospel has been presented to us as the message and the way of life that God desires. Do you believe that God's plan and the values of a life of quality are found in the Gospel? – *Yes, I believe.*
- We often value our human dignity: our abilities and aspirations. Do you believe in yourselves, in your goodness deep down, in your renewed faith, in your mystical service for the Kingdom of God? – *Yes, I believe.*

## Prayer of the Faithful

- For men and women of good will, that they may continue to act with sensitivity and to set a good example to those around them, *let us pray to the Lord.*
- For the Church, that it may be a community of those who are conscious of their baptism, *let us pray to the Lord.*
- That the qualities of Jesus may be evident in all those who are baptised, *let us pray to the Lord.*
- That our surroundings may improve, thanks to the example of those who are baptised, *let us pray to the Lord.*
- For all of us, that we may be lively and responsible members in the life of our people, *let us pray to the Lord.*

## Offerings

- *Receptacles for oil and chrism or glass of oil:* Father, anointed with the power of the Spirit, Jesus went about doing good. Our anointing in the sacraments reminds us that you are with us and you send us to spread the word.
- *Cross and laurel crown:* We offer you, Father, the symbols of the life of Jesus: the service, sacrifice and victory of the one who fulfils your will as a beloved Son.
- *Certificate of baptism:* Receive, Father, our commitment to remain followers of Jesus, working for your Kingdom.

## 4. RITE OF COMMUNION

### Introduction
To communicate with Jesus is to become like him to such an extent that we set a good example wherever we go. Let us strengthen our following of Jesus with this communion.

### Hymn

### Prayer
Blessed are you, God our Father,
who, at the Jordan, presented your beloved Son to us,
lowly as a sinner,
but conscious of a mission: to be the Lamb who takes away the sins of the world…
You wanted him to be sharer and redeemer,
making him descend like a penitent sinner,
anticipating in his baptism the manner in which he would be stripped in his passion.
You have delivered him to us, re-clothed with the Spirit to reconcile us and raise us up,
as the greatest of gifts, fallen from heaven,
as the greatest of blessings that you have ever spoken.
Now, Father, send down your Spirit again,
like you did upon Jesus by the Jordan,
and shore up our weakness
with resurrection and with hope.
Bestow your blessings among this community,
so that, with our neighbours, we may go forward with the ever challenging project of the Gospel.
United in our commitment to your Kingdom
we say to you: Our Father…

### Sign of Peace

### Distribution of Communion: Hymn

### Act of Thanksgiving
- We give you thanks, good Father, because in the baptism at the Jordan you manifested yourself in the anointing of Jesus, bathing him in the Spirit and introducing him to history as your beloved and trustworthy Son.
- We thank you for our own experiences of baptism, a bathing inspired by the Spirit, an experience of death and resurrection, the tension of being laid bare and of commitment.
- We thank you for the followers of Jesus, anointed by the Spirit, who devote themselves to the service of others and bring the example of Christ vitally close to us.

## 5. CONCLUDING RITE

### Resolution
To continue in the footsteps of Jesus: to proceed on our way doing good and saving those influenced by the evil one.

### Blessing

### Conclusion
To accept baptism in its fullness is not a matter for children. To realise its full significance and to maintain the dignity of those who are baptised, it is necessary to be adults in the faith and to provide ourselves with a liberal dose of the Gospel.

The baptised must live the liberating adventure of the Beatitudes with others: to create brotherhood as a consequence of choosing poverty and service, to speak up for justice, to work for peace and for liberty, to cultivate purity of heart… For that which is already in itself a human responsibility, one must be strengthened by the baptism of the Spirit.

### Final Hymn and Dismissal

# The Season of
# LENT

# Ash Wednesday

## 1. SETTING THE SCENE
- In a prominent place, a silhouette of Jesus walking (it can remain there for the whole of Lent).
- Cardboard feet on the ground, with the values of conversion (they can be replaced during Lent).

### Poster with texts like:
- "Conversion is a daily task"
- "God walks with me"

## 2. INTRODUCTORY RITES

### Introduction
With Lent, we begin our preparation for Easter, the most significant and challenging time of the year for Christians. Today, we begin Lent: this is a time of challenge and training, with constant reference to Jesus Christ, risen from the dead.

In Lent, we remember that conversion is a task for the whole year. Day by day, we should meditate on the exemplary and virtuous model of Jesus, who made his way through life with steadfastness and without faltering. Conversion is a fundamental task for the Christian

Ashes are the external sign that characterises this day. They symbolise that we are sinners and that we must change.

We present the *symbols* that are the focus for this celebration:

- *Candle and ashes:* Before the symbolic light of the candle, ashes are a symbol of something that has been extinguished.
- *A flowering plant and ashes:* Next to the sprouting life of the plant, the ashes are a symbol of death.

### Hymn

### Greeting
Brothers and sisters, together let us praise the Lord, who calls us to conversion.

### Prayer
God, good Father, we know that you love us and that you are faithful to your promises. Please continue to look down upon this community with affection and strengthen in us the presence of your Spirit. May he enlighten us, so that we may live with wisdom, with energy and in faithfulness.
And may the encouragement that we give to one another help us to bring to a happy conclusion the hopes and the desires for sanctity, that we feel as followers of Jesus. Through the same Christ…

## 3. LITURGY OF THE WORD

### Introduction to the Readings
Any time is suitable for the acceptance of salvation. Lent expresses it and reminds us of it. It invites us to change profoundly, to be pure in heart, to be consistent with the mercy of God. If we look into the very depths of our being, we will discover that we have some or many things to reform, stamp out or change. In Lent, we are constantly reminded that we have to take hold of the old man. "Now is the time of grace," says Saint Paul, "now is the day of salvation". Let us live, then, with the sincerity and repentance that the Word of God reveals to us today.

### Readings
Joel. 2:12-18. *Psalm.* 2 Cor. 5:20-6:2. *Acclamation.* Mt. 6:1-6. 16-18. *Brief silence.*

## Reflection

With Ash Wednesday, we begin preparation for Easter. We prepare ourselves to live through, as is befitting, the great event of the history of salvation: Christ's passing from death into life, with all its transcendence and purpose. The Church reminds us that this preparation consists in seeking an increasingly sincere and perfect conversion, by means of profound meditation on the Word of God, the life of the sacraments, prayer, voluntary privation – of which fasting and abstinence are an example – and renouncing selfishness. It is a matter of bringing all the means into play, in order to advance further and more deeply in the Christian life.

Lent is a most suitable opportunity for strengthening convictions and commitments: for example, austerity in relation to consumerism, thinking well of others instead of talking badly of them, not thinking of ourselves as the best but rather thinking that we are the ones at fault, etc. We would do well, furthermore, if we considered the Beatitudes (Mt. 5:2-12); in them, Jesus encapsulates the Christian ideal. According to them, what do we lack, what do we have in excess?

Next to the ashes, in addition to the Easter candle reminding us of our change into new beings, we have a flower that symbolises a renewed, pure, regenerated life. Conversion means following Jesus of Nazareth, allowing ourselves to be transformed by his Spirit.

Life provides us with opportunities for improvement. Lent and Easter remind us of the quality of renewal that we must maintain throughout the whole year. (*Silence for internal reflection.*)

## 4. PENITENTIAL RITE

### Introduction

Ashes, in our Lent tradition, symbolise human frailty and sin. Receiving ash on our heads, at the beginning of Lent, is a public recognition of our sinful state.

When the ash is put on, we are told: *Turn away from sin and be faithful to the Gospel.* In this way, we identify it with repentance and reconciliation.

The first penitents covered their heads with ash, in order to indicate publicly that they were sinners, that the dirty dust of their sins exuded from their inner being. We recognise with the ashes that we have also destroyed something, we have *reduced someone to dust.* But ashes are also the remains of a cleansing fire and the beginning of new life.

Now is the moment to publicly recognise our failings and to set ourselves to lead a new life. Receiving ashes is a sign of conversion, asking for forgiveness and trust in the mercy of God.

### Penitential Rite

We recognise that our lives are tainted by weakness and sin. Conscious of the evil that we do and of the good that we fail to do, let us express our sorrow, trusting in the mercy of God:

- That you may forgive all our sins, *Lord, have mercy.*
- Because we need your help in order to change, *Christ, have mercy.*
- Because we want to prepare for Easter, genuinely converted, *Lord, have mercy.*

### Giving of Ashes

*A leading member of the community puts ashes on all those present who come forward; to each one, he says:* Turn away from sin and be faithful to the Gospel. *The first or one of the first, who approaches to receive the ashes, comes with chains upon his body. When the ashes are put on him, he lets the chains fall to the ground.*

### Hymn

## 5. RITE OF COMMUNION

## Introduction

Communion with Jesus should be the cause and effect of our working daily for conversion. We come to communion because we need the strength and support of the saints.

## Hymn

## Prayer

Blessed are you, Christ laid bare,
who, being of divine state,
did not cling to your equality with God,
but descended to the condition of a slave,
obedient unto death, and a death on the cross.
Jesus, the memory of you has not been wiped out.
You are not a stranger in this town.
You keep your radiance;
for which many look to you with wonder
and many others run out to meet you.
How good it is to have known you!
How precious to experience you within!
We proclaim your worth,
we sing to you in gratitude;
we cry out to any who wish to hear us
that they may learn to follow your counsel,
that they may come to know your story,
that they may discover your essence, without fear,
and may truly see what you are: your human and brotherly quality.
Jesus, we join our voice with yours,
to say together to the Father: Our Father…

## Sign of Peace

## Distribution of Communion: Hymn

## A Motivating Reflection
### (in the Act of Thanksgiving)

Lent is about overcoming, an open window on life,
an experience of austerity, a reason for belief,
the spark of conversion, the plan for goodness,
the horizon of the liberating feast of Easter.

Lent is meditation on Jesus,
a new, simple and natural man,
One among many, although *different*:
an evangelist stepping forward towards his destiny…
Lent is an experience of salvation,
living with honesty, reconciliation,
the message of the *crucified one who knows all*
who shocks and unnerves…
only the simple appreciate how he revives and saves.
Lent is always life, and a life of quality.
All conversion is already a sign of *new life*.

## 6. CONCLUDING RITE

### Resolution

To meditate on the Beatitudes (Mt. 5:2-12) and to make a resolution of your own choice for the whole of Lent.

### Blessing

### Conclusion

Lent is a preparation and training to live the Resurrection. At the same time, it reminds us of the task and the daily responsibility of conversion. May we not squander the grace that accompanies us. Let us remember that conversion is to make our way through life with a clean conscience, faithfully developing our calling to holiness, in imitation of Jesus.

### Final Hymn and Dismissal

# First Sunday of Lent

## 1. SETTING THE SCENE

### Poster with one of these texts:
- "No to temptation"
- "To worship? Only God"
- "Jesus also was tempted"

To the *symbols,* which may remain throughout the whole of Lent, are added the ones proper to this day, indicative of current temptations:

- Bottle of alcoholic beverage.
- Tray with money.
- Basket with fruit, attractive to the eye.

## 2. INTRODUCTORY RITES

### Introduction
We come together to celebrate our faith and to get as close as possible to Jesus. The underlying meaning of Lent is conversion of heart. And this is a daily task.

Today, we are going to become aware that temptation is a real part of life. Sometimes, it deceives us and drags us down. To be conscious of our failings and our sins is good, because in this way, we can correct them.

Temptation can always be overcome. Jesus, too, in this respect, is a clear example.

### Hymn

### Greeting
Brothers and sisters, let us bless God, who is rich in mercy.

### Penitential Rite
- You, who have conquered the Tempter: *Lord, have mercy.*
- You, who sympathise with our weaknesses: *Christ, have mercy.*
- You, Saviour of all: *Lord, have mercy.*

### Prayer
God, our Father, we human beings are your favourite creatures; we carry in our being the mark of your Spirit. But we are as fragile as clay and we are exposed to every kind of temptation. Strengthen us with your Word, so that we may be worthy of being chosen by you. Through Christ...

## 3. LITURGY OF THE WORD

### Introduction to the Readings
Many and various are the temptations that try to ensnare us through life, some from within and others from without. There are three ways in which they particularly confront us: in the desire to possess, in the desire to attract attention and in the desire for power.

The Gospel recounts to us some of the temptations that Jesus suffered. Nothing is so human as temptation; as we say: we are flesh and blood. But also, there is nothing so dehumanising as temptation, when it deceives us and brings about our fall.

### Readings
Gen. 2:7-9; 3:1-7. *Psalm*. Rom. 5:12-19. *Acclamation*. Mt. 4:1-11. *Brief silence.*

## Reflection

Human beings are lustful (cf. Rom. 7:14-25). They are overcome by seduction, riddled with temptation (cf. Gal. 5:17). This is like a dark shadow that accompanies every person on his or her journey through life. We all experience this tension between *living according to the flesh or living according to the spirit* (cf. Gal. 5:16-17; Rom. 8:5-8.12-13). Jesus himself, who was a human being like any one of us, also suffered the ravages of temptation. However, he always wished to be faithful to his own self (to his conscience), honoured by others and obedient to God. This *being the same and different* is one of the features that make him appealing.

In fact, in all of us, there are tendencies towards life and instincts of death. All of us, some more and others less, are subject to the environment of error and evil that is the origin of personal sin. The failings of each one of us have a negative influence around us. That is why Jesus, like you and I, did not have it easy.

He had to draw heavily on his spirituality, so as not to be drawn along by the current, not to be dragged down by any temptation. It is human to suffer temptation. What dehumanises us and undermines our dignity is to give in to it, become entangled and fall into it.

There are temptations of an intimate nature, as though springing from inside us, which bring fundamental values into play. Jesus experienced this kind of temptation in solitude. However, in addition to this, he suffered from external temptations, accosted by enemies who often put him to the test in order to make him slip up (cf. Mk12:13-17; Jn 8:3-11). They were those who thought that he was possessed (cf. Mk 3:22-30). Even his closest friends tempted him (cf. Mt. 16:21-23). But he, with sensitivity, prayer and clear-headedness, had the knowledge and ability to thwart any temptation that came his way. He was a profoundly spiritual person.

We are also equally aware that temptation challenges us from within and from without. We are able to overcome it. The example of Jesus gives us this assurance. To achieve this, he proposes that we should be vigilant and pray. In his prayer, he expresses this important intention: "Lead us not into temptation…" (*Silence for internal reflection.*)

## Creed

## Prayer of the Faithful

## Let us pray together:

■ Lord, we feel weak, like creatures of clay; free us from the many temptations that lie in wait for us.
■ We want to live in holiness of life, so that the Church may be faithful, and so nourish the seeds of goodness in society.
■ We pray to you, Lord, for our community and for our town, that we may all support a life of quality.
■ Inspire us with that mercy that flows from you, so that we may know how to understand and encourage those who have fallen under the weight of temptation.
■ And may you accept all our intentions.
*Let us pray to the Lord.*

## Offerings

■ *Loaf of bread and Bible:* Father, we need bread each day in order to live; but we also need to nourish our spirit with your Word.
■ *Various individual names on a paten:* With our names, we offer up to you, Lord, our own lives. We do not want to follow the influence of evil, but that of the Gospel.

## 4. RITE OF COMMUNION

### Introduction
Communion with Jesus is a powerful aid to overcoming temptation. Jesus enlightens us, so that we may live with sensitivity and awareness, as befits Christians.

### Hymn

### Prayer
Bountiful Father, it is a duty to bless you,
even more when temptation surrounds
us like a shadow.
We are caught up in a great tension.
We are children of a sterile society,
parched of human values and holiness.
But we also experience the healthy current
of a history of salvation, strongly inspired by Jesus.
He, the Son of Light, rejected all temptation,
extinguished the influence of sin
and offered us the wholesome alternative
of the resurrection.
Through the obedience of faith
we receive the abundance of your gifts;
your blessing surrounds us completely
and impels us to unfold the mystical spirit of those
who are converted.
We recognise, Father, that you follow on foot
behind your offer of salvation
and you look to us to quicken our pace of goodness.
Aware of your mercy and desirous to fulfil your will
we unite with all those who pray to you:
Our Father…

### Sign of Peace

### Distribution of Communion: Hymn

### Act of Thanksgiving *(spontaneous)*

## 5. CONCLUDING RITE

### Resolution
To live each day in alertness, vigilant, so as not to fall into any temptation, nor to be the cause of temptation for anybody else.

### Blessing

### Conclusion
What we have shared and celebrated in this gathering should encourage us to overcome the many temptations that occur in life. Situations tempting us to moral lapses will continue to present themselves. The logical course, as genuine Christians, is not to fall victim to them. The scene of Jesus being tempted reminds us that nobody escapes temptation. But this gospel scene also shows us that temptation can be overcome. We rely on the Spirit to achieve this.

### Final Hymn and Dismissal

# Second Sunday of Lent

## 1. SETTING THE SCENE

### Poster with one of these texts:
- "Here is my Son. Listen to him."
- "God blesses us through Jesus"

### In addition to the symbols for the whole of Lent, there can be:
- Alb only, or a cross draped with a white cloth.
- Walking stick: "Leave your country".

## 2. INTRODUCTORY RITE

### Introduction
My brothers and sisters, we are called together in faith which we experience as a gift. Last Sunday, we contemplated Jesus, confronting the fundamental temptations of life, holding out against them and adopting a worthy and faithful response. Today, we are going to witness the promises and revelations, with which God brings his Word into action.

This alternative experience that inspired Jesus and filled him with energy caused great wonder in his disciples. Three of them experienced it spectacularly, on one occasion, when they went up a mountain with him, to pray.

### Hymn

### Greeting
Brothers and sisters, we bless God the Father, who confirms Jesus as his beloved Son and as the true Word that we must heed.

### Penitential Rite
- You, who were tested by suffering:
  *Lord, have mercy.*
- You, who make the light shine within us:
  *Christ, have mercy.*
- You, the radiance of the Father's glory:
  *Lord, have mercy.*

### Prayer
Holy Father, you present to us again the great gift of your Son, your Light and your Word, so that we may listen to him and heed him. Like him, we want to be missionaries on foot, walking among the people with the urgency of the Gospel. Accept our desires to be messengers of your Kingdom. Through Christ…

## 3. LITURGY OF THE WORD

### Introduction to the Readings
The first news that we have of the history of salvation already tells us of promises, blessings and covenants. God has always been the same. His offerings of grace can always be more effective, if they find acceptance and responsibility within us. So it was, in the case of Abraham, and the same can happen with any other believer: the presence and love of God transform one's life. The three disciples, who went up the mountain with Jesus, experienced it in an exemplary way.

### Readings
Gen. 12:1-4a. *Psalm.* 2 Tim. 1:8b-10. *Acclamation.* Mt. 17:1-9. *Brief silence.*

## Reflection

A believer is the kind of religious person who listens to the plans that God traces out for him and puts them into practice, in the form and manner that he feels God is indicating to him, although he may not be able to understand all the implications and risks of the yes that he declares. This is the example that Abraham and all the great believers leave us with. God said to Abraham: "Leave your country". And "Abraham departed, as the Lord had spoken unto him". In the history of the people of God, he is recognised as the *father of believers*. His faithfulness, put into practice, is of the highest order.

This account of Abraham's calling, as with other similar ones in the Bible, reveals to us that the biblical God often *destabilises* us, in a healthy way. We all run the risk of *becoming set in* or of *focusing on* various interests and plans that are not of prime importance, from the viewpoint of the Kingdom of God. It is very probable, then, that the Spirit may try to change our criteria and *upset us*, in the interest of a greater solidarity or a greater service to the Kingdom. The believer, who responds with faithfulness to these guiding interventions of God, feels his presence and his blessing. In the obedience of faith rests his security and his confidence. This conviction is essential, if one is to put one shoulder to the wheel, while toiling hard for the Gospel.

The experience that the disciples have at the top of the mountain amazes them. God refers to Jesus as his chosen Son. Later, he will be the great Prophet and the new Law. With him, a new history begins. With him, the fullness of the Revelation comes to pass. So great was the impact on them that they wanted to remain on the mountain. Jesus, for his part, invited them to come down, to return to crude and harsh reality, because one has to continue pulling one's weight, in arduous toil for the Gospel. To remain up on high would be an escape. In this way, mystical experiences are valid, if they prove

regenerating and encourage commitment on behalf of the Gospel. (*Silence for internal reflection.*)

## Creed

## Prayer of the Faithful

- For all those who strive for the transformation and improvement of this world, *let us pray to the Lord.*
- For those who govern, that they may bring about the development of all people, *let us pray to the Lord.*
- For all those of us who form the Church, that we may find, in prayer, the light and energy of committed Christians, *let us pray to the Lord.*
- For all those who suffer, that they may come to understand the Christian value of suffering, *let us pray to the Lord.*
- For all of us who want to follow Jesus, that the message of the transfiguration may give us courage in moments of difficulty and in the darkness of life, *let us pray to the Lord.*

## Offerings

- *Working overalls and Gospels:* Lord, we want to put our vocation into action and to take part in the task of spreading the Gospel.
- *Sandals:* Lord, we want to be missionaries and to spread the Gospel beyond the confines of our community.

## Hymn

## Symbolic Representation

*Someone hands out Gospels to different people, while saying one of these texts:*

- Spreading the Gospel is a gift.
- Our vocation is to preach the Gospel.
- Before preaching the Gospel, let us pray with the Gospel.

# 4. RITE OF COMMUNION

## Introduction
In anything connected with Jesus, surprise and wonder have no limits. Let us renew, in Holy Communion, the pure breath of the Spirit.

## Hymn

## Prayer
Let us join together our sentiments and our voices
to give you thanks, Father, for your chosen Son,
that final and supreme word, that you invite us to hear.
He is the Prophet, sprung from your breast,
the messenger of the new Law,
the foundation of a new society.
We give you thanks, because you have called us
to take part in this adventure:
you have made us sharers in a vocation
and you entrust us with the task of spreading your word.
Father, following Jesus is an experience
that brings us our greatest personal fulfilment.
In the light of your calling,
we understand ourselves better.
United in faith and desiring to serve you,
we say to you: Our Father…

## Sign of Peace

## Distribution of Communion: Hymn

## Motivating Reflection
(*in the Act of Thanksgiving*)
Brothers and sisters and friends,
we invite you sincerely to develop,
with courage, the calling of faith.
Do not sin at the table of life.
Do not give in to the call of pleasure.
Do not allow yourselves to be carried
along by indifference.
Do not waste time, nor let yourselves be dragged
down by pessimism.
Do not let the spirit become blunted.

Friends, it is the time to live a different way.
Your ability is great: believe it!
The time has come to accept the challenge of living.
Nothing new will we find ready made.
The Gospel message is always timely and surprising,
so divine, that it converts and mobilises us.
It challenges us like the wise one from Nazareth.
Take heart! The greatest disaster is to live a wasted life.

# 5. CONCLUDING RITE

## Resolution
To pray that we may transmit what has earlier been the subject of our prayers: nobody gives what he does not possess.

## Blessing

## Conclusion
The religious experience always awakens hopes and expectations, but this will not stop us from encountering problems and periods of darkness. What is important about faith, is that it makes us stand on our own feet and gives us the courage to face the meaning of life realistically. It is very important to nurture the Christian experience. Thanks to it, our level of aspiration is raised.

## Final Hymn and Dismissal

# Third Sunday of Lent

## 1. SETTING THE SCENE

### In addition to the symbols for the whole of Lent:

- Jug or other suitable receptacle, with the following text on its exterior: "Give me a drink".

## 2. INTRODUCTORY RITES

### Introduction

Welcome, brothers and sisters, to this celebration. We who gather together, through the impulse of faith, are conscious of our goodness, but also of our sin. The good news that always flows from God's revelation is that he loves us, and this should influence us, so that we do not harden our hearts.

On the journey through Lent, we are frequently invited to be converted. This has to be demonstrated, by being put into daily practice. Just as we are preoccupied with efficiency, in different aspects of life, we should analyse if we behave in the manner that God and others expect of us.

### Hymn

### Greeting

Brothers and sisters, let us praise the Lord together, who invites us to open our hearts to him and to worship him in spirit and in truth.

### Penitential Rite

- Because we have not been faithful to our conscience, *Lord, have mercy.*
- Because we have not always followed the promptings of the Spirit, *Christ, have mercy.*
- Because sometimes we have spurned the water of life, *Lord, have mercy.*

### Prayer

God, our bountiful Father, in Jesus, you have appeared among us.
In him, we find the Way and the Covenant so that we can live joyfully in communion with you.
We praise your concern and your efforts for us to be able to experience you as Abba.
In the lap of our mother Church, we give you thanks for the experience of Christian life, and we bless you for gatherings of faith and salvation.
Strengthen us in our desire to be the living Gospel so that we may know how to communicate the experience of Christian people. Amen.

## 3. LITURGY OF THE WORD

### Introduction to the Readings

Often, when faced with the hardships and reverses that we suffer in life, we ask ourselves if God is on our side. This happened to the people of old, in their journey towards liberation.

Jesus also experienced different kinds of hardship. The Gospel today reveals him to us sitting down, tired, asking help from a Samaritan woman: Give me a drink. This page in the Gospel is beautiful, meaningful and full of significance. It tells of a meeting with the Saviour, full of nuances and questions relating to conversion.

### Readings

Exod. 17:3-7. *Psalm*. Rom. 5:1-2. 5-8. *Acclamation*. Jn 4:5-42. *Brief silence.*

## Reflection

In his meeting with the Samaritan woman and, later, with his apostles, there is a rich dialogue, with a variety of revealing implications. Although he is tired from his journey and in need of food and drink, Jesus makes it clear that for him, there are some fundamental values that rank above any other requirement.

Jesus, with his habit of breaking certain conventions that were senseless or contrary to reason, achieves a profound communication with that woman who, quite apart from not having a very savoury reputation, belonged to a rival nation. He converses with her, in a human way, without attaching apparent importance to her moral state, bringing out the best in her, not bringing out her negative points, but encouraging her positive side, making her see that it is not only in the temple that we worship God, but everywhere, in such a way that we live in the Spirit and the Truth.

Let us notice Jesus' capacity to penetrate deeply into people's hearts and to help them change from within. That woman, who came with a pitcher to draw water, finally has it in abundance. And in the end, she comes to understand the language of Jesus, accepts it and finally announces joyfully the transformation that he has produced in her being: from having gone through life in a great void and without any moral equilibrium, she comes to feel a spring of living water rising up from within her, which revitalises and inspires her until she is full to overflowing. The Samaritan woman ends up becoming a missionary. (*Silence for internal reflection.*)

## Creed

## Prayer of the Faithful

- For the universal Church, that it may not cease to present, throughout the world, the image of an understanding God who is close to us, *let us pray to the Lord.*
- For governors, educators and all those who have any social responsibility, that they may promote a culture in the service of human dignity, *let us pray to the Lord.*
- That the faith may drive us increasingly towards commitment of life, *let us pray to the Lord.*
- That we may know how to respond to the questioning and doubts of those who are asking from the depths of their hearts, *let us pray to the Lord.*
- For all of us, that we may continue being committed to personal and community renewal, *let us pray to the Lord.*

## Symbolic Representation

*Some lighted candles are handed out and circulated, while each person says to the other:* The faith urges us to be witnesses.

## 4. RITE OF COMMUNION

## Introduction

Meeting with Jesus strengthens our lives. An intense and frequent meeting is that of Holy Communion. Let us profit from it today, so that we may live in truth and with authenticity.

## Hymn

## Prayer

We bless you, God, for our meeting with you,
because you bring us closer to the truth and you
set us on the right path by means of your Spirit.
Many laugh at us because we still believe
and because we preach the purposes of the Gospel.
But we praise you, Father,
because you have encouraged us in Jesus,
who inspires us to be witnesses,
like the Samaritan woman,
among the people of our town.
Aware of and grateful for the gifts we have received
we say to you in brotherly communion: Our Father…

## Sign of Peace

## Distribution of Communion: Hymn

## Act of Thanksgiving

- We give you thanks, good Father, because we have shared in this religious assembly that strengthens our community.
- We give you thanks for the experiences that give us strength on our daily path.
- We bless you for our meeting with you and with Jesus in the Spirit.

## 5. CONCLUDING RITE

### Resolution

To strengthen with deeds, signs and words, our missionary message and Gospel witness.

### Blessing

### Conclusion

As we finish, let us remember the teaching on conversion that the Gospel story wished to leave us with. God is understanding and patient. If he has created us with the ability to be creative in different areas of life, it should also be evident in the realm of Christian witness. A Christian has to go through life spreading a good example and the Gospel, like Jesus, bringing all his energy and passion into play, in order to improve this world. May the Lord be with us.

### Final Hymn and Dismissal

# Fourth Sunday of Lent

## 1. SETTING THE SCENE

### Poster with one of these texts:
- "Jesus enlightens us"
- "Jesus wishes us to see"

### In addition to the symbols for the whole of Lent:
- Receptacle with water and a little towel.
- Dish with clay.
- Sunglasses.

## 2. INTRODUCTORY RITES

### Introduction
We have come together, once more, because we have a similar personal and community motivation: we are motivated by our religious beliefs, our faith and membership of this Christian community.

The powerful message of today is expressed in the contrast of light and darkness. The symbolism of light is frequent in biblical literature. Faith brings light. Without faith, we can go through life as if in darkness. The Gospel, also, reveals more: perhaps we need God to cure us of a certain blindness, so that we may know how to get to the heart of the mystery of life and to see others clearly.

### Hymn

### Greeting
Brothers and sisters, let us praise the Lord together, who has called us to lead a life of vibrant faith.

### Penitential Rite
- Because you are the Light of the World, *Lord, have mercy.*
- Because we have often been unwilling to see, *Christ, have mercy.*
- Because we are blinded by sin, *Lord, have mercy.*

### Prayer
God, bountiful Father, who has given us life and enriched it with the faith of baptism, preserve in us our youth and strength of spirit, so that we may go forward as worthy sons and daughters of light, and so build your Kingdom, in communion with all, sons and daughters in common commitment. Through Christ…

## 3. LITURGY OF THE WORD

### Introduction to the Readings
To walk as *sons and daughters of light* is the logical thing for all Christians and all people of good will. But this requires looking not only with our eyes, but, above all, from within our hearts. The message of the readings stresses the illuminating significance of the faith.

### Readings
1 Sam. 16:1b. 6-7. 10-13a. *Psalm.* Eph. 5:8-14. *Acclamation.* Jn 9:1-41. *Brief silence.*

### Reflection
We have surely heard, more than once, statements charged with wisdom, such as these: *What is essential can only be seen with the heart; there is no one more blind than he who does not wish to see…* In that vein, the first reading, encapsulating biblical wisdom, advises us: do not dwell on appearances;

do not be deceived by external appearances. "The eyes of God are not the eyes of man, because man looks at appearances, but the Lord looks into the heart." Perhaps because of this, God loves us unceasingly. Because he knows that, deep within each human heart, some good sentiments and noble aspirations are to be found. Nobody is so perverse, or so obstinate, as to shut himself away completely from the light.

Nevertheless, the darkness of evil example and deceit are always there, as a risk and a threat. Even we ourselves have possibly been a stumbling block to others. The author of the letter to the Ephesians exhorts us: "Once you were darkness, but now you are light in the Lord". Therefore, seek what pleases him, denounce what displeases him and choose what strengthens human dignity. This is the dynamic of baptism that the gospel text symbolises. The gift of God begins with "open your eyes", in order to clear your mind and become balanced emotionally. If anyone with a bad conscience is not open to the Gospel, he will stumble through life like a blind man, because he keeps his mind and heart in darkness. (*Silence for internal reflection.*)

## Creed

## Prayer of the Faithful
- Let us pray, brothers and sisters, to God the Father, for all those who seek him, that they may be enlightened by the light of faith.
- Let us pray for all those who are blinded by the problems of life and fail to see the mercy of God.
- We pray for the intention of the Church, that it may become purified and be a shining symbol to the world.
- Let us pray also for the Christians of our community, that we may cleanse our hearts and be able to see ourselves with clear and penetrating eyes.
- Let us pray for each other, that our eyes may

always be a clear mirror, reflecting a worthy and honourable soul.
- For these and all our intentions, *let us pray to the Lord.*

## Offerings
- *Paschal candle alight and small lighted tapers around:* Father, receive our baptismal commitment to follow Jesus as sons and daughters of light.
- *Mask that is burnt in the flame of the Candle:* Lord, you do not look at outward appearances, but into our hearts; accept our resolve to invite the spirituality of the Gospel into our hearts.

## Hymn

## Symbolic Representation
*Someone stands up in sunglasses. He goes up to the receptacle with water in it, washes his eyes, dries them and returns to his place without the glasses that he was wearing.*

## 4. RITE OF COMMUNION

## Introduction
Let us feed ourselves on *the bread of life.* Jesus offered himself to us as nourishment. Communion with Jesus helps us to see into the heart of things and to be *sons and daughters of light.*

## Hymn

## Prayer

We bless you, Father, because you remain by our side
favouring us, with the light of your Spirit,
so that we may not wander from the path of life.
We praise you because you have planted in our history
a human example, brimming with clarity and
charged with reason.
Jesus, a flash of your light,
reveals to us the mystery and meaning of life.
His way of being and talking carries so much
evidence and conviction
that it has brought in the era of Man made new.
In him, there shines a new and complete solidarity.
Driven on by his example, we lift up our hearts
and say to you with one voice: Our Father…

## Sign of Peace

## Distribution of Communion: Hymn

## Act of Thanksgiving (*spontaneous*)

## 5. CONCLUDING RITE

### Resolution

To walk as sons and daughters of light.

### Blessing

### Conclusion

The light of Christ has appeared upon our way. His
person is an example with everlasting appeal. He
spent his time doing good. And this is how God has
envisaged that our lives can be.

May we grasp what we have celebrated in its very
depths and may the Lord help us during the week,
to assimilate what has most touched our hearts.

### Final Hymn and Dismissal

# Fifth Sunday of Lent

## 1. SETTING THE SCENE

### Poster with one of these texts:
- "Without the Spirit, what is left for us?"
- "The Spirit brings life"
- "Christ helps us to live"

### In addition to the symbols for the whole of Lent:
- Brazier with earth and, in the middle, a receptacle with flammable spirit.

## 2. INTRODUCTORY RITES

### Introduction
As we journey through Lent, we become increasingly aware that Jesus can transform our lives radically with his Word and his actions.

This conversion, that we speak of so much, is a life-giving renewal which can happen, if we live with the breath of the Spirit. Jesus helped many people. Deep down, his overriding concern is for people to live, but to live in the Spirit, with the greatest sensitivity. That is how to find meaning in the present and beyond death. The Gospel of the resurrection of Lazarus gives us an indication today of what Jesus wants.

### Hymn

### Greeting
Brothers and sisters, let us bless the Lord, who inspires us to raise up our lives.

### Penitential Rite.
- You, who desire our conversion:
  *Lord, have mercy.*
- You, who raise up our moral being:
  *Christ, have mercy.*
- You, who nourish our wish to live:
  *Lord, have mercy.*

### Prayer
We pray to you, Lord God, that your grace may help us, so that we may always live in that same love that moved your Son to deliver himself up to death, for the salvation of the world. Through Christ…

## 3. LITURGY OF THE WORD

### Introduction to the Readings
What we are going to listen to in the readings should resonate powerfully in our spirit, so often timid and withdrawn. When we find ourselves in a powerless or depressed state, sad or disenchanted, sunk low or embittered, our spirits must be raised by affirmations such as "I am the resurrection and the life", "I will fill you with my spirit and you will live". Today's readings bring consolation, encouragement and transcendence.

### Readings
Ezek. 37:12-14. *Psalm.* Rom. 8:8-11. *Acclamation.* Jn 11:1-45. *Brief silence.*

### Symbolic Representation
*When the words "Lazarus, come out", are proclaimed in the Gospel, an adult, wrapped up in sheets, is presented to the assembly. His sheets are unfastened and taken off; he himself lights the flammable spirit of the brazier.*

## Reflection

Spirituality is a natural condition in people's lives; it affects our health and has a lot to do with improving our surroundings. There is nothing better than being spiritual, if one is to be profoundly happy. If human beings are spiritual by nature, it means that living from a divine perspective is essential for life and inspiration. Without the Spirit, human existence lacks something special that uplifts it and endows it with great capacity.

In this way, human beings have a spiritual calling. Deep down in every person lies this necessity. It is an exciting dimension, that compromises and complicates, but that also improves our quality of life. If we listen to the Spirit, we live. If we ignore it, we deteriorate.

One does not reach maturity, if one *allows oneself to be borne along by the flesh.* It is true that we live our spirituality under the threat of licentiousness. But someone is truly mature when they are docile to the Spirit, when they persevere in the conversion of their mind and heart, when they have a radical commitment to God and to the world, that is to say, when their life overflows with charity.

In the Church, we will always have, in Jesus, a reference point for true spirituality. He was supremely spiritual, he allowed himself to be led by the Spirit. Conquering the weakness of his own flesh, he became the Redeemer of the frailties in others. This was possible through the death and resurrection experience that his whole life was marked with. Because of this, it is appropriate and healthy to bring our spirituality face to face with that of Jesus. He did not live it only within, but expressed it in the street, it impelled him towards a missionary and social commitment. (*Silence for internal reflection.*)

## Creed

## Prayer of the Faithful

- That respect and service for life may grow in the world, *let us pray to the Lord.*
- For all believers, that we may foster a pure and spiritual demeanour that corresponds with the Gospel, *let us pray to the Lord.*
- That solidarity and development among the people of our town may be furthered, *let us pray to the Lord.*
- For those who have a social responsibility, that they may understand their service as a commitment on behalf of those who need it most, *let us pray to the Lord.*
- For all of us and for our intentions, *let us pray to the Lord.*

## Offerings

- *Plant in a poor state, but with one vigorous part or shoot:* Father, we are sinful flesh, but also spirit, and we wish to live.
- *Some identity cards on a tray:* Lord, we offer you ourselves, with the intention that our whole being may be pleasing to you.

## 4. RITE OF COMMUNION

## Introduction

Jesus is the living bread come down from heaven. Whosoever eats of this bread shall live for ever. He is the life of the world. Let us receive Jesus with gratitude.

## Hymn

## Prayer

With our eyes uplifted and our hearts eager
to do your will we praise you, Father.
And linked by the faith to those who have gone before us,
we recognise that the saviour you gave to us is

following on foot.
We hear the call of life from the four corners
of the earth.
We know that you have opened all the tombs
and that your plan to restore life is unchangeable.
Blessed are you, Father, for the plentiful
redemption that you have spread abroad,
so that the balance of history may not be broken.
Blessed are you for that Spirit infused within us,
so that our souls may be kept in expectation.
We thank you for the constructive impulses that
you inspire us with.
Heartened by the generous and
life-giving example of Jesus,
we say to you: Our Father…

## Sign of Peace

## Distribution of Communion: Hymn

## Act of Thanksgiving
- ■ We give you thanks, Father, because you have taught us to appreciate the message of Jesus and to live with the flow of the Spirit.
- ■ We thank you that you bless us with the incomparable gift of the Spirit, that helps us to avoid so many pitfalls and to rise up from so many graves.
- ■ Because you always give us a fresh opportunity, we thank you for that "time of grace" which began in Jesus, and we promise you that we will walk in the way of the just who follow in the path of the Spirit.

## 5. CONCLUDING RITE

## Commitment
To raise up our lives within ourselves and around us, combining mercy and solidarity.

## Blessing

## Conclusion
The tears that Jesus shed for the death of his friend Lazarus reveal his sensitivity. Jesus is moved by human suffering, he is sensitive to its very depths. But, besides weeping, Jesus revived Lazarus: he raised him from the grave. Today, also, he can raise us from many graves: routine, vulgarity, despair, fear, sadness, selfishness… To live and to help others to live, is the most beautiful and exemplary thing that we can do.

## Final Hymn and Dismissal

# Palm Sunday

## 1. SETTING THE SCENE

### Poster with one of these texts:
- ■ "Jesus is Lord"
- ■ "Jesus, the triumphant martyr"

### Symbol:
- ■ Cross with a laurel crown.

## 2. INTRODUCTORY RITES

### Introduction
With the liturgy of Palm Sunday, we begin the greatest week of the whole year, what we call Holy Week. This week is great and holy, because we remember and celebrate very important facts about the faithful and devoted life of Jesus. During these days, we can relive with admiration his standing in faith and commitment until the end.

The setting for everything that we are going to consider was Jerusalem, the capital to which Jesus was drawn, in order to show his face before the authorities and throw out the riff-raff for God's cause. Today, among other things, we are going to consider the two faces of people: on the one hand, they acclaim Jesus and applaud him; but soon, on the other hand, the same people are rejecting him and crying for his death.

As for us, let us place ourselves, as Holy Week begins, as believers, not as spectators. These are days full of action and charged with meaning, in our present time as well.

## Commemoration of our Lord's entry into Jerusalem
If it is judged fitting, this rite may be performed outside the place of worship, in order to make an entrance in procession with palms. In this case, the above introduction is made, once the assembly is gathered. The rite includes prayer, proclamation of the Gospel and the procession entering with palms:

### Prayer
Lord, increase the faith of those who wait for you, and listen to the prayers of those who attend you, so that those of us today, who raise our palms in honour of Christ, may remain steadfast with him, bearing fruit in abundance. Through Christ…

### Gospel
Mt. 21:1-11

### Processional Entrance: Hymn

### Prayer
God, bountiful Father, who in the person of Christ have given us an supreme example of sensitivity, painful sacrifice and dignity, help us in our life to follow in the steps of so many believers who dedicated themselves to your Kingdom, growing day by day as witnesses of the Gospel. Through Christ…

## 3. LITURGY OF THE WORD

### Introduction to the Readings
The first reading tells us of the Servant of Yahweh, that symbolic personage, obedient to God, with a prophetic mission, who suffers for the people and in place of the people.

Jesus is the authentic Servant of Yahweh. Without holding on to his divine rank, he took on a simple way of life, obedient and suffering unto death and death on the cross. For having lived like this, for the benefit of the people, we recognise him today as Lord of history.

## Readings

Is. 50:4-7. *Psalm.* Phil. 2:6-11. *Acclamation.* Mt. 26:14-27.66 (*It can be proclaimed by three people*). *Brief silence.*

## Reflection

This Sunday is the beginning of Holy Week, which embodies signs and symbols of great Christian significance. It is a week for meditation and direct encounter with Christ. It leads towards Easter.

This Sunday's message recalls a paradox suffered by Jesus: first he is acclaimed and applauded, and afterwards, he is rejected. The people recognise the prophetic and human quality of Jesus: he had taught with authority and had helped many; but he also criticised and declared truths that displease them, especially the most influential of them. These succeeded in stirring up the people. For this reason, it is also the Sunday of suffering. Sometimes, among any community, this two-faced behaviour and attitude come to the forefront.

In communion with the experience of the letter to the Philippians, every believer must truly and rightly applaud the Servant Jesus, who, through being faithful unto death, even death on the cross, is also Lord of heaven and earth. The supreme sacrifice, not turning his back on suffering, although unjust, is a good example for us to focus on, at the beginning of this great week. In Jesus, we find a school of humanity that today also is paradoxical. What use is it to gain the whole world, if we ruin our lives? Today, like yesterday, to be a Christian is to fulfil the memory of Jesus. For this reason, Holy Week is a unique occasion for us to

deepen our experience of the profundity of the love of God, which passes through the depths of pain. (*Silence for internal reflection.*)

## Creed

## Prayer of the Faithful

- For the Church, that it may be generous and faithful to the last, like Jesus, *let us pray to the Lord.*
- That there may be no abuse of power and that human rights may be respected among nations, *let us pray to the Lord.*
- That we may confront everything around us that enslaves people, *let us pray to the Lord.*
- For those who suffer, that they may not fall into despair, *let us pray to the Lord.*
- That we Christians may celebrate these days that we call holy in a holy way, *let us pray to the Lord.*

## Offerings

- *Laurel branch:* We offer you, Lord, this branch, professing that in Jesus lie the meaning and purpose of life.
- *Gospel:* We present to you, once more, the Gospel of Jesus, because it always represents a challenging and wholesome alternative.

## 4. RITE OF COMMUNION

## Introduction

Jesus invites us to live in a Gospel frame of mind. His whole person is an example and nourishment for our spirituality. Let us share in Holy Communion, in order to live like Jesus.

## Hymn

## Prayer

Blessed are you, God our Father,
who in your exceeding mercy
have loved us passionately in Jesus Christ, who was
made lowly and stripped bare in his obedience to you.
Yes, Father, blessed are you for the human lesson
that you have left us in the Redeemer of history.
Recognised and applauded by some,
beaten and struck down by others,
he experienced, to the full, the wrongs of injustice.
He, who had uplifted the hearts of so many,
tasted the dust of shame
and suffered rejection by those said to be religious.
But whosoever trusted completely in you
could not remain confounded.
Because you never went back on your word, you
raised him from the tomb
and lifted him on high.
conferring on him a name-above-all-names,
proud of his chosen path.
Father, we bend the knee, in wonder and joy,
and we proclaim that Jesus is our Lord, to your
great glory,
the supreme example of liberation through love.
Joining in his triumph and sharing the great vision
that he leaves us,
we say to you in gratitude: Our Father…

## Sign of Peace

## Distribution of Communion: Hymn

## Act of Thanksgiving

God, good Father, we give you thanks
for the spirituality that we have shared.
We are here for you, with our hearts open to Easter.
We are here, ready to shine forth the light of the Gospel.
Grateful for your redeeming mercy,
we return to our lives with the power of witnesses.
Come with us into the street, to our work,
into our family life, places of recreation…
All our plans seek the same objective:
your Kingdom and your will.

## 5. CONCLUDING RITE

## Commitment

To live the lessons of Holy Week fervently.

## Blessing

## Conclusion

We recognise that Jesus is Lord, for the glory of
God and for our dignity. We emphasise that Jesus'
victory comes through obedience and suffering.
Lessons of love and suffering have now been
learned, so that, throughout this week, wherever
we might be, we may deepen our experience of
Christ's way of life. It is an especially significant
week, because it gives us the most outstanding
example of Jesus.

## Final Hymn and Dismissal

# The
# EASTER TRIDUUM

# Holy Thursday

## 1. SETTING THE SCENE

### Poster with one of these texts:
- "Love never passes away"
- "He loved us to the end"

### Symbols:
- Table with household tablecloth, loaf of bread and large glass or jug of wine.
- Chairs around the table.
- On another table, a wash-basin, a large pitcher of water and a towel.

## 2. INTRODUCTORY RITES

### Introduction
Holy Thursday speaks of love, sacrifice, selfless and humble service, communion, solidarity… values that we appreciate.

Today, we give special consideration to the fact that God is love; in Jesus, he has loved us to the end. Just as Jesus is overflowing with feelings, signs and words, so may we learn to love each other, according to the example and witness that he left us. Today, a day of brotherly love, we remember Jesus' instruction to us: "Love one another as I have loved you."

### Hymn

### Greeting
Brothers and sisters, let us bless the Lord, who loves us with boundless love.

### Penitential Rite
- Lord, you are our faithful Friend: *Lord, have mercy.*
- Lord, you are the Servant of all: *Christ, have mercy.*
- Lord, you are our Master teaching us by your example: *Lord, have mercy.*

### Gloria

### Prayer
Lord, our God, you have called us together today to celebrate that memorable supper in which your Son, before giving himself up to death, entrusted the Church with the banquet of his love, the new sacrifice of the eternal covenant; we pray to you that the celebration of these holy mysteries may bring us to the fullness of love and life. Through Christ…

## 3. LITURGY OF THE WORD

### Introduction to the Readings
The readings on this day show the decisive influence that the Jewish Passover, like the Christian Passover, has had throughout history. They were memorable events, which we cannot forget because of the great significance that they have had and continue to have. The Gospel recalls the amazing scene of Jesus washing the feet of his disciples. It was a revealing and exemplary action. If Jesus, the Master, humbles himself to the extent of washing their feet, it is because a very important value is at stake. As followers of Jesus, we must serve and help in a similar manner.

### Readings
Exod. 12:1-8.11-14. *Psalm.* 1 Cor. 11:23-26. *Acclamation.* Jn 13:1-15. *Brief silence.*

## Reflection

The biblical and theological significance of this day are very thought-provoking. Jesus was keen to celebrate the Passover with his disciples. The feast of the Passover was very important for Jews. It was the commemoration of God's act of salvation, in liberating the people from the oppression of Egypt. But Jesus gives it a new meaning, its proper meaning. At that supper, he opened his heart, speaking with the deepest warmth. He spoke much of the Father. He described himself as the Way, the Truth and the Life. He washed the feet of his disciples, expressing, in this symbolic act, the teaching that distinguished him. He delivered a testament to love: "Love one another as I have loved you." In what was the first Eucharist, he celebrated his sacrifice in a sacramental manner and recommended to his disciples of all times: "Do this in remembrance of me." Offering oneself up, even unto death, is the hallmark of Christians and the new form of worship of the Church.

But on this day, we recall something further. After having supper, Jesus went out with his friends to take a stroll. He went straight into the countryside, because he was very keen to pray. In the middle of a garden, he began to pray so intensely, that he trembled before the death that loomed ahead of him and he reached a point where he began to sweat blood. His friends were not able to pray with him; they had fallen asleep. At that point, armed men arrived and arrested him. His friends fled in fright… (*Silence for internal reflection.*)

## Symbolic Action:
## The Washing of Feet

## Prayer of the Faithful

- That enmity between all human beings may be overcome, *let us pray to the Lord.*
- That we Christians may live in solidarity with one another, like Jesus, *let us pray to the Lord.*
- That nobody may feel alone or abandoned in our town, thanks to everyone's help and the sharing of resources, *let us pray to the Lord.*
- That great store may be placed by all of us upon the value of service, *let us pray to the Lord.*

## Offerings

- *Small tray with wedding rings on it:* We renew before you, Lord, our commitment to love, as spouses and parents.
- *Daily utensils of service:* We offer you, Lord, these instruments of service. May our efforts become redoubled, thanks to the faith.
- *Book of Charity, action programmes for the town:* We present to you, Lord, some signs of love for our town.

## 4. RITE OF COMMUNION

### Introduction

God is love. Jesus leaves us the instruction, as a summary of his whole life, that we should love as he does. Let us share in this, obeying Jesus' words: "Do this in memory of me."

### Hymn

### Prayer

With men and women of good will,
who represent the new way of brotherhood,
service and communion,
we praise you, Father, on this Holy Thursday.
The example of so many witnesses who love even unto sacrifice,
within and outside the Church,
is an incentive for us who celebrate Jesus.
He, the Master, who even washes the feet of others,
the Servant, ready even to give up his own life,
the Priest of the new covenant,
because he transforms life into worship
and the rite of love into sacrament,
leaves us an example, so that we may live with quality and passion.

**Eucharistic Services for Sundays & Feast Days**

He truly lived for others and loved us to the end.
He bore witness that genuine love
is often transformed into sacrifice,
always into giving and generosity without limit.
May we receive, Father, the great example of Jesus
and, united in his memory, we say to you:
Our Father…

## Sign of Peace

## Distribution of Communion: Hymn

## Act of Thanksgiving
(*personal and in silence*)

## 5. CONCLUDING RITE

## Resolution
To bring about reconciliation if enmity exists
between us. To increase our capacity for love
and service.

## The Blessed Sacrament is transferred to the Altar of Repose: Hymn

## Prayer before the Altar
"Lord, make me an instrument of your peace.
So that where there is hate, may I bring love;
where there is offence, may I bring forgiveness;
where there is discord, may I bring unity;
where there is doubt, may I bring faith;
where there is error, may I bring truth;
where there is despair, may I bring hope ;
where there is sadness, may I bring joy;
where there is darkness, may I bring light.
Good Father, make us seek not so much
to be consoled, as to console;
not so much to be understood, as to understand;
not so much to be loved, as to love.
For it is in giving that we receive,
in pardoning that we are pardoned
and in dying

that we are born to eternal life."
(Francis of Assisi)

*Silent exit, for the benefit of the quiet recollection of those who wish to remain in prayer.*

# Good Friday

## 1. SETTING THE SCENE

### Poster with one of these texts:
- "He loved us to the end"
- "Into your hands, Lord, I commit my spirit"

### Symbols:
- Christ on the cross.
- Posters of various martyrs.

## 2. INTRODUCTORY RITES

### Introduction
Before Christ, death was something full of mystery, fear, doubts. It was a parting… With Jesus, death was transformed into life, with the promise of resurrection. Just as God the Father cannot allow eternal death in his incarnate Son, neither can he contemplate it for ourselves, who are also his children.

Jesus will be human until the end and he will convert the death of parting, into the death of meeting, the beginning of true life in God for ever after. He dies like us, so that with his death, he may sow the seed of the promise of eternal life, which our Father offers us, in accordance with redemption. Jesus' message on Good Friday is: I die for you, so that you may live again with me. *Brief silence for personal prayer.*

### Prayer
God, Holy Father, who through the Passion of Christ, our Lord, have destroyed death, the consequence of original sin, that comes to all of us; we pray that you may make us like to your Son; so that we, who are, by our human nature, the image of Adam, the man of the earth, may become through the action of your grace, the image of Jesus Christ, the heavenly man. Through Christ…

## 3. LITURGY OF THE WORD

### Introduction to the Readings
The ravages suffered by Jesus, his anguish and faithfulness, are frequently associated with the image of "the Servant of Yahweh". Here is a figure from the Old Testament, who is the incarnation of all human suffering. But it is a suffering that redeems, because it is taken on by someone innocent, who trusts in the victory of God.

The second reading presents Jesus as an authentic New Testament priest. And Jesus' priesthood was not a privilege, but a vocation of obedience and sacrifice.

In the account of the Passion and death of Jesus, we contemplate one who fulfils all his promises to the very end. He died in a violent way, because he would not go back on his word that he was the Prophet of the Kingdom of God.

### Readings
Is. 52:13-53:12. *Psalm*. Heb. 4:14-16; 5:7-9. Acclamation. Jn 18:1-19:42 (*it can be proclaimed by three people*). *Brief silence.*

### Reflection
Why did Jesus die unjustly and in such a violent way on the cross? Why did they repay him with evil, when he had loved so greatly, bringing salvation? Does sorrow have so much meaning? Is our salvation really in the cross?

Jesus left us many teachings and an impressive example of the path that we must follow.

Today, all its meaning is captured in the sign of the redeeming crucifixion. The cross and the Crucified One are a great symbol for Christians, a symbol that for some is mad, for others a foolish thing, while for true believers, it is the power and wisdom of God (cf. 1 Cor. 1:18-24).

The martyrdom of Jesus was the logical result of his commitment, the culmination of a process of constant attacks on him. He, out of honour and faith, had to break barriers: he received sinners and ate with them; he received prostitutes, lepers…; he criticised the way worship was thought of, the business dealings at the temple…; he presented himself as the witness and Son of God Abba; he spoke the truth with absolute sincerity… Jesus hinted that with his way of acting, he was *inviting* martyrdom. He kept going, in awareness and freedom: I have to go up to Jerusalem, he said, although there, the Son of Man will be condemned to death (cf. Mt. 16:21); but "no one will take my life from me; I will give it of my own free will" (Jn 10:18). "If a grain of wheat does not fall to the ground and die, it remains alone; but if it dies, it bears much fruit" (Jn 12:24). And Jesus died forgiving his enemies …

To be like Jesus is not popular. Many people wear a cross on their breast, but it may, perhaps, be more of an adornment than a Christian symbol of the crucified Redeemer. Sometimes it seems that, within the Church, also, the cross is unpopular, which is a great scandal and a very bad example, because there can be no following of Jesus, without the cross (Mt. 16:24). The rejection of the cross is an obstacle to understanding Jesus and his Gospel. Neither is it possible to build the Kingdom of God, without accepting the cross.

And one final point. Mary, the co-redeemer, said to God in her youth: "Let it be done in me, according to your word" (Lk 1:38). Now, in the terrible dying moments of her son, she maintains her attitude of prayer that she has kept throughout her life: "Let it be done, Lord". And there she is, beside the cross, faithfully fulfilling her role and confirming her "amen" as a believer. (*Silence for internal reflection.*)

## 4. UNIVERSAL PRAYER
### (*according to the Missal*)

## 5. ADORATION OF THE CROSS

### Introduction
On one day in the year, at Christmas, we worship the Child Jesus, in the joy of his birth, the promise of salvation. Now we are going to worship him on the cross, in the suffering that redeems us, with gratitude and veneration.

Let us share in the meaning of his self-giving. Look, we are not alone in our duty of bearing the cross each day. He has gone before us, as a guarantee that no suffering is pointless.

He who is crucified will be revealed to us and we will be invited to contemplate him, that is to say, to penetrate the mystery that he embodies: There is no greater love than to give one's life… The cross is uncovered.

### Symbolic Action
Contemplating the cross and worship.

## 6. RITE OF COMMUNION

### Introduction
Jesus sacrificed himself completely. He gave his life freely for us. Let us unite ourselves with Jesus, so that we may live with him in faithfulness and commitment.

### Hymn

## Prayer

Blessed are you, Father, for Jesus Christ the Redeemer, brought down because of love, baptised in blood, because he made a liturgy of his life that always pleased you.

His devotion unto martyrdom culminated in him being laid bare, stripped of everything, apparently powerless, misunderstood, rejected, abandoned, even by his own.

In his crucifixion, he leaves one last lesson: true power does not reside in strength but in the *weakness* of love, which is loyal and sacrificing to the very end.

We confess, Father, that his roots have remained in history and they have grown again thanks to the Spirit. The rebel Redeemer has descended into the abyss and he has roused those who were sleeping the sleep of death.

He has awakened them with authority and said to them: Rise up! I am the life of those who are dead.

Yes, Father, nothing of yours dies.

We know that hopes which take hold on earth have influence and life for ever.

Blessed are you, because you save us from apparent disaster, because you conquer in a powerless way and because you bring life out of death.

In communion with all who are redeemed, we praise you: Our Father…

## Distribution of Communion: Hymn

## Act of Thanksgiving

- Thank you, Father, for Jesus the Redeemer, because he gave up his life as an expiation for our sins.
- Thank you, because both the incarnation of your Son and the redemption are *foolish things* that only have one explanation: love.
- Thank you also, because the redemption is an offering of love and you call us to receive it in freedom.

- You look on us and you forgive us, in the compassionate actions of Jesus. May your blessing descend in abundance upon this community and upon this town; may your mercy descend upon us and may you guide us towards salvation.

## 7. CONCLUDING RITE

### Resolution

To live in awareness and with the exemplary life of the redeemed.

### Blessing

May the Lord bless this community, who have celebrated the death of his Son, in the hope of his sacred resurrection; may his forgiveness and consolation come down upon us. Through Christ…

### Conclusion

We began this celebration in silence; in the same way, we conclude it in silence. Let us meditate on the mystery of our redemption, considering the changes that must take place within us, so that we may confirm in the Easter Vigil that we want to live as new creatures in Christ.

### Exit in silence

# Holy Saturday: Easter Vigil

## 1. SETTING THE SCENE

### Poster with one of these texts:
- "Alleluia! He is risen"
- "Easter means to raise up our lives"
- "Easter means to be raised with Christ"
- "He is living among us"

### Church arranged and decorated

### Symbols:
- Paschal candle-stand adorned.
- Baptismal font adorned.

Pastries and drinks for a reception at the end in church, outside or in the parish hall.

### Opening address
Brothers and sisters, the resurrection of Jesus is the central event of our faith. Christ has conquered death, that is to say, evil, hatred, injustice, disunity, sin.

This celebration, the most important of the year, unfolds in four parts: the Service of Light, the Liturgy of the Word, the Liturgy of Baptism and the Rite of Communion. We bring together in this celebration our deepest Christian feelings.

## 2. SERVICE OF LIGHT
*(It takes place outside the place of worship. The church remains in darkness. Wood is prepared for the fire and a piece of wood with nails in it, for the symbolic action.)*

### Introduction
With the Service of Light, we are going to reaffirm our commitment: we evoke symbolically our desire and our promise to leave behind what is negative in ourselves, in order to live in the way that Jesus teaches. We start with a symbolic act, with which we begin our *Easter journey*: the stripping away of our faults, so that we may re-clothe ourselves with the spiritual quality of people made new.

*The fire is lit.*

### Prayer
May the Lord bless this fire and kindle within us so great a desire for heaven, that we may be able to come with a clean heart to the feast of Eternal Light. Through Christ…

### Symbolic Action
*Slips of paper are nailed to the piece of wood with the faults written on them that we wish to burn in the fire of renewal.*

*The paschal candle is lit from the fire. The minister says:*
May the light of Christ, that brings us gloriously to life, dispel the darkness of our heart and spirit.
*The others light their tapers directly from the candle or from each other's.*

*Entrance procession led by the paschal candle.*
*The lights of the church are put on.*

### Easter Proclamation
Awake, brothers and sisters!
Enjoy the presence of the Light!
Immerse yourself in a symphony of pure fresh air!
The resounding greatness of God is speaking to you.
Life kisses your forehead with its lips.
Live, love, share! Feel loved, brothers and sisters!
Touch the veins of the earth with your roots.
Grasp time and history.

March like a torrent, full of strength and vitality.
The Light of God is a challenge of new life,
of great hope,
of the Spirit radiated by the rebel from Nazareth.
He says to you: "I am".
I am the day, I am the Light.
I understand neither shadow nor darkness.
Because of this I have duties for the morrow,
springtime labours,
an undertaking of constant renewal.
Behold him, brothers and sisters!
Look how he approaches.
Open all your windows,
break down your doors,
smash down walls,
illuminate every corner,
feel full of goodness:
you have many battles to win,
many shadows to drive away…
You also have to fulfil your obligation to the Light.
The streets, the houses, the people are waiting for you…
It is an urgent matter, brothers and sisters!
You will have to give of yourself until all becomes
fresh and clear,
until all is resurrection
and the Promised Land is everywhere.

*The candles are put out.*

## 3. LITURGY OF THE WORD

### Introduction to the Readings
With the solemn proclamation of Easter, we have already entered the holy night of the resurrection of the Lord. By the light of the new paschal candle, we are going to relive the history of salvation, a history whose beginnings are recounted to us in the readings of the Old Testament, and that reaches its culmination in the experience of the resurrection of Christ, narrated by the first witnesses. The Word of God wishes to motivate us in faith, in renewal and in commitment.

### Readings from the OT
Exod. 14:15-15:1. *Psalm*. Is. 55:1-11. *Psalm*. Ezek. 36:16-28. *Brief silence.*

### Gloria

### Prayer
O God, who illumines this holy night with the glory of the resurrection of the Lord, keep alive the spirit of your sons and daughters in your Church, so that, renewed in body and soul, we can devote ourselves fully to your service. Through Christ…

### Readings from the NT
Rom. 6:3-11. *Alleluia*. Mt. 28:1-10.

### Reflection
Friends, this world can be restored. Everything has a remedy, because in the resurrection of Jesus Christ, our morale and our zest for life are raised up, our human energy is strengthened and all our hopes grow towards infinity. God is confident of this. There is a solution, if we responsibly take the steps that Easter marks out for us: to pass from death into life, from the primitive state to the spiritual plane.

The story of Jesus is a symbol for all of us, who are also children of God. Easter reminds us, and lays before us once more, the genuine and honourable Christian way of life. For this reason, particularly on this night, it is logical and necessary to ask oneself: What *steps* do I have to take? What do I have to let go of? We must always be encouraged by that experience in faith that is summed up very well by Saint John's Gospel: "God loved the world so much, that he gave his only Son, so that no one who believes in him might perish, but might have eternal life" (Jn 3:16). As he aptly describes, the responsibility is in *going towards the light*. Those who do not want salvation, detest the light, and do not go towards the light, so as not to see themselves accused on account of their works. On the other hand, if we long for the truth, we go towards the light, because we have no qualms about our actions being revealed (cf. Jn 3:20-21).

Let us remember that in this consists the *original retribution* of our God: he has the holy *mania* that society should be different. The Promised Land is possible with the spirit of the Beatitudes. This is the best and the most wholesome form of rebelliousness. No other compares with the risen Lord.

Friends, the springtime of the Gospel is in sight. Living in springtime brings one to the Christian experience of Easter. (*Silence for internal reflection.*)

## 4. LITURGY OF BAPTISM

*(This takes place next to the baptismal font. If space does not permit, a receptacle of water is put in a prominent place.)*

### Introduction

On this special night, we are going to recall again the meaning of our baptism. Through it, we are incorporated into the paschal mystery of Christ. This is, therefore, the most suitable setting and the proper moment in which to renew our baptismal promises. It is towards this objective, that all our undertakings in Lent have been directed: to incorporate ourselves completely, through faith and by decision, in the new life of the risen Lord. Let us reaffirm, then, our vocation to be like Jesus.

### Blessing of the Water

Lord our God, on this night when we celebrate the marvellous act of our creation and the even greater marvel of our redemption, may you bless this water so that we may now be brought to life again and able to participate in the joy of Easter. Through Christ…

### Renewal of Baptismal Promises

Brothers and sisters, through the mystery of Easter, we have been buried with Christ, so that we might live a new life. Now that Lent is over, let us renew our baptismal promises.

- Do you renounce all that goes against Christian values, such as selfishness, rancour, despair, misunderstanding, envy, bad temper, intolerance, laziness…; do you renounce your old self, so that you may live in freedom as children of God?
- *Yes, I renounce it.*
- Do you believe in God, the Father Almighty, Creator of heaven and earth?
- *Yes, I believe.*
- Do you believe in Jesus Christ, who died, rose to life and sits on the right hand of the Father?
- *Yes, I believe.*
- Do you believe in the Holy Spirit, who helps us on our Christian journey?
- *Yes, I believe.*

God, Father of our Lord Jesus Christ, who gave us new birth with water and the Holy Spirit, keep us in your grace for eternal life. Amen.

### Symbolic Action

*A prominent member of the community takes water from the font and makes the sign of the cross on the foreheads of several of the faithful, saying at the same time:* X., I mark you and seal you with the sign of Christians. *At the end, the same person sprinkles the whole assembly.*

## 5. RITE OF COMMUNION

### Introduction

Communion with the risen Jesus embodies his message of love and sacrifice. Let us share together in Holy Communion, in order to strengthen our faith and to proclaim that Jesus continues to live within us.

### Hymn

## Prayer

Father, we lift up our hearts and voices
to toast you in a song of praise
because, year after year, we marvel
at the joyful experience of liberation.
In truth, God of our fathers,
you have acted with greatness towards us.
We are glad for the light brimming forth in Jesus,
that illumines and regenerates every situation.
This night is as clear as day.
The song of our faith
and the music of our hope
unite in acclaiming you:
Alleluia, God the liberator!
Alleluia for the Redeemer, risen from the dead,
symbol of a land made new!
Alleluia for our baptism,
confirmed in the warmth of community!
And alleluia for our town
heartened by the reverberations of Easter!
In the intimacy of the Spirit who breathes in us
and in festive communion with the whole Church,
we say to you: Our Father…

## Sign of Peace

## Distribution of Communion: Hymn

## Act of Thanksgiving

- We give you thanks, Father, because you are full of love and mercy.
- We give you thanks for Jesus, risen from the dead, ideal and figurehead for new beings, who trust in the Spirit, who sow the seeds of health in history and leave a trail that draws in others to follow in their wake.
- And we give you thanks for our own selves, redeemed and remade so that we may advance your Kingdom, in communion with all men and women, who foster hope and the struggle for what is right.

## 6. CONCLUDING RITE

## Resolution

To live like new beings.

## Blessing

## Conclusion

With the Easter Vigil, we have celebrated the *Passover* towards a new life. All that is negative has been left behind. We have resolved to change. Let us not forget it. Jesus has left us the example of his sacrifice and he assures us of transcendence next to him and next to the Father. For all of which today we wish to offer to Jesus our most sincere applause: Thank you, Jesus! (*Applause.*)

And now, we will have refreshments together and make a toast to the resurrection.

## Final Hymn and Informal Dismissal

# The Season of
# EASTER

# Easter Sunday

## 1. SETTING THE SCENE

### Symbols:
- Those of the Paschal Vigil remain.
- Large cross with a poster: "He is not here; he is with us". At the beginning, it is covered by a white sheet.
- Bowl with earth in it and a large open flower.

### Background music

## 2. INTRODUCTORY RITES

### Introduction
Brothers and sisters, Christ is risen. Alleluia! We are celebrating the central event of our faith: the resurrection of Jesus through the intervention of God the Father. Let us express our faith with joy in the resurrection and affirm that love has triumphed: Christ has definitely conquered death and sin for ever.

### Symbolic Action
*Someone uncovers the cross and proclaims the text of the poster. The sheet remains on the ground, next to the cross.*

But we recognise that Jesus' victory is not finished. Our collaboration is needed, so that the plan God envisaged may be fulfilled: to set the world to rights, destroying the corruption of evil ways. Here is the *Passover* that is proposed to Christians: from evil to good, from what debases to what brings personal dignity.

### Hymn

### Greeting
Brothers and sisters, let us bless the Lord, who calls us to a new life.

### Penitential Rite
- You have conquered death: *Lord, have mercy.*
- You are the life of the world: *Christ, have mercy.*
- You intercede on our behalf: *Lord, have mercy.*

### Gloria

### Prayer
Lord God, who on this day have opened to us the gates of life, through your Son, the conqueror of death; grant to us, on celebrating the solemnity of the resurrection, that, renewed by the Spirit, we may live in the hope of our future resurrection. Through Christ…

## 3. LITURGY OF THE WORD

### Introduction on the Readings
The Readings contain testimonies of the resurrection of Jesus. It is, without doubt, the central event of our faith, not only for what it tells us about the life of Jesus, but also for what it symbolises for us too. To enter into the dynamic of the resurrection brings with it a demanding logic: to seek treasure above, not what is below.

### Readings
Acts 10:34a. 37-43. *Psalm*. Col. 3:1-4. *Alleluia*. Jn 20:1-9. *Brief silence*.

## Reflection

What is of the essence is invisible to the eye, but can be seen with the heart. The Easter resurrection is an experience of faith, which helps us to affirm ourselves in what is honourable in life and to grasp the alternative way of the Gospel. It is to open one's life completely to salvation: to receive it as a gift and take it on as a task. Jesus will always be our guiding example: he went about doing good and healing… because he was anointed by the power of the Spirit and God was with him.

Therefore, Easter is placing oneself on the side of life, being witnesses and bringing mankind closer in the building up and improvement of society. Many people in the Church set an example by caring for those less fortunate, looking after the underprivileged, supporting and healing those who are wasted by illness, terminally sick… Few civil institutions support these situations in the way that the Church does.

Easter means looking for the *treasures from above* in everything, that is to say, whatever promotes dignity in people, raises morale and maintains the adult stature of faith.

Now, in this present time, we are the witnesses, moved by faith, to communicate the truth of Jesus and the power of his resurrection. We have to know how to express in words and deeds that Jesus is the beginning of a new history, the cornerstone of a new social order. He who listens to his words and puts them into practice, builds on solid ground…
*(Silence for internal reflection.)*

## Creed

- We believe in the nearness of God.
- We recognise that Jesus is the worthiest of human beings, the first-born of the *New Creation*, with such a radiance that it could not be extinguished by the ravages of history.
- We are inspired by his way of life, because he took the plans of God seriously and because his existence has a ring of truth, selfless love, redemption, freely chosen poverty, freedom, the giving up of one's very self, a transformation of priorities...
- We understand faith as a daily adventure, prompted by the Spirit, which we experience in public life, where pluralism is increasing and where the rising clamour can be heard of those who suffer the most.
- We admit that the Church presents an image that is far from perfect. But nevertheless, we are joined to Christ the Saviour.
- We believe that Easter is the nucleus of all Christian dynamism, the key event that opens up an unexpected horizon of personal destiny.
- We believe that love is the great testament to Jesus and that it falls to us to communicate it, for the good of humanity.
- We experience that the spiritual life is the best means to freedom, and we believe that spiritual power is the main driving force in history.
- We know that having more does not make us happier, but rather, learning to need less.
- We value the Christian sense of the mystery and the plurality of gifts and personal qualities.
- And like many believers, with a sense of urgency, we commit ourselves to that idealistic and much needed goal – a restored humanity.

## Offerings

- *Glasses:* Accept, Lord, our firm resolution not to go through life like blind people. We want to keep our eyes wide open and our sensitivity finely tuned.
- *Walking boots:* Lord, like Jesus, we are treading life's path; may it be for the benefit and help of others.
- *Large candle alight:* We offer you, Lord, our desire for renewal at Easter and to be a light in the midst of the daily bustle of life.

## Hymn

## Symbolic Action

*A prominent member of the community, having dipped his fingers in the water of the baptismal font, approaches different people and makes the mark of the cross on their foreheads, expressing the confirmation of their faith and their adherence to Jesus. He says to them:* May the Spirit come upon you, so that you may be a Christian who bears fruit.

## 4. RITE OF COMMUNION

### Introduction

To communicate with the risen Jesus means supporting life and growth at all levels. The Easter resurrection represents a growth in enthusiasm and morale.

### Hymn

### Prayer

In order to praise you with our whole being
we are here, good Father.
We show our gratitude to you
by re-clothing ourselves in the Light and the Spirit
on this new morning of the resurrection.
The night has been speckled with flaming stars
which anticipate a dawn of celebration
throughout the world
for the saving Redeemer.
The spring clothes itself in green, amidst the
applause of life and triumph.
There is a burning rhythm because a
firm hope shines forth
forged in you, God of mercy.
In a circle of brothers and sisters,
we celebrate love and liberty,
A passion for living and solidarity,
because Jesus Christ is the first-born of
the New Creation,
the burgeoning shoot, bursting with
reason and triumph,
he who fulfilled your will so completely

that you have enthroned him at your right hand. Father, we want to fill our lives with the Gospel and to go through life doing good like Jesus. Receive our prayer with love: Our Father…

## Sign of Peace

## Distribution of Communion: Hymn

## Act of Thanksgiving (*spontaneous*)

## 5. CONCLUDING RITE

### Resolution

To bring the Easter message into daily life.

### Blessing

### Conclusion

We have shared joyfully in the resurrection of Jesus: his message and his challenge. Inspired by it, we have the duty to be a lively community. May we be witnesses to what we have celebrated and spread this spirit among our neighbours. May the grace and love of God go with us. Alleluia!

## Final Hymn and Informal Dismissal

# Second Sunday of Easter

## 1. SETTING THE SCENE

### Poster with one of these texts:
- "The believers lived in unity"
- "They shared everything in common"
- "Nobody was left in want"
- "Faith, unity and testimony"

### Symbols:
- Lighted paschal candle. A phrase stuck to a strip of cardboard: "Peace be with you".
- Various lighted candles and an unlit one next to the paschal candle. This is lit at the proclamation of the Gospel: "My Lord… happy are those who have not seen and yet believe".

## 2. INTRODUCTORY RITES

### Introduction
We gather together around Jesus, restored to life by the experience of Easter within us. For committed Christians, Easter is more than just a day, or a few weeks; one must be under the influence of salvation for the whole of one's life and with the aim of measuring up to Jesus' standard. His spiritual presence, within the community, is the main incentive to following the Christian ideal.

Let us celebrate this Easter gathering with the same sense of unity that the early Church experienced.

### Hymn

### Greeting
Brothers and sisters, let us worship in union with the Lord, who invites us to live in the atmosphere of Easter.

### Penitential Rite
- You have risen again and will live for ever: *Lord, have mercy.*
- You are the conqueror of sin: *Christ, have mercy.*
- You are the first-born of the New Creation: *Lord, have mercy.*

### Gloria

### Prayer
Blessed are you, Father, for all Christian communities
who are a sign of Gospel unity
in faithfulness to the example of Jesus.
Taking up the example of the best tradition,
we wish to understand our vocation as disciples
and to look at ourselves in the mirror of the Beatitudes.
May your Spirit purify us
so that we may be a community that bears witness
in the midst of this town. Amen.

## 3. LITURGY OF THE WORD

### Introduction to the Readings
The great argument in favour of the resurrection is the way of life that can be observed in Christians. Those who formed the first community in Jerusalem manifested this way of life in a very powerful way. Because of this, the people *began to talk about them.*

The Gospel reminds us that faith is a gift and a spiritual experience. For this reason, it is a mistake to ask for a different kind of proof… Whoever attempts this, like the apostle Thomas, is demanding something out of place. Faith cannot be grasped by the hands, but only by the spirit.

## Readings

Acts 2:42-47. *Psalm.* 1 Pet. 1:3-9. *Alleluia.*
Jn 20:19-31. *Brief silence.*

## Reflection

The book of the Acts of the Apostles describes the atmosphere of the early Church, inspired by the Holy Spirit. It is a vibrant, graphic and condensed text, with a descriptive summary of the authentic, genuine and valid ideal of the first Christians of Jerusalem. Today we have to say that the sense of community has not lost its relevance. The different human sciences continue to affirm that human beings become people, by remaining in communion with others. Theology points out, in the same way, that God's plan is communal and not individual. Common adherence to Jesus Christ leads to profound communion.

According to the book of the Acts, that community in Jerusalem built up its strength in "common unity", in such a way that "they lived united, they held everything in common and shared according to the needs of each one". That community also nourished itself "with the teaching of the apostles, in the breaking of bread and in prayer".

It is clear that the plans and foundations of the Kingdom of God collide head on with individualism, at all times. That is why we are urged on by missionary zeal. The words of Jesus are poignant today: "As the Father has sent me, so am I sending you. Receive the Holy Spirit."

We live within history. And the Christian objective is to bring about the ideal of the first reading, as far as possible, in our own day. The good thing about the ideal is that it has a never-ending appeal. Not all parishes and communities fulfil this ideal. If we try to, we will be giving practical expression to the resurrection. (*Silence for internal reflection.*)

## Creed

## Prayer of the Faithful

- We pray, Lord, that social justice and peace may grow among us.
- We pray that our Church may be a joyful witness to the Gospel and the risen Lord.
- We pray to you, Lord, for all newly-born children, that they may enjoy the benefits of a beautiful world.
- Lord, we wish to walk in the path of the Christian ideal and so to serve our town.
- We present to you our personal intentions. *Let us pray to the Lord.*

## Offerings

- *Bowl with earth in it:* Lord, we offer you this earth, a symbol of fertility. Just as new life grows up within it, we pray that the new life of Easter may grow within us, under the influence of the Spirit.
- *Flowers:* We offer you, Lord, these flowers, a symbol of the colour and joy that your living presence inspires in us.

## Hymn

## Symbolic Action

*To make a collection for a common purpose.*

## 4. RITE OF COMMUNION

## Introduction

Easter flowers call us to the challenge of redemption. God wishes to save us if we allow him to do so. May communion with Jesus give us strength when confronting our frailties and empower us to preserve in ourselves a high level of spiritual and moral life.

## Hymn

## Prayer

In the community of the redeemed,
Father, we address our prayer to you.
The thrilling experience of Easter inspires us.
We know that you dwell within us and that your
love goes with us.
We are the continuation of that original Church
in which the signs of redemption flowed,
the signs of your loving presence.
This community, Father,
rejoices in you, for the wonder of Jesus, risen
from the dead.
He encourages us, binds us to him
and urges us towards the daily miracle of unity.
This community applauds you
for calling us to enlarge your people,
working tirelessly for your Kingdom.
You have left us, in Jesus, the most convincing
example of human life
and in your community, an ideal which challenges
us to mutual service, openness and mission.
In communion with all those who share this ideal
accept, Father, the prayer that seals our faith:
Our Father…

## Sign of Peace

## Distribution of Communion: Hymn

## Act of Thanksgiving

Lord, we feel your presence living and acting
among us.
We are your community.
We want to work in unity for the cause and for the
mission that the Gospel insists upon.
We have learnt many values from you.
Now we will go forward with our people.
Keep us alive in spirit
and grant us the deep sensitivity of those who are
brought back to life.

## 5. CONCLUDING RITE

## Resolution

To create the solidarity, the people and the
Kingdom of God.

## Blessing

## Conclusion

We have celebrated the presence of Jesus among
us. We have emphasised that faith is, above all, a
spiritual experience, that enables us to go through
life, with vigour and without deceit. We are very
blessed in being able to go forward in life with the
experience of the risen Lord within us. For this
reason, let us bear witness to the faith and let us
present the Christian ideal to other people, as a
feasible daily way of life.

## Final Hymn and Dismissal

# Third Sunday of Easter

## 1. SETTING THE SCENE

### Poster with one of these texts:
- "Stay with us, Jesus"
- "They recognised him in the breaking of bread"
- "Where are we going to?"

### Symbols:
- Walking shoes.
- Open Bible.
- Broken bread.
- Paschal candle alight and two candles that are lit at the proclamation of the Gospel: "their eyes were opened and they recognised him".

## 2. INTRODUCTORY RITES

### Introduction
The experience of the resurrection not only raises our hope, but also gives us strength and courage, when confronting everyday life. Each day we have to be faithful, or to correct our behaviour, as the case may be. Jesus was like that: he did not give credence to anybody, if it meant straying from the will of God. We must continue to nourish our faith at the Easter fountain.

### Hymn

### Greeting
Brothers and sisters, let us bless the Lord, who wants to raise us up with Christ.

### Penitential Rite
- Because we do not open our hearts completely to your Word, *Lord, have mercy.*
- Because we frequently do not see the signs of your presence, *Christ, have mercy.*
- Because we are slow to understand you, *Lord, have mercy.*

### Gloria

### Prayer
God, bountiful Father, you have called us into life, in order to make this world into a great and pleasant home, an experience and anticipation of your Kingdom. We give you thanks for the opportunity to live and for our good fortune in living in your company, like children, who already taste on earth the life that one day we hope to attain in fullness. Amen.

## 3. LITURGY OF THE WORD

### Introduction to the Readings
The experience of the resurrection moves the apostles to announce and testify that the awaited salvation has been completely fulfilled in Jesus of Nazareth. The Gospel presents a beautiful doctrine: Jesus often surprises us on life's journey, helps us to resolve crises and urges us on to be witnesses.

### Readings
Acts 2:14. 22-33. *Psalm.* 1 Pet. 1:17-21. *Alleluia.* Lk. 24:13-35. *Brief silence.*

### Reflection
The experience of the resurrection instils in the apostles the urgency of proclaiming Jesus. This is what Peter does with the eleven disciples and this is what we must also do, at the present time. We have been saved at the price of Christ's blood. Our

salvation has been at great cost, so we should not take our path through this life lightly.

But the most notable thing about this Sunday is the story in the Gospel. The experience of faith and harmony in the community are threatened by crises that each person has at a particular moment.

Those disciples who were on their way to the village of Emmaus are going away from the community. They appear to be some of those who were wavering, those who were *losing focus*... They only have beautiful memories of Jesus: "He was good, powerful in his works and in his words; but he has been dead for three days." Nevertheless, as they walk, they have inner doubts and questions, which they need to continue giving voice to. Due to the anxiety that they feel and the lack of clarity that they have, they are seeking, discussing... They need to release their tension.

With these feelings and as they turn their backs on the community, Jesus comes up to them and joins them on their journey of desertion. At the beginning, he listens to them. Those disciples are still uneasy. It seems that they want to get to the heart of the truth: Has he really risen from the dead? Is he the Messiah, the Saviour awaited by the people? Is there any point in following him?

Listening to them and in tune with their *mental and existential confusion,* Jesus grasps the essence of their crisis, gets to the bottom of their problem. He tries to enlighten them with the Word, following the line of reasoning that they have adopted: "We were hoping that he might be the future liberator..." Curiously, he does not invite them to pray. They still do not recognise him.

The conversation becomes more and more interesting. The minds of Jesus' companions are becoming clearer and their hearts filled with warmth. The feeling of empathy grows, to the point

that they say to him: "Stay with us." And it is in the symbol of the unity of the table, in the act of breaking bread that they recognise him. By now they are burning within and they can see with total clarity. Like all those who are truly touched and convinced by the impact of God, they feel that he *turns them upside down*, they understand that they must retrace their steps and return to the community. The latter is preparing for its mission.

The *road to Emmaus* is an extraordinary teaching, real and applicable to many people. (*Silence for internal reflection.*)

## Creed

## Prayer of the Faithful

- That the Church may feel strengthened by the experience of the risen Lord, *let us pray to the Lord.*
- That the blessing of God may reach all households, *let us pray to the Lord.*
- For those who experience a crisis of faith or of community, that they may recover their faith and be strengthened in their witness, *let us pray to the Lord.*
- For those who do not feel that God is like a Father, that we may help them to discover and understand the great revelation of the Gospel, *let us pray to the Lord.*
- For all of us, that we may uphold Jesus' human way of life, *let us pray to the Lord.*

## Offerings

- *Withered plant:* We present to you this withered plant. It evokes the personal situation that we are often in, when we are ensnared by crises and doubts, with our will demoralised and our energies flagging.
- *Watering can:* We also offer up, Lord, this watering can, a symbol of the spiritual watering that we need to maintain our Easter growth.

## Hymn

## Symbolic Action

*The same person who has presented the watering can takes it back from the place of offerings, pours a little water over the pot with the withered plant and says:*
In order to be alive within and healthy without, an intense communion is needed with one's own self and with God, who lives within us.

## 4. RITE OF COMMUNION

### Introduction

To commune with Jesus is to want to live in the fullness of redemption. Let us receive the Eucharist of the Lord, with the joy of believers who carry themselves with dignity.

### Hymn

### Prayer

God, Holy Father,
we give you thanks, because you have
come forth to meet us.
In Jesus, you have done this in a wonderful way.
You invite us to a familiar and friendly communion,
with you at the centre, as a link of unity
and a call for balance amidst diversity.
You are not an awkward presence for us,
although you may make demands of us and correct us.
When we experience your company,
the Gospel inspires us even more.
Blessed are you, Father, for your revelation!
As you help us so much,
we ask you to show yourself to those who seek you,
that they may enjoy and develop, like us,
the meaning of life that you teach so surely.
Rely on us to make a *bridge*.
With all those who invite you into their hearts
we say to you: Our Father…

### Sign of Peace

### Distribution of Communion: Hymn

## Act of Thanksgiving

■ We give you thanks, Father, for the experience of meeting with you and with Jesus in the Spirit.
■ We give you thanks for Jesus, the Way and the Covenant, in the name of all those who seek you.
■ We also give you thanks for the help of the community and of the Church; for what it brings to us and for what we can share within it.
■ Rely on us to bring the Gospel closer to our people.

## 5. CONCLUDING RITE

### Resolution

To know how to support those who suffer a crisis of faith or a crisis in relationships in the community.

### Blessing

### Conclusion

Faith in the resurrection of Jesus is the solid foundation of the Christian life. It is also the powerful experience that motivates us to follow him each day. The optimism of the faith does not remove life's difficulties, but it does give them meaning and makes them bearable.

May the conviction of knowing that we are accompanied by Jesus inspire our journey. Let us go through life bringing to others the experience of Easter. It is a guarantee of the fullness of life, that is to say, of an everlasting springtime.

### Final Hymn and Dismissal

# Fourth Sunday of Easter

## 1. SETTING THE SCENE

### Poster with one of these texts:
- "Jesus, the Good Shepherd"
- "Come and follow me"

### Symbols:
- Shepherd's crook, pouch and sandals.

## 2. INTRODUCTORY RITES

### Introduction
Brothers and sisters, we continue in this Easter time, with the challenge of the new life before us. This means living a conscientious and responsible life. Jesus, the Good Shepherd, wants us, his followers, to be responsible. He goes before us offering life, and he expects us to commit ourselves to the same adventure.

### Hymn

### Greeting
Brothers and sisters, let us bless God the Father, who has sent us Jesus as the Good Shepherd.

### Penitential Rite
- Lord, you took on the burden of our sins: *Lord, have mercy.*
- Lord, you have saved us: *Christ, have mercy.*
- Lord, you are the Good Shepherd for everyone: *Lord, have mercy.*

### Gloria

### Prayer
God, bountiful Father, who have given your Church the immense joy of the resurrection of Jesus Christ; grant us the happiness of the Kingdom of your chosen ones, so that in this way the tender flock of your Son may take part in the wonderful victory of your Shepherd. Through Christ…

## 3. LITURGY OF THE WORD

### Introduction to the Readings
In the early days of the Church, there is a growing awareness of the special importance of Jesus and his message. The Gospel describes the Good Shepherd, as he goes on his way, concerned for the life of his sheep. We can put our trust in this shepherd: he opens the gates of salvation to all.

### Readings
Acts 2:14a. 36-41. *Psalm.* 1 Pet. 2:20b-25. *Alleluia.* Jn 10:1-10. *Brief silence.*

### Reflection
The fourth Sunday of Easter focuses our gaze on Jesus, the Good Shepherd. The figure of the shepherd is a helpful way for biblical writers to talk to us about God. Jesus, also, makes use of this image to show us his way of acting and his feeling. He is the sincere and faithful shepherd, who gives the utmost care: he looks for the lost sheep; he goes out in search of those who are missing; he offers the values of the Kingdom, in abundance, to everyone; and he waits by the door in an attitude of cordial and special welcome, because he is interested in people, as individuals – he knows each one by their name and he is very familiar with their personal stories…

This image of Jesus, as the Good Shepherd, has left its mark on the consciousness and memory of the Church. From the beginning until now, the tremendous lesson of this shepherd has been emphasised: his graceful generosity, his liberating sacrifice – "I have come, so that they may have life and may have it to the full".

Christian communities, of all periods, have a great example in this model of a shepherd. It is a clear example of how we should live out our responsibilities within the community and how we should be missionaries, who go out in search of those who are not among us. It is a motive for intensifying our solidarity, within and without, so that life may be overflowing in abundance. This shepherd invites us today to share in his values, so that we may continue to worship God in the way that pleases him, walking in the ways of unity and service.

The Gospel is the voice of this Good Shepherd. Any other message that does not go along these lines must represent for us a *strange voice*, which we should take no notice of, like someone hearing rainfall. The profound voice of the Good Shepherd resonates with spirituality and personal truth. This is what marks out the difference between the true disciples, who have recognised him, and those who act from other motives. (*Silence for internal reflection.*)

## Creed

## Prayer of the Faithful

Let us turn in prayer to the Lord, confident that he will hear us.

- Let us pray for all the people of God, that they may faithfully follow the voice of the Good Shepherd.
- Let us pray for improvement in the quality of life. May those in government be inspired by the wisdom of the Gospel to address civic problems with effectiveness and decisiveness.
- Let us pray for all those who suffer and for those who wander like sheep without a shepherd, so that through the closeness and support of their brothers and sisters they may find hope.
- Let us pray, also, that Jesus may be the Shepherd for everyone, and that we may be good witnesses.
- Let us pray for each other, but especially for adolescents and young people, that they may open their hearts to the call of God, discover the needs of the Church and respond with generosity.
- For these and for all our intentions, *let us pray to the Lord.*

## Symbolic Action

*Someone goes to a prominent place and says:* We the followers of Jesus are not a flock of vice-ridden people who go where people drag them down. In following Jesus, we are seeking the Kingdom of God.

## 4. RITE OF COMMUNION

### Introduction

The Church has always recognised Jesus as the Good Shepherd. As we unite ourselves with his person, let us renew our commitment to follow him.

### Hymn

### Prayer

It is fitting, Father, that we praise you for Jesus Christ whom you have sent as a Good Shepherd
to fill us with life, and with his abundant grace.
He has gone before us, providing guidance.
Sensitive people listen to his voice and follow him because Jesus draws their admiration.
He speaks with a firm and convincing voice;
he seeks direct and plain dialogue with each person;
no personal story is strange for him;
he knows each one by their own name…
We give you thanks for such an attentive and dutiful shepherd

who waits up for the sheep that has gone astray,
who goes out in search of those who are missing
because he desires that his redeeming voice
should reach out to all.
Father, we bless you for the longing of
this shepherd
to reunite us in one single Church.
Because we are drawn to his voice and we wish to
follow his call,
because we have experience of his redemption,
we say to you with uplifted hearts: Our Father…

## Sign of Peace

## Distribution of Communion: Hymn

## Act of Thanksgiving

- Father, we make our prayer of gratitude as a
  community. We unite in the faith of those who
  came before us and we say to you: "The Lord is
  my shepherd, I shall not want" (Ps. 23:1).
- We give you thanks because you have sent us
  Jesus, to lead us in respect and dignity.
- We confess that this Good Shepherd has risked
  everything even to the point of giving up his
  own life for his sheep.
- Borne up by such an example, we strengthen
  our communion and reaffirm that we want to
  follow him.
- And when we go out into the street, we will be
  witnesses to the one who guides us with such
  sureness, so that everyone may recognise the
  Shepherd, the pioneer in the art of giving up
  one's life.

## 5. CONCLUDING RITE

### Resolution
To generate life and enthusiasm, like the Good
Shepherd.

### Blessing

## Conclusion
We have celebrated Jesus as the Good Shepherd
who gives up his life. According to his own words,
no one has greater love than he who is capable of a
similar sacrifice. Jesus desires abundant life for all
his sheep. Here and now, this depends on us also.

## Final Hymn and Dismissal

# Fifth Sunday of Easter

## 1. SETTING THE SCENE

### Poster with one of these texts:
- "All service is of value"
- "Services complement each other"
- "Jesus is the Way, the Truth and the Life"

### Symbols:
- Mirror.
- Cornerstone.

## 2. INTRODUCTORY RITES

### Introduction
The resurrection of Jesus, that we celebrate in this season of Easter, also gives us reasons for welcoming each other into this celebration today.

We come together now, after another week of work, study, and relationships with family, friends and neighbours. We are going to share the Word and the signs of unity, so as to strengthen the qualities of care and service, that must always distinguish us, through our vocation and through following Jesus, in the midst of our people.

### Hymn

### Greeting
Brothers and sisters, let us together praise God the Father, who has offered us Jesus as the Way, the Truth and the Life.

### Penitential Rite
- You, Lord, are the Way: *Lord, have mercy.*
- You, Lord, are the Truth: *Christ, have mercy.*
- You, Lord, are the Life: *Lord, have mercy.*

### Gloria

### Prayer
Lord, you have deigned to redeem us and have made us your children. Look upon us always with a father's love and ensure that we who believe in Christ, your Son, may reach true freedom and our eternal inheritance. Through Christ...

## 3. LITURGY OF THE WORD

### Introduction to the Readings
In the organisation of the first Christian community, they soon saw the need for sharing out services and tasks. Among ourselves also, this principle should be fulfilled: it is better that many people should do a little rather than a few people doing a lot.

The other readings remind us that Jesus is the cornerstone upon which the edifice of the Church stands. He is also the Way, the Truth, the Life and the great symbol for recognising God.

### Readings
Acts 6:1-7. *Psalm.* 1 Pet. 2:4-9. *Alleluia.* Jn 14:1-12. *Brief silence.*

### Reflection
The Christians realised immediately, through the Gospel teaching and through the imperatives of life, that service is an essential and defining aspect of the Church: a Church that does not serve, has no value.

For this reason, in a Christian community, there must never be lacking the practice of love, through mutual service, above all for the most needy.

This attitude of service is ingrained in human consciousness and reinforced by the example of Jesus, who left a long list of acts of service to his name. He did not come to be served, but to serve and he wanted to be in the midst of his own people, as someone who serves. Nothing teaches better than example. Jesus is the cornerstone of the Church, because he made service his way of life.

From the beginning, the sharing out of services, responsibilities and tasks has been a function of the Church. At the present time, we emphasise also that we are all able to offer some service; in this way we can all make community life more dynamic. Participation and co-responsibility are two fundamental values in a community.

Focusing on the passage in the Gospel, we notice that Jesus speaks of himself in the first person, with bold and direct assertions: "I am the Way, the Truth and the Life. Nobody can come to the Father except through me." This is not vain pride, nor the cult of personality, but sincerity and the service of a teacher.

Among the many offerings and models that are presented to help one make one's way in life, for many years now the Gospel has been proposing the alternative way of Jesus: an ideal steeped in human mysticism and divine revelation. This proposed way of Jesus is even more daring and heartening when our plans have been overturned, or when we are weighed down with disillusionment. Above all, it is then that Jesus is the Way, the Truth and the Life.

It seems that, after three years of living together, the apostles Thomas and Philip had understood very little regarding Jesus' message and identity. He wanted to be the mirror and witness to the Father: "He who has seen me, has seen the Father."

But sometimes words say little; deeds express more. That is why Jesus comes to say: Believe, at least, through my works. (*Silence for internal reflection.*)

## Creed

## Prayer of the Faithful
- Let us pray that all of us who undertake to humanise this world may unite our efforts.
- Let us pray for the Church, that love may always be the sign that distinguishes Christians.
- Let us remember the people who suffer for different reasons, may they attain the justice and peace that they need and which is their right.
- Let us pray that the culture of solidarity may make progress, with expressive and effective acts of service.
- Let us pray that we may do good out of conviction and without tiring.
- For these and all of our intentions, *let us pray to the Lord.*

## Offerings
- *Bricks and stones:* We present to you, Lord, these bricks and stones representing each one of us. United in Jesus, our cornerstone, we want to build a new Church and a new society.
- *Photographs of Christian witnesses and a poster of Jesus:* We present to you, Lord, these images of witnesses, in which we perceive your presence and a great commitment of life.

## Hymn

## Symbolic Action
*Various people go up to a prominent place. One has a mop, another a tray of medicines, another a book of doctrine, another the Bible, another a lighted candle, etc. Upon reaching the appointed place, they say:* Jesus fills us. We are all able to perform some service.

## 4. RITE OF COMMUNION

### Introduction
We have experience of Jesus' guidance and of the quality of his example. In receiving Holy Communion, let us choose to be guided by his truth.

### Hymn

### Prayer
Good and loving Father,
in gratitude, we make a common prayer that
comes from our innermost heart
recognising that you have called and chosen us.
We are your People, your Church.
Like so many believers, we feel the need
to proclaim your wonders:
to confess that you intervene on our behalf,
that you have unleashed the strength of your saving
arm and that you invite us to continue following Jesus.
He is the Way that many reject,
the Truth above all other truth,
the Life of holiness sifted even unto martyrdom.
In Jesus and in his Gospel, we have the cornerstone
and the solid foundation to build a new humanity.
Encouraged by the authentic nature of many witnesses
and desiring that life may express what we pray for,
we say to you: Our Father…

### Sign of Peace

### Distribution of Communion: Hymn

### Act of Thanksgiving
- We give you thanks, Father, for Jesus, the human symbol of what you are for us.
- We give you thanks for the exemplary path, traced out and experienced by Jesus, that you propose for everyone.
- We give you thanks, because we realise that in you is found the guarantee of how much meaning is given to our lives. May we be enlightened, so that we may know how to communicate to others how good you are.

## 5. CONCLUDING RITE

### Resolution
To express in word and deed that Jesus is the Way, the Truth and the Life.

### Blessing

### Conclusion
Once more, we have reminded ourselves that Jesus is the great symbol for reaching God and the cornerstone that gives a sure foundation to the Church. With our faith strengthened, let us be worthy signs to the outer world of God the Father, of Jesus and of the Spirit. May it be a good week for everyone and may the Spirit of the Lord go with us.

### Final Hymn and Dismissal

# Sixth Sunday of Easter

## 1. SETTING THE SCENE

### Poster with one of these texts:
- "We know because we believe"
- "The Spirit is with us"

## 2. INTRODUCTORY RITES

### Introduction
The coming feast of Pentecost is evident in today's message. Although life is often complicated for us, it is crucial to open ourselves to the Holy Spirit, who enlightens us and leads us to the truth. Thanks to him, we are able to understand Jesus better and to live the Gospel.

### Hymn

### Greeting
Brothers and sisters, let us bless the Father and Jesus, because they have sent us the Spirit of truth.

### Penitential Rite
- You, Lord, are our goodness: *Lord, have mercy.*
- You, Lord, are mercy: *Christ, have mercy.*
- You, Lord, remain with us always: *Lord, have mercy.*

### Gloria

### Prayer
God, bountiful Father, you accompany us and defend us with the Spirit of truth and strengthen our hope. May the power of the faith have an effect in our lives. Through Christ…

## 3. LITURGY OF THE WORD

### Introduction to the Readings
In the early Church, there was a great enthusiasm for preaching the Gospel. The presence of the Holy Spirit empowered the believers. They experienced Jesus' promise that he would send the Spirit as defender and comforter.

### Readings
Acts 8:5-8.14-17. *Psalm.* 1 Pet. 3:15-18. *Alleluia.* Jn 14:15-21. *Brief silence.*

### Reflection
Frequently, we say that hope is the last thing one loses, and so we are re-emphasising the decisive importance of this virtue. Without hope, everything withers away, the horizon becomes cloudy, it is impossible to be motivated. Like faith and charity, Christian hope leans on direct relationship with God. It encompasses and fulfils the meaning of all human hope.

One cannot imagine any Christian vitality, without considerable experience in the theological virtues. A profound and direct relation exists between the three. They are bathed in the water of the same fountain: God. Saint Peter exhorts us "always be ready to give a reason for your hope", that is to say, let it be seen when you are motivated by your relationship with God.

Friends, how important spirituality is for human beings! It is essential in order to enter into and taste the human mystery itself, just as it is for confronting life's difficulties and setbacks. From the standpoint of spirituality, everything can be understood from a better perspective. That is why Saint Peter says: "it is better to suffer for doing good, if that is the will of God, than to suffer for doing evil".

All human spirituality is strengthened by the Spirit of truth that Jesus leaves us with, as a great gift. This Spirit is a presence: "it lives with you and is in you", and is an incentive to "keep the commandments", that is to say, to live the values that ennoble us, give us dignity and make us worthy. The Spirit that constitutes and invigorates Jesus is the same one that makes us an advocate, a counsellor, a comforter…, that leads to complete truth. Thanks to this Spirit, we discover the mentality of the Gospel more profoundly. He always brings a breath of air, if one allows him to enter in. (*Silence for internal reflection.*)

## Creed

## Prayer of the Faithful

- For a healthy and vigorous society, *let us pray to the Lord.*
- For the Church, that it may incarnate the Kingdom of God in all cultures, *let us pray to the Lord.*
- That the presence of the Spirit may stand out in Christian communities, *let us pray to the Lord.*
- For the sick and for all those who suffer the ravages of pain, that they may find care and compassion, *let us pray to the Lord.*
- For all those who enjoy good health, that they may know how to appreciate it as a gift, to look after it in a responsible way and to generously serve others, *let us pray to the Lord.*
- That we may commit ourselves with all our neighbours to the improvement of our own town, *let us pray to the Lord.*

## Offerings

- *Small bare cross or a crucifix:* Father, we present to you this symbol imbued with wisdom, because "it is better to suffer for doing good, if that is your will, than to suffer for doing evil".

- *Chrism:* We present to you, Lord, the chrism that reminds us of our confirmation and the commitments we assume, whenever we renew our faith, enlightened by the Spirit of truth.

## 4. RITE OF COMMUNION

### Introduction
In order to live in communion with Jesus, nothing helps us as much as the Spirit. Let us allow him to prepare us and let us be grateful to Jesus for such an extraordinary gift.

### Hymn

### Prayer
Good and loving Father, you desire to renew the life of the Church and of the world
by means of the Spirit of truth.
In him, you base the defence of all that is honest.
You offer him to us as an alternative way,
so that we may persevere in doing good, even at the cost of suffering.
Many are not able to receive him
because they make no effort to breathe in his Spirit.
We however, have experienced the gift of the Spirit:
he guides us with the wisdom of the cross.
Father, receive the honour that we offer you in tribute.
We want to live an honest life,
to be workers in the building up of your Kingdom,
collaborating with men and women of good will.
Clothed in the Spirit and united in Jesus,
we say to you: Our Father…

### Sign of Peace

### Distribution of Communion: Hymn

## Symbolic Action

*After the communion, someone takes the cross, raises it before the assembly and says:* Brothers and sisters, with the Spirit of Jesus, we are able to give a reason for our hope.

## Act of Thanksgiving

- We give you thanks, Father, for the experience of the faith that helps us so much and challenges us so much.
- We give you thanks, because we can share it and nourish it together in our community.
- We want to live our faith with enthusiasm, so that we may imbue it with words and deeds.
- Help us to live in the Spirit of truth, so that we may raise the human quality of our own town.

## 5. CONCLUDING RITE

### Resolution

To do good, although it may cost us suffering.

### Blessing

### Conclusion

As Christians, we have a fundamental duty, to give a reason for our faith and our hope. This we do with words, but also, and above all, with our actions. For this, we count on the great gift of the Spirit. Thanks to him, we grow in dignity and are able to make great progress. Let us listen to the Spirit and not put any obstacles in his way. With God's help let us live the week in a positive manner.

### Final Hymn and Dismissal

# Ascension of the Lord

## 1. SETTING THE SCENE

### Poster with one of these texts:
- ◼ "Go and make disciples"
- ◼ "Go and proclaim the Gospel"
- ◼ "I am with you always"
- ◼ "Heaven is the work of a lifetime"

## 2. INTRODUCTORY RITES

### Introduction
We reach the culmination of the Easter period, with the feast of the Ascension of the Lord, a very important and symbolic truth of our faith. Jesus is the mirror in which the destiny of all mankind can see itself reflected. Heaven is our hope, and the world our responsibility. Because the fullness of heaven does not come about in a moment, we commit ourselves to the improvement of the earth, raising the level of humanity to the fullest.

Let us concentrate today on the meaning of the Ascension of the Lord, who sheds light on our horizon and on our everyday journey.

### Hymn

### Greeting
Brothers and sisters, let us bless the Lord, who calls us to fullness of life.

### Penitential Rite
- ◼ You, Lord, lift up our lives: *Lord, have mercy.*
- ◼ You, Lord, intercede for us: *Christ, have mercy.*
- ◼ You, Lord, understand us more than anyone: *Lord, have mercy.*

### Gloria

### Prayer
Grant us, bountiful Father, that we may exult with joy and give you thanks, because the ascension of Jesus Christ, your Son, is already our victory, and he, who is the head of the Church, has gone before us to the glory to which we are called, as members of his body. Through Christ...

## 3. LITURGY OF THE WORD

### Introduction to the Readings
Jesus passed through this world in a responsible manner. His existence is recognised and applauded by those who want to live a truthful life. But if we admire Jesus, it is not by remaining with our arms folded, but by deepening our passion for the Gospel even more. God has given us the gift of Jesus, so that we may grow in our commitment to liberate the world.

### Readings
Acts 1:1-11. *Psalm*. Eph. 1:17-23. *Alleluia.*
Mt. 28:16-20. *Brief silence.*

### Reflection
The ascension of Jesus is the culmination of his resurrection. It is also the symbol of the complete salvation of all humanity. It reaffirms that our life rises up again with his, in spite of death. Human destiny is one of triumphant transcendence.

The ascension of Jesus is accompanied by praise on the part of God the Father: he exalted him and granted him the *Name-above-all-names*; he granted him the title of *Lord* and he seated him at his right hand for ever, as an example and standard for human existence.

For ourselves who are on the journey of life, the Ascension is a moment of admiration for Jesus; but it also provokes us to get on with the work. Jesus gives us the command: "Go and make disciples of all peoples…" Then the spreading of the Gospel in the Church began. And now, it falls to us. We can not remain rooted to our spot, staring at the sky. To preach the Gospel is an urgent task for us; it is the nucleus and priority of the Church, because the Church lives for the Gospel. Small communities and parishes, as visible and close-knit organisms of the Church, exist, above all, to evangelise. This is their reason for being and it should govern all their life and activity.

John XXIII stressed this, at the beginning of Vatican II: "What is expected of the Church today, is that it may introduce into the veins of society, the perennial virtue, the divine virtue of the Gospel." John Paul II tells us why there is the need for a *new evangelisation.* It is because the Gospel is the people's inheritance, for all humanity; its goodness belongs to everyone, a public message that we must learn how to interpret through signs, gestures and words.

As the second reading states, may the Father of our Lord Jesus Christ give us "a spirit of wisdom and perception of what is revealed", so that we may understand the inheritance that comes to us and the task that we have before us. Jesus commits himself to being in our company: "I am with you always, until the end of the world". (*Silence for internal reflection.*)

## Creed

## Prayer of the Faithful
- That the values of the Kingdom of God may be promoted among all peoples, *let us pray to the Lord.*
- For those who threaten the lives of others, that sensitivity and respect may grow in them, *let us pray to the Lord.*
- That our Church, encouraged by the human story of Jesus, may fulfil the beautiful mission of the Gospel, *let us pray to the Lord.*
- That our community may respond to the challenge of a new evangelisation, *let us pray to the Lord.*
- That we may all have a clear awareness of our vocation and destiny, *let us pray to the Lord.*
- For all of us, that our faith in Christ may drive us on to show forth the goodness of God, *let us pray to the Lord.*

## Hymn

## Symbolic Action
*Someone goes to a prominent place, displays a New Testament and says:* Jesus passes on to us the task of being witnesses. Go and make disciples. *Afterwards, he goes up to a person in the assembly and says to them:* X., the Kingdom of God urges us on. *Next, he goes up to someone else and says to them:* X., the Kingdom of God begins here.

## 4. RITE OF COMMUNION

## Introduction
Communion with Jesus is always an inspiration for life. Receiving communion today has the added incentive of encouraging us to seek all that comes from above.

## Hymn

## Prayer

Lord, our God,
in communion with those who work for the
Promised Land,
the realisable promise of your Kingdom,
we offer up this prayer of blessing to you
for the wonder of your solidarity with us.
We bless you for so many witnesses of selfless love
who have built up brotherhood throughout history
leaving us the inheritance of heaven, here on earth.
We praise you for the fearlessness of so many believers
who sacrifice their health and their energy
on humanitarian projects inspired by the Gospel.
Thousands of voices and signs assure us
that your Kingdom is of this world:
the definitive age of your grace has dawned
which shakes up the structures that do not accord
with your heavenly kingdom.
And we raise our arms in a sign of victory
because you have exalted Jesus Christ
and you have seated him at your right hand,
satisfied with his journey through life.
For us, he is the first among many,
the symbol of humanity's fulfilment,
the first-born of the New Creation
for your glory and our guidance.
Good and loving God, you have placed in our hands
the flowering of life upon earth,
the possibility of living as worthy members
of your Kingdom.
With Jesus and with all those who bless you
in heaven and upon earth, we say to you: Our Father…

## Sign of Peace

## Distribution of Communion: Hymn

## Act of Thanksgiving

■ We give you thanks, Father, because we
experience within us the seeds of indestructible
life, our hope of fulfilment.

■ Our faith increases and our responsibility grows
as we celebrate the story of Jesus: simple and
great, serving and free, demanding and merciful.

■ We give you thanks, because you have entrusted
us with the promotion of your Kingdom, which
is ours also. We wish to begin within ourselves
and through our community, so that we may
support the presence of heaven on earth with
the witness of our lives.

## 5. CONCLUDING RITE

### Resolution

To fulfil the will of God on earth, as it is already
being fulfilled in heaven.

### Blessing

### Conclusion

The ascension of Jesus is a symbol and guarantee
of our human adventure. We are not in the hands
of blind destiny. The Christian faith assures us, that
our deepest desires cannot be frustrated. We are
created in order to reach fullness. That is heaven.
While we walk upon this earth, we are called upon
to take up Jesus' role. Let each one of us see how
we can put it into practice at home, in the street, at
our workplace or places of recreation.

### Final Hymn and Dismissal

# Seventh Sunday of Easter

## 1. SETTING THE SCENE

### Poster with one of these texts:
- "All joined in continuous prayer"
- Eternal life is to know the only true God

## 2. INTRODUCTORY RITES

### Introduction
Traditionally the period of nine days between Ascension Day and Pentecost has been marked as a time of waiting in prayer. Today's first reading gives the clue, for we are told there how after the Ascension the apostles, together with several women, including Mary the mother of Jesus, went back to Jerusalem and "joined in continuous prayer". Of course they were waiting for the promised coming of the Holy Spirit, who would lead them to "all truth". It is from this period of intense prayer that the Christian tradition of the Novena (Nine Days of Prayer) arose.

Like the apostles and the companions of Jesus we continue to wait in expectation of the Lord to fulfil his promises to us. This is the ideal time to think again about our prayer lives. It is not that God needs to know what we need, rather that we need to be ready to receive what God is offering.

### Hymn

### Greeting
Brothers and sisters, let us bless the Lord, who continually pleads for us before his Father.

### Penitential Rite
- You, Lord, are our help: *Lord, have mercy.*
- You, Lord, are the stronghold of our lives: *Christ, have mercy.*
- You, Lord, prepare us for the gifts of the Spirit: *Lord, have mercy.*

### Gloria

### Prayer
Heavenly Father, as we rejoice in the Ascension of Christ your Son, open our hearts to receive the gifts of the Spirit and renew our hope that we too will rise in glory to enjoy the fullness of life in your kingdom. We make our prayer through Christ …

## 3. LITURGY OF THE WORD

### Introduction to the Readings
The apostles had learnt the importance of prayer because they had often observed Jesus praying. In today's Gospel we are privileged to listen in to Jesus praying to his Father on our behalf. The wonder of it is that we can be caught up in the glory of God. Jesus, having finished his work on earth, is able to pray about the fact that because his disciples believed in him, he is glorified "in them". They too belong to the Father. The same is true for us, for in the same prayer Jesus goes on to say: "I pray not only for these but also for those who through their teaching will come to believe in me" (v.20). What greater incentive do we need to deepen our faith?

## Readings

Acts 1:12-14. *Psalm.* 1 Pet. 4:13-16. *Alleluia.*
Jn 17:1-11. *Brief silence.*

## Reflection

Instinctively little children imitate their parents. Indeed even as they grow older they may retain mannnerisms which they are unaware of, but which identify them as children of their parents, and of course imitation is the sincerest form of flattery. We know that the disciples were intrigued by Jesus' habit of prayer and after observing him they asked him to teach them how to pray. On that occasion he taught them the 'Our Father'. There must have been other occasions when they overheard Jesus praying to his Father and in chapter seventeen of St John's Gospel we are privileged to listen in to his priestly prayer at the Last Supper.

When they were gathered in the upper room after Jesus had returned to the Father and they were awaiting the coming of the Spirit, they would not have had to work out what to do or how to pray. They had learnt how to be in communion with God in the quiet of their inner being and in the spoken word that came straight from the hearts. Did they have a rota to ensure that the continuous prayer went round the clock or did they meet from time to time for communal prayer and spend the rest in quiet retreat? Whatever St Luke meant in describing the prayer as continuous we can be sure that it was life giving and vibrant.

It is a shame if we overcomplicate prayer. When adults take up a reverent posture for prayer the little child will be drawn into the awe and mystery of God's presence. It will be like the disciples watching Jesus as he withdrew to a lonely place. When the adult prays with the child about the ordinary things of life, the child will begin to realise that God is interested in everything. As we await the coming feast of Pentecost we might try to imitate the disciples and be prepared for all the Lord will ask of us. (*Silence for internal reflection.*)

## Creed

## Prayer of the Faithful

- For a lively faith and the gift of prayer, *let us pray to the Lord.*
- For parents, guardians and teachers; that they may be worthy role models for our children, *let us pray to the Lord.*
- For our bishops and clergy; that they may imitate the apostles and lead the church in faith and hope, *let us pray to the Lord.*
- For those who share in the sufferings of Christ; that they may also share in his glory, *let us pray to the Lord.*
- For all family, friends and parishioners who have gone before us, especially those who have had some part in teaching us how to pray; that they may now be sharing in the eternal banquet, *let us pray to the Lord.*

## Offerings

- *Lighted candles:* Father, we present these candles as symbols of our prayer. As they continue to burn may they be a reminder of our desire to be in continuous union with you, through Jesus Christ our Lord.
- *Incense:* Father, as we continue to rejoice in the ascension of Jesus, may this sweet-smelling incense symbolise our prayers as they rise into your presence, united with the prayers of Jesus. (*Candles and incense are left in a prominent place before the altar.*)

## 3. RITE OF COMMUNION

## Introduction

There is no greater prayer than the one which unites us perfectly with Jesus at the eucharistic table. Let us pray that we may be ready to receive the gift of the Lord himself.

## Hymn

## Prayer

God our Father, these are precious moments.
The world cries out for justice and peace, yet often men and women do not realise that their cries go out to you.

We thank you for the faith that brings us together today, and for the prayer which unites us through your Son, Jesus Christ, with you and with one another.

Hear our prayer for all those who are dear to us and have asked our prayers;

for all those who have a special claim on our prayers;

and for all those who have still to discover the power of your loving presence.

Make us worthy to receive Holy Communion this day. May we be charged with renewed vigour to continue the mission of Jesus in our own time and place, and be signs of justice and peace to all around us.

Fill us with a deep spirit of prayer, remembering that it is by the power of the Spirit that we are able to say: Our Father …

## Sign of Peace

## Distribution of Communion: Hymn

## Symbolic Action

*After communion, members of the congregation are invited to come forward and place a few grains of incense on the charcoal, saying:*
Lord, may my prayer rise before you like incense.
*(Another hymn may be sung during this time.)*

## Act of Thanksgiving

■ Father, we thank you for the gift of your Son, Jesus, to our world.

■ Jesus, we thank you for teaching us how to pray and for uniting us in this great gift of the Eucharist.

■ Holy Spirit, we thank you for your mighty gifts. May they strengthen us for all that stands before us in the coming week.

## 4. CONCLUDING RITE

## Resolution

To be faithful to prayer during this special Novena.

## Blessing

## Conclusion

We are a community of believers, and we are the inheritors of a great tradition of prayer, handed on from the apostles through each generation.
Prayer is not an extra, but touches into every aspect and corner of our lives. St Paul teaches us that it is not so much that we pray, but rather that the Spirit prays within us. Let us give the Spirit free rein during the coming week.

## Final Hymn and Dismissal

# Pentecost Sunday

## 1. SETTING THE SCENE

### Poster with one of these texts:
- "United in the same Spirit"
- "No one inspires us like the Spirit"

### Symbols:
- Fire in a fireproof receptacle.
- Basket with varied fruit (the fruit of the Spirit).

## 2. INTRODUCTORY RITES

### Introduction

Today, the day of Pentecost, we recall a very important experience: the Spirit descends upon the apostles, fills them with courage and launches them on the Gospel journey, giving witness to the Lord Jesus. We are at the very beginnings of the Church. Thanks to the Spirit which the Father and Jesus have sent us, the Christian movement has continued up to the present day.

In our community, the Spirit is also present, working within our conscience and giving us a passion for the Gospel. And it is because Pentecost represents such a decisive experience that, for a Christian, all that is good is summed up by following the inspiration of the Spirit.

Let us joyfully celebrate this gift in our community. There is no question that we are sinners; but the Spirit is enlightenment, our driving force, certainty and generosity.

### Hymn

### Greeting

Brothers and sisters, thanks to the Holy Spirit, we know that we are children of God. Because of this, let us bless the Lord.

### Penitential Rite
- The Spirit is the one who assures us that God is our Father. Forgive us, Lord, because we have not always behaved like your children.
- Freedom is the result of accepting the Spirit. Forgive us, Lord, because we have become enslaved by many things, rules and people, and we have undervalued the gift of Christian freedom.
- The Holy Spirit seeks to conform our way of thinking to that of Christ. Forgive us, because we have preferred to follow other ideas and other advice, which have not brought us happiness.
- The Spirit shares his gifts with each of us, for the benefit of the community. Forgive us, Lord, because we have buried your gifts and we have not made sufficient effort to engage our talent and concern in the building of your Kingdom.
- Finally, forgive us, Lord, because the works of the flesh are more abundant in us, than the effects and fruits of the Spirit.

### Gloria

### Prayer

We place ourselves, Lord, where your Spirit may blow, the Spirit that blows where it will,
free and liberating,
conqueror of the Law, of sin and death.
By your Spirit, we live, Lord: the Spirit
that lived in the heart and in the womb
of a young woman from Nazareth.
In your Spirit, we journey, Lord: the Spirit

that empowered Jesus
and sent him to announce the Good News,
mercy and liberation.
To your Spirit, we open ourselves, Lord. The Spirit
who took away at Pentecost
the prejudices, doubts, fears of the apostles,
and opened wide the doors of the upper room
so that the community of Jesus' followers
might always be sensitive to the world,
free in their speech,
faithful in their witness
and unconquerable in their hope.
In your Spirit, we come together, Lord. The Spirit
who always takes away the fears of today in the
Church,
who burns up all forces in the Church which are not
service
and purifies it with poverty and martyrdom.
Your Spirit, Lord,
who reduces all vices to ashes,
nourishes all good values
and is the soul of the Kingdom,
is the spirit that we obey, Lord. Amen.
(*Prayer found in a parish community*)

## 3. LITURGY OF THE WORD

### Introduction to the Readings

Thanks to the Spirit, the Gospel could not be buried, or reduced to silence. It continues to live, to enlighten the people and to instil a challenge and healthy revolution in society.

The revolution of the Spirit is always in favour of justice and what Christians understand as the Kingdom of God. Like the apostles gathered together, we too invoke the Spirit of Jesus, so that we may take up the challenge and contribute to the common good. Pentecost means sensitivity and commitment.

### Readings

Acts 2:1-11. *Psalm.* 1 Cor. 12:3b-7.12-13. *Alleluia.* Jn 20:19-23. *Brief silence.*

### Reflection

Today, we celebrate the feast of the Holy Spirit. We have always heard that the Spirit is the *Soul of the Church*, but we must also admit, not without a certain sadness, that he is to a large extent unknown.

The Gospel presents him today, in a way that is simple and beautiful at the same time: Jesus, risen again, passes on the Spirit to his friends. He breathes upon them and says to them: "Receive the Holy Spirit." Jesus, the perfection of man and the fullness of life, communicates to us the most beautiful and profound aspect of his resurrection: the Spirit, who makes us new people, valiant men and women, who take up the challenge, with a new way of life, which stems from a Gospel that is reflected upon, shared and put into practice by the community.

Yes, the Spirit is justice, brotherhood, peace, joy, it drives us forward on our mission: "As the Father has sent me, so I am sending you." We, Jesus' friends, are now the communicators of the Gospel, we are the presence of God, in the little corner of the world where we live, and we have the mission of clearly revealing the God who sets us free, so that people may recognise his act of salvation, and so we may work together, in the building of a different and better society.

In the first letter to the Corinthians, we are also told that we Christians have been entrusted with a mission within the community: "in each person, the Spirit manifests itself for the common good". Today, like yesterday, the parishes in question are those in which life is fertile and alive, new projects and realities are emerging, and we Christians in the world are the protagonists of the creative activity in the community. For this reason, we remember that parish work is everybody's task. The Spirit calls on everyone to work together. No one is so poor that he does not have something to bring, nor is anyone so rich that he does not have anything to learn. If someone excludes himself, he causes poverty within the group.

Now we continue this celebration and we pray that God may enlighten us. May the Spirit fill us with his wisdom, so that each one of us will do the best he can. (*Silence for internal reflection.*)

## Creed

## Prayer of the Faithful

- God, good Father, we give you thanks for the Spirit who disturbs us, enlightens us and invites us to work for the common good.
- We confess that Jesus was a supremely spiritual man and, because of this, honourable, brave in the struggle and valiant even unto martyrdom.
- As Christians, we wish to live the experience of the Spirit, the gift of baptism and confirmation, fervently.
- And as Christians, we seek the unity that Jesus desired and the early Church tried to find: a single heart and a single spirit.
- For this reason, we pray to you, Father, for all our people, that our daily life together may be even more human and fraternal.
- We also pray to you for all those who suffer, that they may find in Christians a hand outstretched to help them.
- For these and all our intentions,
  *let us pray to the Lord.*

## Hymn

## Symbolic Action

*Two people approach the symbols, raise them up, while another person proclaims:* Holy Spirit, clothe us in the Gospel again, so that Jesus' plan may be made flesh. May our community know how to understand, serve and love our people, offering them the choicest fruits of redemption.

## 4. RITE OF COMMUNION

## Introduction

The Spirit helps us to give depth and quality to life. Let us receive communion in this same Spirit.

## Hymn

## Prayer

Holy Father,
a song of praise rises from our hearts
because you have scattered upon the world
the Spirit of the risen Lord
to breathe encouragement into the march of history
and so that we may live together in dignity and brotherhood.
In a circle of brothers and sisters, we celebrate such life-giving company
who moves us to go forward in solidarity,
opening our hearts completely to our fellow men and women.
Father,
we believe that the Spirit is also acting in our time,
revealing himself through signs and witnesses
to transform history into a Kingdom of solidarity.
We confess that, in spite of our resistance,
You never withdraw the Spirit from us;
You continue to offer him in abundance
so that we may come to the profound conviction
that there is no other freedom, nor better life
than when we follow your counsel.
With Jesus among us, we bless you,
and with an open heart, we say to you: Our Father…

## Sign of Peace

## Distribution of Communion: Hymn

## Act of Thanksgiving

We give you thanks, good and loving Father,
for the Spirit that you have given us
to renew the life of the Church and of the world.
In the light of the Spirit, we grow in our
desire to serve you
and to promote all the values of the Gospel.

We give you thanks for helping us to know that
we are temples of the Spirit;
for his profound and permanent effect
on our sensibilities,
because he enlightens and renews our life.
We experience that he prays within us
and he whispers to us that we are your children and
you our Abba.
Help us, Father,
to be as honest as the Spirit marks us out to be,
to live a spiritual life like Jesus,
to strive for the Promised Land
like so many saints who have come before us
in the Church.

## 5. CONCLUDING RITE

### Resolution
To live according to the Spirit.

### Blessing

### Conclusion
Following the Spirit is a never-ending task. He
commits us to spread the Gospel to every corner of
the earth. Let us permit him to accompany us on the
projects of his choosing and let us follow in his steps.

### Final Hymn and Dismissal

# SOLEMNITIES
# OF THE LORD

# Most Holy Trinity

## 1. SETTING THE SCENE

### Poster with one of these texts:
- "We are God's people"
- "We are God's family"
- "God, the open family"
- "Bless the Lord"

## 2. INTRODUCTORY RITES

### Introduction
Whenever we gather together as a Christian assembly, we greet each other in the name of the Father, the Son and the Holy Spirit. Today, on the feast of the Most Holy Trinity, this is especially significant. God's family is closely bound together and they open themselves to us with overflowing love. Let us remember that at our baptism, we were marked by the seal of this God. We reaffirm our membership of this family, sharing in this fraternal meeting.

### We set the scene for this celebration by presenting these symbols:
- Icon of the Most Holy Trinity.
- Globe of the world (God the Creator).
- Paschal candle (Christ the Saviour).
- Picture of a dove  (The motivating Spirit).

### Hymn

### Greeting
Brothers and sisters, let us praise God the Father together through the Son and in the Holy Spirit.

### Penitential Rite
- Because you are all mercy: *Lord, have mercy.*
- Because you are our Redeemer: *Christ, have mercy.*
- Because you are the soul of the Church: *Lord, have mercy.*

### Gloria

### Prayer
God, bountiful Father, you have sent into the world the Word of truth and the Spirit of holiness, in order to reveal your wondrous mystery to all; grant that we may profess the true faith, that we may know the glory of the eternal Trinity and worship your unity. Through Christ…

## 3. LITURGY OF THE WORD

### Introduction to the Readings
Throughout history, a fundamental religious experience has been constant among people who believe: the continual presence of God giving inspiration into life. The Gospel captures this experience in an extraordinary text that everyone can understand: "God loved the world so much that he sent his Son, not to condemn the world, but that it might be saved by him."

### Readings
Exod. 34:4b-6. 8-9. *Psalm.* 2 Cor. 13:11-13. *Alleluia.* Jn 3:16-18. *Brief silence.*

### Reflection
Our God is not a boring, far-away and distant being, nor a cruel castigator, nor a bully, nor a stopgap, nor any of the numerous false images that abound everywhere in the popular consciousness. Our God reveals himself as a family, as a community of love and communion. When we pronounce the name of

the Christian God, we are referring to a divine community, in whose image we are made, and who has approached us through revelation and redemption.

The God of the Trinity is unique to Christianity. In this vital nucleus, the unfolding of all that exists originated. We come from a powerful spring of life and love. The Most Holy Trinity is the personal and loving God who is living with us, who offers us an extraordinary freedom and invites us to collaborate with him in the marvellous work of Creation. The three members of the Trinity are seriously involved in the history of salvation, to such an extent that the Son became one of us and gave up his life for all mankind.

This God of the Trinity is both origin and destination. His mystery is revealed by his Son, made human. He speaks to us of a Father brimming over with love. His own incarnation is a way of coming close to us that can only be explained by love. But, besides this, the Son, God-with-us, is the mediator for the sending of the Spirit, whom he has given us as a comforter, guide and one who reveals the whole truth. This spirit is the one who assures our spirit that we are the children of God (Rom. 8:16).

The way to draw near to our God is by spirituality and life in the faith which is developed by the Gospel, and not by philosophy, nor by other forms of knowledge. Someone wrote: God is like the sun; whether you see him or not, he appears or is hidden, he still shines. If you cannot prevent the sun from shining, still less can you prevent God from pouring his mercy upon us. (*Silence for internal reflection.*)

## Creed

## Prayer of the Faithful

- That we may set ourselves free from idols and all false images of God, *let us pray to the Lord.*
- That Christian communities may proclaim the Good News that God is a family, who loves us

and welcomes us, *let us pray to the Lord.*
- For believers of all religions, that they may testify to their faith with signs and words of freedom, *let us pray to the Lord.*
- For those who have come to the faith or who have left it, that they may find a good example in those who profess to believe, *let us pray to the Lord.*
- For ourselves who share in the Gospel, that we may behave like brothers and sisters in every situation, *let us pray to the Lord.*

## Symbolic Action

*A person presents the baptismal font (if there is a portable one) or a large receptacle of water. Another brings up some beautiful flowers that are put into the font or receptacle. One of the two says:* Baptism is the fountain of life. We were baptised in the name of the Father, the Son and the Holy Spirit. *Then the assembly is sprinkled with holy water.*

## 4. RITE OF COMMUNION

## Introduction

God the Father sent his Son into the world, in order to save it. Communion with Jesus is a sign of opening ourselves to salvation, the greatest gift the Most Holy Trinity has given to us.

## Hymn

## Prayer

We praise you, Father.
We feel deeply loved by you.
You are the origin and the goal of the
great march of history
and of our own personal history.
Blessed are you, who uplift us with a divine vocation
and lovingly open the door for us,
to your house of the Trinity.
We recognise that everything springs from your fountain of love:
your thoughts for us are for a boundless universe,

you created us for life
and you left us the task of growing and advancing.
Such was your inspiration.
We feel, Father, that you penetrate us like water
penetrates a sponge,
that you have redeemed us through the human
story of your Son
and you have restored us to life with your
Spirit of holiness.
Now you invite us to put the Gospel into practice,
so that the earth may resemble heaven as
much as possible.
Infuse us with the mysticism of the prophets
and the sensitivity of the pure in heart.
Rely on our commitment.
We thank you for having communicated to us
the experience of your family
and for including us in the real and necessary work
of your Kingdom.
In communion, we say to you with Jesus: Our Father…

## Sign of Peace

## Distribution of Communion: Hymn

## Act of Thanksgiving

- We give you thanks, our God, for the experience of the faith, thanks to which we can better understand your revelation.
- With Saint Paul, we confess that we live, move and have our being in you.
- We sense that you are infinitely greater than we are able to imagine. The whole of Creation is a collective symbol of your presence.
- We thank you for having sought us out, for having come to meet us.
- Thank you for the invitation to be one of your family and to share a destiny of fullness with you.

## 5. CONCLUDING RITE

## Resolution
To live with the qualities that are fitting for children of God.

## Blessing

## Conclusion
This day, especially dedicated to our God, reminds us of the first commandment in our tradition: "To love God above all things".

We have celebrated the mystery of the Trinity and we have affirmed that he is good, that he keeps the door of his house open and that he is close to us all, intimate with every believer.

On account of this relationship with God, we must be in favour of everything that is worthy and human. Genuine faith is a guarantee of all that is good. We believers can be the greatest witnesses to that.

## Final Hymn and Dismissal

# Corpus Christi

## 1. SETTING THE SCENE

### Poster with one of these texts:
- "I am the Bread of life"
- "Jesus is the bread broken for us"
- "Jesus is the blood poured out for us"

### Symbols:
- Loaf of bread.
- Large glass or jug of wine.
- Basket of food (an expression of sharing).

## 2. INTRODUCTORY RITES

### Introduction
Today, we celebrate the feast of the Body of Christ. Throughout history, Christian people have valued the Eucharist so much that they have dedicated a special day to it.

Celebrating the Body of Christ is to remember Jesus' Last Supper and the meaning of that first Eucharist. It means to incorporate, in ourselves, the power of devotion forever.

To honour the Eucharist, as the presence of Jesus, also means solidarity with our most needy brothers and sisters, since it is with them that Jesus especially identifies.

### Hymn

### Greeting
Brothers and sisters, let us bless the Lord, whose sacramental presence is with us in the Church.

### Penitential Rite
- You, Lord, are the definitive Word: *Lord, have mercy*.
- You, Lord, are the Bread of life: *Christ, have mercy*.
- You, Lord, are the new Covenant: *Lord, have mercy*.

### Gloria

### Prayer
O God, who in this wonderful sacrament have left us the memorial of your passion; grant us to venerate the sacred mysteries of your Body and your Blood, that we may constantly experience within ourselves the fruits of your redemption. You who live and reign…

## 3. LITURGY OF THE WORD

### Introduction to the Readings
The Eucharist soon took a strong hold among the first Christians. The ample richness of its symbolic meaning spread rapidly among the first communities. The Eucharist is the living bread that nourishes and the blood of a redeeming sacrifice, which inspires generosity; it is the love that unites members of the community, so that they may dedicate themselves in attentive service to all their neighbours.

### Readings
Dt. 8:2-3.14b-16a. *Psalm.* 1 Cor. 10:16-17. *Alleluia.* Jn 6:51-58. *Brief silence.*

## Reflection

Corpus Christi is the celebration of the Eucharist, the nourishment offered to believers to encourage them to persevere on life's journey. Jesus strengthens us with his whole person and his whole message. The highest form of giving is to offer oneself as food and drink: "My flesh is real food and my blood is real drink."

There is a document attributed to Saint Justin, according to which we are able to appreciate how the Eucharist was already being celebrated in the second century: "Both those of us living in the cities as well as those from the countryside gather together; the commentaries of the apostles or the writings of the prophets are read. Afterwards, the person presiding exhorts everyone to the imitation of these examples. Next, we offer up our prayer. Then, we share in the bread and wine of the Lord, and distribute the gifts that have been brought. Those who possess goods give them in order to help the needy." An inspiring description!

At the present time, we Christians, who are organised into little communities or parishes, continue meeting together in accordance with Jesus' command: "Do this in memory of me" (Lk. 22:19); that is to say, so that we may share in the symbolic actions and the dynamic commitment of that Supper. In these meetings, we proclaim the Word of God, celebrate the life of Jesus, above all his act of self-giving, and our communion in his devoted love, even unto sacrifice; one of us exhorts the congregation to follow the example of Jesus and that of the saints, his greatest followers; we pray together; we repeat the symbolic act of nourishing ourselves with the Body and Blood of the Lord; we make collections to distribute and to help the needy.

Corpus Christi is a journey of nourishment: "I am the living Bread which has come down from heaven: whoever eats of this Bread, will live for ever." The most fundamental and genuine quality of Jesus is his complete giving of himself: as bread that is broken and shared out and blood that is poured out in mercy. The story of his life is aptly demonstrated in the sharing of bread and the cup being handed round. Similar graceful acts should be brought out in us, by the commitment in that phrase: "love is paid for by love". The Eucharist and loving union go hand in hand.

Our community, like the Church, is the body of Christ. Without our service, without our sharing, there can be no real sacramental act. Because we live what we celebrate, we too, in communion with him, must become a bread that is shared and a life that is offered. That is why we have a basket with a variety of foods among the symbols. Today, Christian charity is being stressed, so that we may share what we are and what we have, and live in a growing spirit of service. (*Silence for internal reflection.*)

## Creed

## Prayer of the Faithful

- Let us unite our prayer through the intercession of Jesus. He gave himself, even unto the sacrifice of his own life.
- Let us pray for divided peoples, for broken families, for those who feel their dreams have been shattered, for lost friendships...
- Let us pray also that the commitment of Christians may be capable of changing the unjust structures of society.
- Let us increase our generosity, so that it may express itself without limit and that in this way, the needs of those who live beside us may be addressed.
- Let us pray also that our love may be true, genuine, effective and non-condescending, self-sacrificing and generous. *Let us pray to the Lord.*

## Symbolic Action
*Collection for parochial or diocesan charity.*

## Hymn

## Offerings

- *Donor card:* We present, Lord, this symbol that represents a way of thinking about others and of helping them with one's own life.
- *Completed collection:* We also present to you this collection that we have just made, an action with which we express that sharing is better than keeping.

## 4. RITE OF COMMUNION

### Introduction

We unite in the same faith. We share the same bread. We have the same mission. Jesus is our nourishment.

### Hymn

### Prayer

We bless you, Father, gathered together as brothers and sisters
because we are able to help and to be united.
Conscious of your love,
in the company of Jesus and of your Spirit,
we look deeply at this world
and we realise that there are homeless,
maladjusted people,
old people poorly looked after, sick people in isolation,
young people without guidance, unemployed people,
broken families, alcoholics, drug addicts,
people incapable of reflecting…
Not everyone is like that, Lord.
But, confronted by this scene, feelings are not enough.
We pray about these problems
so that you may educate us in Christian solidarity.
You, who are good,
heal the wounds of all who suffer.
Help us to seek that levelling out
which eliminates inequalities and creates the
Promised Land.
We aim for the daily miracle of sharing.
We gather together the work of all those
of upright heart
and in good faith say to you: Our Father…

## Sign of Peace

## Distribution of Communion: Hymn

## Act of Thanksgiving

- Father, we give you thanks for Jesus, our nourishment, our salvation, the prophet of brotherhood, who risked everything for love.
- He who became poor, so that he might enrich us with his poverty, urges us in his wisdom to share.
- May our eyes and our sensitivity remain open, so that we may be a community of welcome and solidarity, above all, for the most underprivileged.
- Enlighten us, Father, so that no one will lack his or her share of spiritual and bodily nourishment.

## 5. CONCLUDING RITE

### Resolution

To increasingly develop service and self-sacrifice.

### Blessing

### Conclusion

Sharing in Jesus' Eucharist is a sign of a wider sharing with all our brothers and sisters, especially the most needy. But let us not confuse Christian charity with a feeling of compassion. May the generosity of Jesus enlighten us, so that we may be in solidarity with the poor.

### Final Hymn and Informal Dismissal

# Sundays in
# ORDINARY TIME

# Second Sunday

## 1. SETTING THE SCENE

### Poster with one of these texts:
- ◼ "Jesus takes sin away"
- ◼ "We can be light"

## 2. INTRODUCTORY RITES

### Introduction
Now that Christmas is over, we begin the period that we call *ordinary time*. But we will see that there is continuity in the message. John the Baptist, convinced that Jesus is the one we must listen to and follow, presents him as "the Lamb of God, who takes away the sins of the world" and invites his disciples to change over to Jesus' group. John has come to realise that in Jesus resides the fullness of the Spirit of God. Therefore, what he has to do is to bear witness to him and devote himself fully to the service of his cause, because it is the cause of God the Father. A great example for the life of any Christian.

### Hymn

### Greeting
Together let us bless the Lord, who loves us.

### Penitential Rite
So that we may take part worthily in this celebration, let us acknowledge our sins. *(Brief silence.) I confess…*

### Gloria

### Prayer
God, bountiful Father, you are proud of Jesus, because he let himself be filled with your Spirit; he did good works and is the Light for all people. Now that we have experienced redemption, we feel compelled to proclaim it. Help us to be witnesses to the Lamb who takes away the sins of the world. Amen.

## 3. LITURGY OF THE WORD

### Introduction to the Readings
Jesus, more than any other prophet, felt the power of God, calling him to be "a light to the people" and a sign of universal salvation. John the Baptist confesses that Jesus is the Son of God. We also believe it. That is why we try to express it in words and with witness of life.

### Readings
Is. 49:3. 5-6. *Psalm*. 1 Cor. 1:1-3. *Acclamation*. Jn 1:29-34. *Brief silence*.

### Reflection
The poems about the *servant of Yahweh* sum up, with great symbolic intensity, God's plans and the attitudes appropriate to believers. According to the first reading, God is proud of this Servant. But he asks more of him: "I will make you a light unto the nations, so that my salvation may reach unto the ends of the earth."

Our community cannot remain satisfied with evangelising only those near to us. Salvation must reach the furthest corners of our society.
God will be proud of us, if we labour tirelessly for the Gospel, widening the horizons of the mission. "Here I am to do your will" is the reply and attitude that befit the true believer. Spreading the Word is a task that always needs addressing.

The Gospel brings into prominence "the Lamb of God, who takes away the sins of the world". John the Baptist has the spiritual capacity to discover in Jesus the person who struggles with all his might against evil and tramples it beneath his feet. In the Jewish tradition, the lamb is a symbol of the Passover: it recalls the liberation from Egypt. Jesus, as the Lamb sacrificed on the cross, redeems us, reconciles us and invites us to live in the paschal way, which consists in being people renewed according to the Gospel.

Following Jesus involves breaking with the "sins of the world", with that way of thinking and living, permeating our surroundings, that does not accord with the Gospel and is like a poison threatening to contaminate us. We Christians have no better undertaking for which to struggle, than that revealed by Jesus. His person and his message have a powerful logic.

This capacity for vision and witness is necessary in every age. Our community must continually strive to enlighten men and women who can bring the culture of the Gospel to their own environment. Furthermore, like John the Baptist, our community must learn how to present him who takes away the sins of the world, to all the people. Will God be proud of us? (*Silence for internal reflection.*)

## Creed

## Prayer of the Faithful
- That the profound experience of faith
  may never be lacking in the Church,
  *let us pray to the Lord.*
- That we Christians may have a dialogue of openness and collaboration with everyone, especially with those who do not think as we do, *let us pray to the Lord.*
- That the gifts and contributions of everyone may strengthen our community, *let us pray to the Lord.*

- That the Spirit of Jesus may help us to be witnesses to all of our people, *let us pray to the Lord.*

## Offerings
- *Gospel:* Lord, we want to carry your Law within our hearts. For this reason, we offer you the Gospel that you, yourself, have given us.
- *Keys:* Lord, we want to be open to your Spirit and to the Lamb who is our Saviour.

## Hymn

## Symbolic Action
*Someone goes to a prominent place holding a large glass on a plate. Another person goes up to the same place, with a jug full of water; he says, facing the assembly:* Are we full of God's grace? Is there room for more? (*He pours water into the glass until it overflows.*) God wants to live inside us until we are overflowing…

## 4. RITE OF COMMUNION

## Introduction
Jesus is the Lamb of God, who takes away the sins of the world, he who points the way for those who worship the Father in spirit and in truth. May this communion be an incentive to give witness to God and to Jesus.

## Hymn

## Prayer
Here we are, Father,
in communion with you and with each other.
This community values your nearness
and recognises that Spirit who identified Jesus.
It is he who gives us the atmosphere of family.
Through him, the Gospel penetrates us
until it becomes a deep experience.
Thank you for this Spirit who is so human

that he brings a breath of fresh air into your Church
and sustains so many Christian people.
He whispers to us that you are our Abba,
he assures us that you love us with tremendous love
and confirms to us that you are mercy and forgiveness.
For all of which, our souls are full of gratitude.
We recall our great commitment
and, united in Jesus, we assure you:
"Here I am, Lord, to do your will".
You do not accept sacrifices that are
not made in solidarity.
"My God, I love and carry your Law within my heart."
I proclaim your salvation before the assembly.
In brotherly communion, we say to you: Our Father…

## Sign of Peace

## Distribution of Communion: Hymn

## Act of Thanksgiving

- Father, we give you thanks for Jesus, your Son among us. Through him, we have come to know your salvation.
- We give you thanks, also, for the gift of the Spirit. Through him, we carry your Law within our hearts.
- Help us, so that your light may shine through our lives and in this way, the understanding of your Gospel may grow.

## 5. CONCLUDING RITE

### Resolution
To pray and carry out the will of God.

### Blessing

### Conclusion
In many places, there are Christians who admire Jesus and follow him as true believers. Following Jesus is a personal experience, but it unfolds within community, bringing people together in brotherhood. For everyone, he is the Light, the Truth and the Salvation, who is above customs and temperaments.

Let us open our hearts wide to create brotherhood. We Christians always have a pressing task: to be witnesses to what we experience and celebrate.

## Final Hymn and Dismissal

# Third Sunday

## 1. SETTING THE SCENE

### Poster with one of these texts:
- "The Kingdom of God is near"
- "They left everything… and followed him"

## 2. INTRODUCTORY RITES

### Introduction
Warm greetings on this day of the Lord. Jesus is in the midst of the community as it gathers together. Today we hear again his resounding invitation to follow him, to live united and to preach the values of the Kingdom of God. Jesus' great passion and preoccupation was the Kingdom of God. He dedicated all his efforts to it. The Kingdom of God on earth is the great human cause in every age.

Let us set the scene for this celebration with the presentation of these symbols:

- *Lighted paschal candle:* The people "saw a great light". For us, the great light is the story of Jesus.
- *Radio cassette with headphones:* Jesus goes on inviting us to work for the Kingdom, but the noise of life and many secondary interests prevent us from hearing his call.

### Hymn

### Greeting
Brothers and sisters, let us bless the Lord, who has called us to live like Jesus.

### Penitential Rite
- We have sinned: *Lord, have mercy.*
- We want to be converted: *Christ, have mercy.*
- You are our hope: *Lord, have mercy.*

### Gloria

### Prayer
Bountiful Father, help us to lead a life according to your will, so that we may be able to bear the fruits of good works in abundance, in the name of your Son, Jesus Christ, who lives and reigns with you.

## 3. LITURGY OF THE WORD

### Introduction to the Readings
The salvation that God offers us, always brings with it the gift of perception and an understanding of life. This salvation comes to us through Jesus, the great sign of God for all of us who believe. That is why Jesus can never be a cause of division, but of peace and collaboration.

### Readings
Is. 8:23-9:3. *Psalm* 1 Cor. 1:10-13. 17. *Acclamation.* Mt. 4:12-23. *Brief silence.*

### Reflection
One of the most damaging testimonies that a community can give is that of division between its members. Paul goes out to face this problem in the community at Corinth: there are rival conflicting groups. Every community should apply the lesson: among Christians, Jesus can only be a cause of unity. If this does not apply, it is because we are not under the influence of the same Spirit. The ideal of unity is to arrive at "one same mind and one same feeling". If this common frame of mind is not reached, unity should still remain amidst the diversity.

Furthermore, deep in all people lies a basic and common desire to have a fuller and better life. For Jesus, this human aspiration to have a fuller and better life has a lot to do with what is understood by the Kingdom of God. The Jews expected that a Messiah would secure the liberation of his people, would establish justice and would bring the peace that they desired. Jesus announces that this longed-for Kingdom of God has arrived already in the form of his own person. That is why it was his great passion, the central message of his teaching and the cause to which he completely dedicated his life. It was so important to him, that he could do nothing less than to leave it enshrined in his fundamental prayer: the Paternoster (the Our Father).

However, Jesus did not want it to be his preoccupation only, but to be the main concern of all those who would follow him. On the one hand, he asks for conversion, so that the Kingdom of God may dwell within people; on the other hand, he seeks fellow workers whom he first trains and then sends out.

It would seem that Jesus calls on the first people that he meets, that he does not seek people with any special qualities. That is to say, everyone is good enough to work for the Kingdom of God. What the Gospel really does make clear is that when Jesus calls someone, they have to give something up… because a choice has to be made.

Jesus is still calling upon us. The response of the first disciples was to drop what they were doing

immediately and to follow him – in preaching the Gospel. Do we respond as speedily as they did?

If the Kingdom of God does not begin in oneself, it is difficult for it to be witnessed to or proclaimed. (*Silence for internal reflection*).

## Creed

## Prayer of the Faithful
- For all peoples, that there may be no factions or divisions among them, *let us pray to the Lord.*
- For the Church, that it may proclaim with fidelity the Gospel that has been entrusted to it, *let us pray to the Lord.*
- For the Pope and bishops, the successors of those fishermen from Galilee, that they may never forget that humble beginning, so full of promise, *let us pray to the Lord.*
- That all Christians may work for the Kingdom of God without fanaticism, *let us pray to the Lord.*
- For our community, that it may be distinguished for its dedication to Jesus and for being a sign of unity and brotherhood, *let us pray to the Lord.*

## Symbolic Action
*A person goes up to the altar dressed in a garment of high quality. He takes out a wallet, shows it to everyone and leaves it there. Next, he takes off the garment and leaves it too upon the altar. He says:* It is worth giving up everything for the Kingdom of God.

## 4. RITE OF COMMUNION

### Introduction
Jesus is the Light and the Way for all who come into this world. May communion with him strengthen our vocation to follow him.

### Hymn

### Prayer
Good and loving God, with gratitude and warmth we open our hearts wide to the Gospel.
You love us with a special love,
you enlighten us with humanity and great light,
you call on us to be your Kingdom and to enlarge it.
What a great mission that is for the Christian!
Everything began, Father,
with experience of baptism.

You left a sign deeply engraved in us:
the redeeming cross of life.
Then, we understood the power of your presence,
the impact of your grace was felt deep in our hearts,
it filled our souls with spirituality
and we discovered a new ideal: the meaning of mission.
Since then, we have given ourselves to Jesus' cause.
The Spirit enlightens us and strengthens
us on our mission.
Your Kingdom is our communal project
from the moment it became our personal project.
Thank you for marking us out with
such a beautiful vocation.
Re-clothe us with courage,
so that we may serve our people.
In brotherhood, we say to you: Our Father…

## Sign of Peace

## Distribution of Communion: Hymn

## Act of Thanksgiving

Father, sometimes we are taken up with
unimportant things. On occasion, these things
become little idols and they influence us more than
you do. Accept our conversion which is renewed by
your continuous call. We give you thanks, because
you do not allow us to think of ourselves. Deep
down, what matters most is your Gospel. That is why
we will leave everything to serve your Kingdom.

## 5. CONCLUDING RITE

### Resolution

Conversion and bearing witness to the Gospel,
drawing upon the wisdom that comes from the
great Christian symbol: the cross.

### Blessing

## Conclusion

Following Jesus and creating the Kingdom of God go
together. The Kingdom of God includes creating
brotherhood. For this reason, it is a task for every day.
Throughout the week, let us meditate upon all this.
May life be good to us and may the Lord go with us.

## Final Hymn and Dismissal

# Fourth Sunday

## 1. SETTING THE SCENE

### Poster with one of these texts:
- "Blessed are the poor"
- "Blessed are the pure in heart"
- "The simple shall come first"

### Symbol:
- Vase of water (sign of the Gospel).

## 2. INTRODUCTORY RITES

### Introduction
Welcome to the celebration. We gather together with our trust in Jesus. We have the opportunity, once more, to purify ourselves by contact with the Word of God. Today, it presents to us the ideal of the Beatitudes. This well-known text encapsulates, like no other, what is essential in the Gospel, reveals our true identity and reminds us of our duty to grow to the fullness of our potential.

### Hymn

### Greeting
Brothers and sisters, let us bless the Lord, who calls us to be happy.

### Penitential Rite
- Because you love us, *Lord, have mercy.*
- Because you went even to martyrdom for us, *Christ, have mercy.*
- Because you fill us with holiness, *Lord, have mercy.*

### Gloria

### Prayer
God, bountiful Father, you want us to be happy and, to this end, you have marked out for us the way of the Beatitudes. Enlighten us, so that we may understand the spirituality that they contain, and so that we may truly witness to the inner joy that they produce in us. Through Christ…

## 3. LITURGY OF THE WORD

### Introduction to the Readings
One of the characteristics of God is that he has this desire to save us. And he does this by means of the simplicity of Jesus, who chooses to live in a humble manner, so that he may be near everyone, yet brimming with the gospel message.

The word of scripture today highlights the fact that God chooses what is small and humble, in order to confound false wisdom and proud attitudes. He prefers poverty of spirit, purity of heart, mercy, hunger and thirst for justice, peace…

It is worth comparing our lives with the Beatitudes and drawing some conclusions.

### Readings
Zep 2:3; 3:12-13. *Psalm.* 1 Cor. 1:26-31. *Acclamation.* Mt. 5:1-12a. *Brief silence.*

### Symbolic Action
*While each Beatitude is slowly proclaimed, different people from the assembly bring up single flowers, if possible, of different varieties.*

## Reflection

The practice of the Beatitudes causes life to flower. They are much more than a beautiful poem, which we recite with pride at celebrations, like this. They contain such revolutionary ferment that they kindle the hearts of some people and drive others to distraction. Human progress is only possible if we put into practice these impressive verses of wisdom and contrasting spirituality.

The Beatitudes sum up the Gospel and Kingdom of God proclaimed by Jesus. They all come together in one sole objective: happiness. They constitute a clarion call of joy. God wants us to be happy. Furthermore, we Christians are called upon to bring happiness into the world, a profound, human, personal and social happiness, which affects the present and future. God and Jesus give us these tools, so that we may create happiness with assurance. There are some people who do not use them. Others are not interested in them; they prefer their own complex lives, preserving their own profitable life-style at all cost, which does not achieve either justice or equality… The result is that they are not happy deep down, nor do they make others happy.

Accepting the Beatitudes presupposes delivering an alternative mentality, because the mentality of the Beatitudes is not the one that our surroundings promote, nor that which is spread by the media. Furthermore, in many situations, it presupposes going against the current, because it implies opting for "the madness of the cross" or becoming "the fools of Christ", as Saint Paul put it. We can find beautiful statements about the Beatitudes; but whoever practises them is frequently left out in the cold and even persecuted.

The Beatitudes express the new Christian spirituality. They complete and go further than the Commandments. They propose a feasible, logical, demanding way of life that is bound up with our most noble aspirations. They describe Jesus' ideal and our ideal. To create the Kingdom of God, there is no other way than that of the Beatitudes. (*Silence for internal reflection.*)

## Creed

## Prayer of the Faithful

- Let us pray for the people, that they may organise themselves according to the wisdom of the Beatitudes.
- Let us pray for all those who try to assimilate the message of the Beatitudes, that they may sow the seed of a new society.
- Let us pray for the Church, that it may be a growing expression of the spirituality contained in the Beatitudes.
- We also pray that the Gospel may stimulate our culture, even to the extent of transforming it with the alternative message of the Beatitudes.
- Let us intercede for each other and let us not forget especially the most needy in our town. *Let us pray to the Lord.*

## Offerings

- *Book of the Little Prince:* Lord, there are books, like this one that teach us how to see what is essential in life in our own hearts.
- *Photograph of an exemplary member of the Community who has already passed away:* Lord, examples influence us. In X's life, we have seen a reflection of the Beatitudes.

## Hymn

## Symbolic Action

*A person goes up to the lectern, takes the Lectionary and, facing the assembly, says:* We are simple people. We do not seek prominence. What we desire is to practise the Beatitudes.

## 4. RITE OF COMMUNION

## Introduction

The way of the Beatitudes should characterise all Christians. To resemble Jesus is to have the spirit of the Beatitudes. Let us pray for this Gospel spirit for everyone.

## Hymn

## Prayer

Father, our admiration reaches its summit
as we experience how much you love us.
You desire our happiness fervently.
You have opened our eyes to the message
of the Gospel.
Through Jesus, you have marked out for us
a path of eternal bliss.
You bless those who choose to be poor.
You proclaim that this chosen simplicity
is the best road to freedom.
You have made it clear that salvation
comes to the merciful,
those who suffer, the pure in heart,
those who work for peace and justice.
Father, this is a powerful logic. You are different.
All the world is absorbed in itself,
seeking self-promotion.
For you, on the other hand, the most selfless
person comes first.
We want to be like you:
to concentrate on the Gospel
and to seek the common good above that
of the individual.
You see that this assembly is not of the wise
or the powerful,
but we have great aspirations and we say
to you: Our Father…

## Sign of Peace

## Distribution of Communion: Hymn

## Act of Thanksgiving

- Blessed are you, Father, for the example of so many men and women whose mentality reflects the Beatitudes in the way they think and live.
- Above all, we are inspired by Jesus' example who lived this ideal to the full and presents it to us with great conviction.
- Father, may we learn how to be those who suffer, the pure in heart, the peacemakers, the simple and merciful, so that we may enrich our surroundings with the Beatitudes.

## 5. CONCLUDING RITE

### Resolution

To practise the Beatitudes.

### Blessing

### Conclusion

We have shared in the Christian ideal: the Beatitudes. Now, the testing ground of everyday life awaits us, so that we may put into practice that wisdom which the Gospel pours forth. May the Lord enlighten and help us. May everyone have a happy week.

### Final Hymn and Dismissal

# Fifth Sunday

## 1. SETTING THE SCENE

### Poster with one of these texts:
- "If you share, you are light"
- "Are we salt and light?"

### Symbols:
- Soup bowl full of salt *(sign of the Gospel)*.
- Tray with some lighted candles *(sign of the Gospel)*.
- Loaf of bread.

## 2. INTRODUCTORY RITES

### Introduction
Greetings to everyone. We meet together again, around the risen Christ, so that we may continue to be, in the midst of our town, an active ferment, the salt of unity for a happy society and the light of hope. The Gospel reminds us today of the value of Christian soldiering. If we live according to the Beatitudes, we strengthen the Kingdom of God among us.

### Hymn

### Greeting
Brothers and sisters, let us praise the Lord together, who calls upon us to be the salt of the earth and light of the world.

### Penitential Rite
- Because you are good and compassionate, *Lord, have mercy.*
- Because you are the light for all, *Christ, have mercy.*
- Because you desire our good, *Lord, have mercy.*

### Gloria

### Prayer
Lord, watch over your family with constant love; protect it and defend it always, since it has put its hope in you alone. Through Christ…

## 3. LITURGY OF THE WORD

### Introduction to the Readings
A clear sign that we are Christians is that we do not close our eyes to the needs of others. The faith shows itself in acts of justice, solidarity and mercy. This is the message of the first reading.

In the second, Saint Paul introduces himself, confessing that he is merely a servant of the Gospel he proclaims. He carries the burden of his weakness and his fears like anyone else. His testimony rests solely in the wisdom of Christ on the cross and in the power of the Spirit.

The Gospel, in relation to what we proclaimed last Sunday, tells us: whoever practises the Beatitudes is the salt of the earth and light of the world.

### Readings
Is. 58, 7-10. *Psalm.* 1 Cor. 2:1-5. *Acclamation.* Mt. 5:13-16. *Brief silence.*

### Symbolic Action
*During the proclamation of the Gospel, the bowl of salt and the tray of lighted candles are brought up to the table of symbols at the appointed moment.*

### Reflection
Sometimes we ask ourselves what we have to do to be genuine Christians. The author of the first

reading states that faithfulness to God is mediated through active love for one's neighbour. This is stressed by Jesus and is forcefully expressed by New Testament theologians like Saint John: "Whoever does not love, does not know God, because God is love… he loved us in the beginning. If someone says: 'I Love God' and hates his brother, he is a liar; because whoever does not love the brother that he sees, cannot love God whom he does not see" (1 Jn 4:8. 19-20).

We Christians are fortunate in being able to rely on the wisdom of the faith, in order to act with sensitivity. Jesus sums up for us the message of the Beatitudes with three convergent statements:

- "You are the salt of the earth."
- "You are the light of the world."
- "Let your light shine before men, so that… they may glorify your Father who is in heaven."

To be salt and light are two valuable images that very fittingly reflect the witness and power of Christians. They are two symbolic expressions of powerful significance, so that our heavenly Father may receive the glory that he deserves. The identity card of every Christian should contain these two items of information. It makes no sense for any of Jesus' followers to be bland, insipid, without taste or flavouring, without vital force. It makes even less sense to see a dull Christian, without any spark or brightness.

To be salt is equivalent to bringing meaning, joy, content and hope to daily life; it is equivalent to living with spirituality, a powerful effect, so that through one's witness and commitment many people may discover and glorify our common Father. To be light means that our life and our speech should shed light in a human and Christian way. The light is the love that we express, the solidarity that we have, the encouragement that we transmit, the services we perform, the spirituality that we breathe, the commitments that we keep, the work that we do responsibly, the joy that we spread, the mystical quality that we communicate, etc. In a nutshell, our life sheds light, if it reflects the spirit of the Beatitudes in a natural way.

To sum up, it is fitting for us to ask ourselves: Are we salt? Are we light? Does our life surprise others, so that they can discover and glorify our Father in heaven? Let us meditate on this. (*Silence for internal reflection.*)

## Creed

## Prayer of the Faithful

- Brothers and sisters, let us pray that among all peoples, efforts may be made to create a peaceful society, the fruit of justice and forgiveness.
- Let us pray that we Christians may fulfil our commitment to be salt and light in the midst of society.
- Let us increase our awareness, so that we may support all initiatives which aim to help those who suffer from being marginalised or unemployed.
- Let us pray for each other, so that our lives may glorify God who was the first to love us.
- For these and for all our intentions, *let us pray to the Lord.*

## Offerings

- *Crucifix:* Father, we reaffirm our faith in the wisdom of Jesus on the cross.
- *Flower or beautiful plant and identity card:* Father, we present to you our best self, so that through our works many may discover you and glorify you.

## Hymn

## Symbolic Action

*Someone goes up to the table of symbols, raises the bowl of salt and says:* One way of being the salt of the earth (*he sets down the bowl and raises the tray of candles*) and the light of the world (*he sets down the tray, takes the loaf and breaks it with his hands*) is to share.

## 4. RITE OF COMMUNION

### Introduction
We Christians must live with such Gospel fervour that we become signs of God's goodness. May this communion strengthen our commitment to be witnesses to Christ.

### Hymn

### Prayer
Our God and Father, we praise you with joy because we can be salt and light in the midst of the people. How wonderful this is! Our life can light the way to you,
can be a symbol of the goodness that you are, communicate the mystic quality of the blessed. Everything is a pure gift from you.
What would we be without your Spirit?
He is the one who inculcates the values of the Gospel in us,
who nourishes us as believers,
who encourages us to share.
The same Spirit drives us on to be children of the light and to be tireless preachers of the Gospel of your Kingdom.
Father, we glorify you with all those who know you. We unite our witness, so that it may better reveal your presence.
The community supports us in our mission.
Although sometimes we are hindered by discouragement and we squander your gifts of salt and light, in hope and as a converted people, we say to you: Our Father…

### Sign of Peace

### Distribution of Communion: Hymn

### Act of Thanksgiving
- Father, we glorify you for the light given to us by the Gospel, so that we may create brotherhood.
- We give you thanks, because we are able to be your symbols in the midst of the people.
- Father, may the value of sharing together grow in our town.

## 5. CONCLUDING RITE

### Resolution
To glorify God with our works in daily life.

### Blessing

### Conclusion
We have stressed our commitment as witnesses to be salt and light within our neighbourhood. We have also highlighted our vocation to symbolise in our lives that God is good. May the knowledge remain ingrained in us of how God relies upon our responsible collaboration. Sharing is the solution to many needs and problems. May the Lord go with us and may the week be positive for us.

### Final Hymn and Dismissal

# Sixth Sunday

## 1. SETTING THE SCENE

### Poster with one of these texts:
- ◼ "Happy is the person whose life is blameless"
- ◼ "…But I say unto you"

## 2. INTRODUCTORY RITES

### Introduction
One of the values that we most appreciate is that of freedom. But this has its risks: we can use it in the wrong way. For this reason, the psalm says: "Happy is the person of unblemished life who walks in the way of the Lord." By means of the Spirit, a wisdom has been revealed to us, so that we may know how to grasp and understand what happens inside ourselves and outside us, and so that we may act resolutely. The Gospel reading of the Sermon on the Mount puts Jesus in the place of one who is the dividing point in history: "You have heard it said… But I say unto you."

### Hymn

### Greeting
Brothers and sisters, let us bless the Lord, who is deserving of all our praise.

### Penitential Rite
- ◼ You, Lord, welcome everyone: *Lord, have mercy.*
- ◼ You, Lord, are the sure and certain path: *Christ, have mercy.*
- ◼ You, Lord, are life in all its fullness: *Lord, have mercy.*

### Gloria

### Prayer
Lord, you are happy to dwell in those who are pure and sincere in heart. Grant that we may live in such a way that we might be worthy of having you with us always. Through Christ…

## 3. LITURGY OF THE WORD

### Introduction to the Readings
We human beings are free. If we say yes to God and to life, it is because we see him in our hearts, he convinces us. Nobody imposes him on us.

God respects our freedom, even when we make ill use of it. But he encourages us to opt for what is good. To this end, he gives us the wisdom of Jesus and of his Spirit. Not everyone, however, knows how to value and, still less, how to incorporate this wisdom into their way of life.

### Readings
Eccl. 15:16-21. *Psalm.* 1 Cor. 2:6-10. *Acclamation.* Mt. 5:17-37. *Brief silence.*

### Reflection
God has made revelations throughout history in many ways. He did this before the coming of Jesus. He did this supremely in Jesus and he continues doing it through the Spirit. Full revelation is concentrated in Jesus. He respects and assumes the religious tradition of his people. He criticises everything that is not helpful to people's personal and collective dignity. But he does not break any tradition that helps people in their lives; furthermore, he wants them to fulfil themselves as far as possible. However, he makes it very clear that we have to motivate ourselves more, to set more demanding objectives,

to take on whatever leads to completeness. He has not come to cast away the past, as though history began with him, but rather to bring fu!filment, because he embodies more wisdom than all the earlier prophets do.

The words of the Sermon on the Mount present Jesus' alternative way of life. He makes it clear that we have to be better than the scribes and Pharisees, to enter into the Kingdom of heaven. Those religious professionals based their idea of perfection on fulfilling the Commandments, something that has been taught to many of us. Jesus does not belittle this, but he knows that it is not enough. He asks more of his followers, he demands a greater level of holiness and of response to the Spirit. One of his followers referred to as "the rich young man" is a typical case of those who fulfil what tradition demands and stop at the Commandments; when Jesus asks something more of him, he is not able to comply. Jesus' message, captured first and foremost in the Beatitudes, is a more radical way of life, which brings completeness and re-clothes everything that came before with a new mystical quality.

Let us pause for a moment of brief, yet profound reflection:

- It is customary to value the culture of progress. But progress is questionable, if it does not reach everyone.
- In society, it is said: *what you have, is what you are worth;* but this is so false!
- Politically, there is too much corruption and it is hard to put aside sufficient for the poor and hungry.
- For many, money is like a god. They continue to have false gods…

## What can we ourselves do?

- Greater austerity: consume less, so as to share more.
- Do not waste or throw things away, without making use of them.

- Influence opinion and take part in campaigns.
- And pray. Without the spirituality of the Gospel, it will be difficult for us to achieve a world of justice and solidarity. (*Silence for internal reflection.*)

## Creed

## Prayer of the Faithful

- Let us pray that progress may be a means for justice and liberation for people and nations.
- Let us pray for those who are in positions of responsibility in matters concerning social justice and the distribution of wealth.
- Let us pray that we may create a culture of solidarity among all people.
- Let us pray that within the Church, the example of a simple life and freely chosen poverty may grow.
- Let us also especially remember in prayer all those who are working in the Third World in the service of the poorest people.
- For these and all our intentions, *let us pray to the Lord.*

## Symbolic Action

*A person presents a young plant; another a small watering can or jar of water. The first person raises up the plant and says:* Lord, may we receive your Word full of wisdom; water us with your Spirit, so that we may grow. *The second person pours the water.*

## 4. RITE OF COMMUNION

### Introduction

Jesus' spirituality nourishes our whole being. Let us live devoutly in communion with him, with each other and with all our people.

### Hymn

### Prayer

Blessed are you, God, our Father.
You have come to us through Jesus

and through him, you have left us an example
rich in doctrine and love.
You invite us to this knowledge
because it is for the wise to fulfil your will.
You give us your own Spirit
for us to understand and receive with greater
appreciation.
This little community thanks you
for the many gifts with which You raise us up.
All the Gospel is filled with grace.
It is the alternative way of the simple
and of those who opt for your Kingdom.
Every day, it is for us
a challenge of holiness, of conversion.
Father, blessed are you for this Word of Jesus
that penetrates to our inmost heart.
Surrounded by your love and clothed by your Spirit,
we say to you: Our Father…

## Sign of Peace

## Distribution of Communion: Hymn

## Act of Thanksgiving
- ■ We give you thanks, good and holy Father, for
  your Word which is a fountain of wisdom. Teach
  us to meditate upon it and to fulfil it.
- ■ With the best intentions, we open our hearts to
  your Spirit that permeates all things. We wish to
  be Jesus' faithful followers.
- ■ And now that we know your Gospel better, help
  us to be good witnesses to it.

## 5. CONCLUDING RITE

### Resolution
"Blessed are they who walk in the will of the Lord."

### Blessing
### Conclusion
What we have lived through in this celebration is

now extended into other areas and among other
people around us. Words like *freedom and solidarity*
have meaning and motivation in the hearts of
everyone. May we be counted among those who
know how to communicate these words.

## Final Hymn and Dismissal

# Seventh Sunday

## 1. SETTING THE SCENE

### Poster with one of these texts:
- "Be holy, because God is holy"
- "We are temples of God"
- "Love?… even our enemies"

## 2. INTRODUCTORY RITES

### Introduction
We come to this celebration in the midst of the tasks and commitments of everyday life. During the week, we have been immersed in responsibilities of a personal kind, as well as those of family, work or our neighbourhoods. This celebration is designed to empower everything that we are and everything that we do. We gather together around Jesus, so that we may express, like him, the wonder we feel for God and to give him thanks for helping us so much.

Our vocation calls us to be loving and holy, according to the example that God has given us. But God's plans do not always coincide with ours. For this reason, we set the scene for this celebration with these symbols:

- *Toy weapon:* symbol of rancour, vengeance and, in general, evil sentiments.
- *Bunch of varied flowers:* symbol of good feelings and of the human values that give a person grace and holiness.

### Hymn

### Greeting
Brothers and sisters, let us bless God, who makes the sun shine on good and bad people alike, and sends down rain upon the just and unjust.

### Penitential Rite
- You, Lord, are holy: *Lord, have mercy.*
- You, Lord, take away the sins of the world: *Christ, have mercy.*
- You, Lord, are merciful: *Lord, have mercy.*

### Gloria

### Prayer
God, good Father, we know that you are holy and your mercy has no end. Sensing your presence is a blessing and moves us to live together and to respect one another. Father, may we Christians know how to proclaim and witness to that alternative way of life that the Gospel proclaims. Through Christ…

## 3. LITURGY OF THE WORD

### Introduction to the Readings
We are all called to holiness. Holiness reflects life. The lessons which we are going to hear describe with clear and practical examples how God wants us to work for holiness. For Jesus, in addition to this, there is a fundamental reason: we are children of God, and God is good.

### Readings
Lev. 19:1-2. 17-18. *Psalm.* 1 Cor. 3:16-23. *Acclamation.* Mt. 5:38-48. *Brief silence.*

## Reflection

"Do you not know that you are temples of God and that the Spirit dwells within you?" This experience, which Saint Paul alludes to, is the best way of understanding Jesus' mentality. Without this religious experience and without wisdom of heart, it is not possible to understand the Gospel, in all its depth and fullness. Jesus tells us that the best reference point for being truly worthy is God the Father himself, so amazingly generous, "that he makes the sun shine upon bad and good people alike and sends down rain upon the just and unjust".

It will be impossible for us to assimilate the Sermon on the Mount, if we act with a different mentality. For example, there exists the dynamic of vengeance: "you have done that to me, but I will pay you back for it"; the mentality of the contract: "you have given me such and such, so how can I repay you for it?" We also hear it said or say ourselves: "no one can ask anything of me, because I do not owe anything to anyone". The spirituality of God is completely different. He is pure giving, overflowing, boundless love: where sin abounded, there is a superabundance of redeeming mercy.

The ideal of the Sermon on the Mount goes deep into the very heart of a person; it places human beings face to face with their honesty, and drives them on towards an endless horizon of perfection; boundless love, even towards one's enemies; mercy and forgiveness without any reservation; total respect; constant example; transparency in everything; a hundred per-cent responsibility; that is to say, vibrating at a frequency in tune with the holiness of God. He is always the model, the measure that has no measurement. Does the Gospel expect too much with such a list? That is the nature of holiness. (*Silence for internal reflection.*)

## Creed

## Prayer of the Faithful

- Let us pray that the values of the Gospel may permeate society by means of the active presence of Christians.
- Let us pray that we may all work for peace, always overcoming the reaction of an eye for an eye and a tooth for a tooth.
- Let us pray that the Spirit may enlighten our communities, so that they may bear witness to the goodness of God who does not tire of loving good and bad people, friends and enemies.
- Let us pray for peace and reconciliation among all people.
- For these and for all our intentions,
  *let us pray to the Lord.*

## Hymn

## Symbolic Action

*Two people go up to a prominent place: one with a weather thermometer; the other with a metal tape measure. The second person, extending the tape measure to a considerable length, says:* God loves us greatly, without measure. *He retracts the tape measure a bit.* We sometimes measure our love. *Next the first person raises up the thermometer and says:* What temperature of Christian love do we have?

## 4. RITE OF COMMUNION

## Introduction

God is good to everyone. Jesus takes him as an example of perfection. He himself went through life doing good. Now, with his Spirit and the nourishment of the Eucharist, we can be worthy children of such a good Father.

## Hymn

## Prayer

We praise you with all our heart, Holy Father.
We are moved by your generous and surprising love.
You make the sun shine upon good and bad people
and you send down rain upon the just and unjust.
How different you are from us, God of goodness!
You do not treat us as our sins deserve
nor do you punish us according to our faults;
on the contrary, you overwhelm us with grace
and tenderness.
Where has such a thing been seen?
Only a mother reflects to any degree your
capacity for love.
Holy Father, you are divinely original:
gentle to a fault,
slow to anger, rich in mercy;
all your feelings are good without exception.
Jesus takes you as an example:
"Be perfect as our heavenly Father is perfect."
It is certain: there is no greater value than that of service
nor greater force than love.
We must put far away from us envy, vengeance
and all the mad things that disturb our social harmony.
We are only saved by refinement of the Spirit
and boundless mercy like yours.
Moved by the tremendous example that you give us,
we say to you with wonder and praise: Our Father…

## Sign of Peace

## Distribution of Communion: Hymn

## Act of Thanksgiving

- Good Father, we give you thanks, because you teach us genuine love: generous, disinterested, without distinction… After purifying our hearts, you remind us that we are the torchbearers of the Gospel in this, our own age.
- Holy Father, we want to be like you in word and deed, in personal witness and in our community witness.

## 5. CONCLUDING RITE

### Resolution

To be perfect like our heavenly Father and to love like he loves us.

### Blessing

### Conclusion

Holiness is our great inspiration. This is a daily commitment. To be perfect like God, challenges us to be gracious and generous, especially with those who are our rivals and with those who treat us badly. As believers, we can show that it is possible "To love your enemies, to do good to those who hate you, and to pray for those who persecute you and speak all manner of evil against you."

### Final Hymn and Dismissal

# Eighth Sunday

## 1. SETTING THE SCENE

### Poster with one of these texts:
- "Does God forget us?"
- "Life is more than food and clothing"
- "Seek ye first the Kingdom of God"
- "Either God or money"

### Symbols:
- Flower or plant from the countryside.
- Basket of food.
- Coat hangers with a suit and dress.
- Tray with money.

## 2. INTRODUCTORY RITES

### Introduction
For us, life is certainly more than working, more than earning money, more than enjoyment… If we are here, it is because there are other values that affect us spiritually. More than any material gain, sharing leads to a deep satisfaction.

### Hymn

### Greeting
Brothers and sisters, let us bless the Lord, who invites us to build his Kingdom.

### Penitential Rite
- Because of the many things that weigh us down, *Lord, have mercy.*
- Because we do not trust in you enough, *Christ, have mercy.*
- Because we do not give ourselves completely to your Kingdom, *Lord, have mercy.*

### Gloria

### Prayer
Father of goodness, you look after us with a mother's tenderness. Help us to understand the priorities of your Kingdom and to concentrate responsibly on them. Through Christ…

## 3. LITURGY OF THE WORD

### Introduction to the Readings
The God of the Bible has the feelings of a father and mother at the same time, he is loving and never abandons us. A mother's tenderness and commitment are but a pale reflection of God's love.

The Gospel confronts us once more with the necessity of choosing. The genuine Christian cannot concentrate on such disparate loves as God and money. If we put ourselves decisively at the service of the Kingdom of God, many burdens that consume our energy every day disappear.

### Readings
Is. 49:14-15. *Psalm.* 1 Cor. 4:1-5. *Acclamation.* Mt. 6:24-34. *Brief silence.*

### Reflection
"No one has ever seen God" (Jn 1:18), says Saint John. We can only speak about him by means of symbols, comparisons or similar descriptions. A symbol we frequently use is that of father. But it is an incomplete symbol. God is also mother; and more than a mother, since, "although a mother might forget her children, I will never forget you", says God.

This maternal sensitivity of God is breathed and communicated especially by Jesus: why are you worried, wondering about what you are going to eat, what you are going to drink, or how you are going to clothe yourself? The radical and trusting believer, who has nowhere to lay his head (Mt. 8:20), is convinced that as people, we are much more important to God than the birds, the grass or the lilies of the field. And if he looks after them, how much more will he look after us.

In his desire to preach the doctrine of redemption, Jesus addresses what is most important and decisive. His first statement is powerful: "Nobody can serve two masters". His proposal is that we should accept God as our only Lord; that nothing, nor anybody, may supplant him. In the following sentence, he gives these two instructions: that we should trust in God, just like the birds and the lilies, and that we should not fill our heads with needless worries. Let us understand this clearly: Jesus has never been in favour of passivity or resignation; on the contrary, he has been as proactive as anyone else. What he proposes is to concentrate one's energy on what is the main, decisive thing: the Kingdom of God and its justice. If God is our only Lord, everything else is secondary.

The person who seeks the Kingdom of God discards other ideals with their cults and adopts the Gospel mentality with its ideals: generous solidarity; dignity and human rights at all times; changing, radically, systems and structures that do not help us to live in contentment, etc. Everything else, however necessary and however much it burdens us, will be something derived from practicality. For example, it is very important to eat; but it is more important to create the conditions, so that all of us can eat, even if some of us may have to eat less.

To sum up, if we are creating the Kingdom of God, we will generate true brotherhood, we will promote true progress, and welfare will be a common, general sharing. (*Silence for internal reflection.*)

## Creed

## Prayer of the Faithful
- ■ That nations may progress according to the justice of the Gospel, *let us pray to the Lord.*
- ■ That we Christians may concentrate our energies on the Kingdom of God and that this may always be a stimulus to us, *let us pray to the Lord.*
- ■ That we may be tireless in doing good, and not expect reward, *let us pray to the Lord.*
- ■ That we may know how to collaborate with all those who are building the Kingdom of God, even though they may have different ideas, *let us pray to the Lord.*

## Offerings
- ■ *Diary:* Lord, we desire that the pages of our diaries may reflect our concern for your Kingdom.
- ■ *Gospel:* Father, the Gospel reminds us that your Kingdom has to be our first responsibility.
- ■ *Calculator and file or disk:* Lord, we value this equipment for our work and business. We want it also to be useful in creating your Kingdom.

## Hymn

## Symbolic Action
*A person goes up to the place for symbols and says:* We cannot serve two masters. Ours is the Kingdom of God and its justice. *The tray of money is taken away.*

## 4. RITE OF COMMUNION

## Introduction
We will be blessed, if we put our trust in God and work for his Kingdom. Receiving Jesus in communion signifies that we are on his side.

## Hymn

## Prayer

Good and loving God, we bless you with all creatures.
You are both father and mother at the same time.
In you, our life finds rest.
You are the foundation and salvation of all.
We human beings are your chosen ones:
you love us in a special way.
Would you be proud of us
if we radiated the truth of the Gospel
and if your Kingdom, that is also ours,
came first in everyone's life?
It is not always like that, good Father.
Everywhere, idols emerge, which drag us down;
there is a lot of publicity that ensnares us;
we are easily influenced by our surroundings…
but we have reasons for trusting.
There are people who set us an example:
they are not burdened by possessions or appearances;
they live by a different scale of values,
the one they have learnt in the Gospel.
Father, we wish to be one of these people.
With them, we call upon you: Our Father…

## Sign of Peace

## Distribution of Communion: Hymn

## Act of Thanksgiving

- Father, we give you thanks, because in the pages of the Gospel, we find profound lessons on humanity.
- We recognise that your Kingdom is the best thing for everyone. Re-clothe us in holiness, so that we may love like you know how to love.
- Instil in us that goodness which you breathe. We wish for you alone to be our God.

## 5. CONCLUDING RITE

### Resolution

To create the Kingdom of God and all else will be added unto us.

### Blessing

### Conclusion

Faith in the God of the Gospel encourages us to take positions. For some time now, we have focused on his Kingdom. Now with these meetings, we take heart, strengthen our convictions and deepen our spirituality. There is no need to worry. We have enough with the demands made of us by the Kingdom of God each day. May everyone have a good week, and witness to the Spirit.

### Final Hymn and Dismissal

# Ninth Sunday

## 1. SETTING THE SCENE

### Poster with one of these texts:
- "The true believer listens and responds"
- "Faith is a great gift"

### Symbol:
- Rough stone.

## 2. INTRODUCTORY RITES

### Introduction
The true believer is not the person who calls upon God all the time, but the person who fulfils his will. Sometimes, we are criticised for having the name of God more on our lips than in our hearts. If commitment does not spring from faith, it is no more than empty words, without credibility. To purge ourselves of this, there is nothing better than to learn from Jesus. He showed how to be a believer in word and deed.

### Hymn

### Greeting
Brothers and sisters, let us bless God, who has spoken to us through Jesus.

### Penitential Rite
- Because we often do not carry out your will, *Lord, have mercy.*
- Because we often keep you far from our hearts, *Christ, have mercy.*
- Because we are guilty of many lapses, *Lord, have mercy.*

### Gloria

### Prayer
Lord, we trust in your providence, which never fails; and we beseech you to keep all evil from us, and grant us those blessings that may help us in our present and future lives. Through Christ…

## 3. LITURGY OF THE WORD

### Introduction to the Readings
To be a believer at all, one has to open one's heart completely. But Jesus goes further: he says that we have to put the message we receive into practice. We may be sure that blessed are those, who hear the Word of God and keep it.

### Readings
Dt. 11:18. 26-28. *Psalm.* Rom. 3:21-25. 28. *Acclamation.* Mt. 7:21-27. *Brief silence.*

### Reflection
The Word of God has to penetrate deeply into the hearts of believers, in order to be effective. It is not enough for it to be listened to. It has to be received to the point where it shapes our lives. "Put my words in your heart and in your soul… put them as a sign upon your forehead", as Deuteronomy tells us. Jesus appeals to our intelligent sensitivity: "he who listens to these my words and puts them into practice… builds his house upon a rock".

How profound and evocative is the ending of the Sermon on the Mount! They do not please God, those who invoke him often, if afterwards they do not obey his will. Jesus rules out this playing to outward appearances. Inconsistency is a great failing that destroys all credibility. Besides, it is a cause of such frequent criticism as: "many go to

Mass and how little it shows"; or: "much beating of the breast, but how little commitment"…

Jesus received admiration for what he said and what he did. His actions were consistent with his words. It is not in vain when he assures us that his "meat and drink are in doing the will" of the Father (Jn 4:34). He was always transparent.

This Jesus is the foundation given to us, so that we may form our personalities and build up the Church. That is why it is pointless for us to seek anyone better… (*Silence for internal reflection.*)

## Creed

## Prayer of the Faithful

- We pray for the Church, that it may fulfil the will of God.
- We pray for all those who enrich social life by their witness, that they may not tire of setting an example.
- We pray for this community, that it may bear witness to what it believes.
- We pray for those who are having a crisis of faith, that they may open their hearts to God, who is love and revelation.
- We pray for one another and for all our intentions. *Let us pray to the Lord.*

## Offerings

- *Book of memoirs or personal diary:* Father, whoever reads these pages can see that you are dwelling within people.
- *Bible:* Father, may your words penetrate our hearts, so that we can put them into practice.

## Hymn

## Symbolic Action

*Someone goes up to the symbol (the rough stone), raises it and says:* A Christian is as unshakeable as a rock in his foundations. He is not worn down by life's difficulties.

## 4. RITE OF COMMUNION

## Introduction

To fulfil the will of God is the ideal of every believer. Jesus would say that this was his principal nourishment. May communion with him inspire us to fulfil the will of the Father.

## Hymn

## Prayer

Good and loving Father, we are in agreement with Jesus:
we are not the better for saying: Lord, Lord,
nor when we are down upon our knees
feeling that we are in touch with heaven,
if afterwards, we do not put our prayers into practice.
Your Kingdom will not be achieved with sacramental rites
if they do not bring sincere commitment.
We do not affirm our personal nature by repeating tradition
or simply carrying out what we are ordered to do.
The rock of human endeavour is Jesus:
he is the ideal and the Gospel.
He blesses your name like no other
because he admirably fulfils your will.
He is the great symbol that reveals your mystery.
Good Father, we confess before you
that we have not found a better foundation
than the words and example of Jesus.
If we praise you now with our lips
it is so that we may continue afterwards to bless you with our works.
Supported by the confidence that you give us,
we say to you: Our Father…

**Sign of Peace**

**Distribution of Communion: Hymn**

**Act of Thanksgiving**
- Lord God, we give you thanks for the words of life contained in the Gospel.
- You have given us Jesus as a foundation for us to build up our lives in solidarity.
- Send us your Spirit, so that we may give good witness to the strength of our faith.

## 5. CONCLUDING RITE

**Resolution**
To demonstrate in daily life that we believe.

**Blessing**

**Conclusion**
The faith is a great gift for which we are never sufficiently grateful. It is a great inspiration for life. If we put it into practice, as Jesus teaches us, we will be constructive witnesses: that is what society and the Kingdom of God need most.

**Final Hymn and Dismissal**

# Tenth Sunday

## 1. SETTING THE SCENE

### Poster with one of these texts:
- "How lucky we are to know God!"
- "God is mercy"
- "I desire faith and mercy"

## 2. INTRODUCTORY RITES

### Introduction
Brothers and sisters, how fortunate we are in knowing God! It is not easy to have clear and reliable knowledge of what this means for us. We run the risk of creating false images for ourselves, or of making the wrong interpretations of how God is and how God acts. Having a true knowledge of God helps us a great deal to live a sensitive and spirited life.

### Hymn

### Greeting
Brothers and sisters, let us praise the Lord together, since he desires to save us.

### Penitential Rite
Let us recognise our sins and receive the mercy of the Lord. (*Brief silence.*) *I confess…*

### Gloria

### Prayer
O God, fountain of all goodness, never cease to hear our prayers; and grant that, by your inspiration, we may consider what is right and fulfil it with your help. Through Christ…

## 3. LITURGY OF THE WORD

### Introduction to the Readings
Only by knowing God will we be able to understand his plans, his choices and his preferences. The Bible, and particularly the Gospel, is the great means by which we may know God and get in touch with his spirituality. He is, above all, mercy and salvation.

### Readings
Hos. 6:3b-6. *Psalm.* Rom. 4:18-25. *Acclamation.* Mt. 9:9-13. *Brief silence.*

### Reflection
The prophet Hosea's message is a great one. It focuses on what is essential and genuine in religion: "let us strive to know the Lord… I want mercy and not sacrifices." In fact, all those who experience God are amazed by his great mercy. If something defines him, it is, above all, mercy. God has no other face.

The merciful person is sensitive to the suffering of others in the physical, psychological, economic, moral sense, etc. Because of this, Jesus was especially attentive to the needy, the unfortunate, the marginalised and sinners of his time. His passion for the Kingdom of God caused him to emphasise that his preference was for those most in need of mercy: "The healthy do not need a doctor, but the sick… I have not come to call the just, but sinners."

Mercy characterises those who work for the Kingdom of God. Driven on by this knowledge, Jesus called upon Matthew to be one of his collaborators. The latter had a bad reputation; he kept the company of traditional religious people to some extent. He belonged to a group, the tax collectors, who were looked down upon. Many of them abused their office and bled people dry economically. Besides, he was in the service of an invading people. Nevertheless, Jesus discerned in Matthew's demeanour that he could be a good disciple. Matthew accepted Jesus' proposal, left his work and joined him in the adventure of the Kingdom of God.

To sum up, the person who knows God is also a person who practises mercy, proclaims that there is room for everyone in the Kingdom envisaged by God and celebrates the feast of communion with those who are in sympathy with this endeavour. (*Silence for internal reflection.*)

## Creed

## Prayer of the Faithful

- That the Church may bring the revelation of God's mercy close to everyone, *let us pray to the Lord.*
- For those who have no hope, that they may find encouragement among believers, *let us pray to the Lord.*
- That we may promote a culture of humanity among all people, *let us pray to the Lord.*
- That we may cultivate our sensitivity to the point of being loving to those nearest to us, *let us pray to the Lord.*

## Offerings

- *Open Bible:* Lord, you have revealed yourself; we want to get to know you more each day.
- *Lighted candle:* We also want to know you through prayer.
- *Posters of Jesus and great believers:* Lord, we admire the great believers.

## Hymn

## Symbolic Action

*Someone slowly presents to the assembly, pew by pew, a placard with the phrase "What I want is mercy". When he has finished, he displays it to the congregation and says:* Brothers and sisters, over and above any sacrifice, God desires mercy.

## 4. RITE OF COMMUNION

## Introduction

Mercy is more important than any sacrifice. May our union with Jesus help us to be merciful.

## Hymn

## Prayer

Loving Father, how lucky we are to have known you!
You have left your mark on the whole of creation, but you come to us, above all, through religious experience.
We give you thanks for having revealed yourself, for having sought us out and convinced us.
It was your initiative:
from the beginning, you have been in the midst of the community.
You have never hidden yourself. Your plan is to reveal yourself.
Some say that they have no sense of you;
they assert that you are not necessary, that they do not need you.
We wonder if they were to look deeply into themselves…
We cannot, nor do we want to live without you.
You have touched our innermost heart
and you have drawn us to you with great mercy.
Raising us to even greater heights, your Spirit uplifts us powerfully
and leads us in beauty upon the path of truth.
What more could you do to assure us that you exist?
Father, receive the praise that we express to you

with our lips and with our hearts.
Mercy is the worship that you expect from us.
We do not want to let you down.
Now, through our experience of you, we say to you:
Our Father…

## Sign of Peace

## Distribution of Communion: Hymn

## Act of Thanksgiving
- Father, we give you thanks, because you are full of mercy.
- We admire Jesus the missionary, who travelled through his land, spreading the Word. We are captivated by the assured manner in which he preaches redemption.
- Father, re-clothe us in the mystical quality of Jesus, so that we may be as loving as he, when we proclaim the Gospel of salvation.

## 5. CONCLUDING RITE

## Resolution
To practise mercy towards everyone.

## Blessing

## Conclusion
Whether we may know it or not, God has poured himself forth in his mercy upon all mankind. Through faith, we know that the best way of pleasing him is for us also to be merciful to others. It will be the great sign that we know God.

## Final Hymn and Dismissal

# Eleventh Sunday

## 1. SETTING THE SCENE

### Poster with one of these texts:
- ◼ "We are the People of God"
- ◼ "The harvest is great, but the labourers are few"
- ◼ "Build the Kingdom of heaven"

### Symbol:
- ◼ Working implements.

## 2. INTRODUCTORY RITES

### Introduction
Our quality as Christians is reflected in the support that we give to the Kingdom of God. Today, as always, the harvest is great and the workers are few. We can all add our weight to this task. Everyone's contribution is valuable.

### Hymn

### Greeting
Brothers and sisters, let us bless the Lord, who has called us by our own name.

### Penitential Rite
- ◼ You want to reconcile us: *Lord, have mercy.*
- ◼ You desire our conversion: *Christ, have mercy.*
- ◼ You accept everyone: *Lord, have mercy.*

### Gloria

### Prayer
O God, the strength of those who hope in you, hear our prayer; and since we are weak and can do nothing without you, grant us the help of your grace, so that we may keep the Commandments and please you in our actions and our desires. Through Christ…

## 3. LITURGY OF THE WORD

### Introduction to the Readings
As Christian communities, we share in the experience of the love of God and the permanent challenge of the Gospel. There is still a lot for us to do, before we can consider that the Kingdom of God is established among us.

### Readings
Exod. 19:2-6a. *Psalm.* Rom. 5:6-11. *Acclamation.* Mt. 9:36-10:8. *Brief silence.*

### Reflection
One of the most relevant religious experiences that the people of the Old Testament live through is the covenant: the Lord is our God and we are his people. The Second Vatican Council recaptured this beautiful image of collaboration, like dance partners in a tango, and its biblical significance, by recalling that the Church is the new People of God. The new covenant has been realised in Jesus, with his way of life and his message of redemption. He really is the Saviour. To be part of the Church is to devote oneself to Jesus' mission: to work for the Kingdom of God.

The Council also says that we are all called upon to form part of this new People of God and to continue the mission that Jesus began. He was a great observer of nature and life's events. Such sensitivity, united with his redeeming conscience, led him to discover people's needs and problems. He observed that many people were ill-treated and disorientated like sheep without a shepherd, because those who should have exercised this task did not fulfil it.

Jesus trained some helpers to assist him with the ever-necessary project of the Kingdom of God. It transpires for this group, in the Gospel, that this preparation is both theoretical and practical, although active training predominates: he sends them out to heal, to encourage, to cast out demons…

In these apostles, all the followers of Jesus are represented. The task of salvation, then, as now, is far-reaching and urgent. Putting one's shoulder to the wheel, collaborating, being a worker in the harvest continues to be a labour of love, prompted by faith, which is the hallmark of good Christians. No one in the community is dispensed from this mission. To evangelise and to build the Kingdom of God are the hallmark of Christians. The response is inevitably individual, but must also be communal, because we evangelise as the People of God and not with each one of us going about it independently. (*Silence for internal reflection.*)

## Creed

## Prayer of the Faithful

- Let us pray that the Gospel of salvation may reach the whole world.
- Let us pray that we Christians may further the Kingdom of God within the activities of civic society.
- Let us pray especially that our community may work with creativity and enthusiasm for the people, as a whole.
- We pray that solidarity and good understanding may not be lacking among our neighbours.
- And, together with these, we add our personal intentions. *Let us pray to the Lord.*

## Offerings

- *Handful of ears of corn:* Lord, we are doing something for your Kingdom. We are ready to keep up our efforts.
- *Tray with the names of people in the community:* Lord, you have spoken our names, you have called us. Rely on us.

## Hymn

## Symbolic Action

*Someone dressed in working clothes and a straw hat goes up to a prominent place, and says:* Brothers and sisters, the harvest is great; there are not many of us to spread the Word. How can we be more effective?

## 4. RITE OF COMMUNION

## Introduction

Communion with Jesus can rekindle our commitment. Let us dedicate our efforts to the Church's mission.

## Hymn

## Prayer

Lord, our God,
you love us with the love of the covenant.
We are a small proportion of your People,
a community who opens its heart to your Word and who wants to follow the voice of the
Good Shepherd.
We proclaim, as one, that your mercy is eternal.
We confess that your fidelity does not fade away with the years.
You rejoice and suffer with us;
it moves you to see us like sheep without a shepherd.
In you is salvation.
Your Kingdom is also ours.
That is why you call upon us to spread your mercy,
to relieve the tensions that disrupt our communal life,
to eradicate whatever disturbs the harmony of life.

Father, what blessing there is in proclaiming your nearness,
what assurance in following the missionary wisdom of Jesus.
United to him, the First among all mankind, we call upon you: Our Father…

## Sign of Peace

## Distribution of Communion: Hymn

## Act of Thanksgiving

- We give you thanks, good Father, because you do not allow us to think of ourselves. you have reconciled us by means of Jesus and you maintain your covenant through pure generosity. This uplifts the life of the community and increases our gospel commitment.
- You expect collaboration and dynamism from us to spread your Kingdom. Bless us, so that we may know how to carry on with the mission. It is well worth giving our all for the Gospel.

## 5. CONCLUDING RITE

## Resolution
To strengthen our evangelising and missionary efforts.

## Blessing

## Conclusion
The work, of improving the life of this town and parish falls to everyone. As Christians, we should feel that a special responsibility rests on our shoulders. Let us remember that the harvest is great… If we do not do something ourselves, it may be left undone. And that would lead to impoverishment. May everyone have a good week. God is with us.

## Final Hymn and Dismissal

# Twelfth Sunday

## 1. SETTING THE SCENE

### Poster with one of these texts:
- "The faith is for the bold"
- "Faith has a price"
- "Witnesses, of great value!"
- "To evangelise is to take risks"

## 2. INTRODUCTORY RITES

### Introduction
Witness of life is the value at the heart of today's celebration. As an inspiration to everyone, one must recognise that in society, there are many good people who give encouragement to others and urge them on in life. The world could not humanly survive without these witnesses, without those prophets of truth, beauty, responsibility and hope. Inspired by them and by Jesus, let us celebrate this meeting.

### Hymn

### Greeting
Brothers and sisters, let us bless God, who loves us deeply.

### Penitential Rite
- You, Lord, love us and you teach us:
  *Lord, have mercy.*
- You, Lord, gave your life to redeem us all:
  *Christ, have mercy.*
- You, Lord, are always on our side:
  *Lord, have mercy.*

### Gloria

### Prayer
Grant us, Lord, that we may always live in respect and love for your Holy Name, because you never turn away your attention from those whom you establish on the solid foundation of your love. Through Christ…

## 3. LITURGY OF THE WORD

### Introduction to the Readings
To remain faithful to the Gospel is an extraordinary sign of a great personality. And when it is done, in spite of the dangers and snares that are around us, it shows an even greater courage. The Gospel recalls our invitation to be witnesses whatever the future may bring. To this end, Jesus assures us of his help.

### Readings
Jer. 20:10-13. *Psalm.* Rom. 5:12-15. *Acclamation.* Mt. 10:26-33. *Brief silence.*

### Reflection
To be a person, to be oneself, is a difficult enterprise that can cause us anxiety, at any time. In this hard task, no cakewalk, religious and Gospel experience are of great value: "The Lord is with me like a mighty hero", said Jeremiah. For him, like us, fidelity is very difficult. We are born into a sinful world. Jesus attracts us, but our conflicting environment often tempts and deceives us. Fidelity can only be achieved with strict standards and with great inner equilibrium. This is the ideal set before us today.

The other issue is witness, something unavoidable in Christian life. An outstanding witness of our time, Mother Teresa of Calcutta, said of herself: "The day that God meets someone stupider and poorer than me, he will do even better things." We may be surprised by the sense of humour with which a person faced her future; this beatitude came to my lips: "Blessed are those who laugh at themselves, because their amusement will never end." Certainly, to be a good witness, besides courage and daring, one needs a good sense of humour.

There are Christians who are ashamed of acknowledging their faith socially, or their membership of the Church. Just as there are people who say that religion now has no relevance and others who devalue it, or reduce it to a private matter, there are also Christians who are afraid of appearing ridiculous. It is clear that neither the Kingdom of God, nor the Gospel, figure strongly in their inner life.

Jesus states firmly: we should not renounce the Gospel, nor be unfaithful to the mission, on account of any idea, or because of any fear. And he adds words of encouragement: the Father, who is aware of the flight of a bird, or the falling of a hair of our head, is watching over you. Do not be afraid; he takes care of your life; nobody can take away from you the deep life within.

Therefore, to reduce the importance of the Gospel would be to deprive history of its greatest gift and to impoverish it radically. Nothing else is so wholesome, revolutionary and humanising. At every moment in history, witnesses are necessary for the health of society and the Church. (*Silence for internal reflection.*)

## Creed

## Prayer of the Faithful

- Let us pray for all men and women of good will, whether believers or not, that their honour and responsibility may be a source of good example.
- Let us pray for the Church, that it may manifest the Gospel values opportunely and with courage.
- Lets us pray for those who are afraid, or ashamed of being witnesses to the Gospel.
- Let us pray for our town, that it may progress in a culture of humanity.
- Let us pray for our community, that it may express, in life, the beauty of Christian sensitivity.
- For these and for all our intentions, *let us pray to the Lord.*

## Offerings

- *Missionary crucifix:* Lord, we are heartened by the courage of many missionaries, who risk everything for the Gospel.
- *Hymnbook:* Lord, we have sinned; but we have reason to sing to You, because you have poured forth your goodness.

## Hymn

## Symbolic Action

*Someone, holding a piece of glass, goes to a prominent place and, lifting it up a little, says:* Brothers and sisters, far be it from us to put Jesus away in a corner; we are for proclaiming him openly and transparently.

## 4. RITE OF COMMUNION

## Introduction

God is love. Do not be afraid to take risks for the Gospel. Many do it daily, strengthened by the Spirit. May communion with Jesus help us.

## Hymn

## Prayer

Blessed are you, O Lord our God.
We praise you, because your blessings never end.
You play the card game of love with us
convinced that you are going to win the round.
You exercise mercy in its fullness
because you sound out and know the intimate
depths of everyone's heart.
The way you weave our existence day by day amazes us
and how much you trust in us.
You take the initiative in everything.
You call us to face the challenge of being witnesses
and you console us with words of confidence:
"Do not be afraid… they cannot kill the soul".
You place the example of Jesus before us:
he faced up to all the risks;
that is why you are proud of him.
Father, our aspirations are great:
they grow in the faith, in the warmth of your Spirit,
and they are strengthened when we meet in your name.
You know that we have taken your side.
Accept our faithful commitment
although it may sometimes be weakened by sin.
With the cross and the resurrection as signs,
we say to you: Our Father…

## Sign of Peace

## Distribution of Communion: Hymn

## Act of Thanksgiving (*spontaneous*)

## 5. CONCLUDING RITE

## Resolution

To evangelise, even though we may encounter risks.

## Blessing

## Conclusion

It is easier to proclaim or listen to the Word of God inside our churches, than to bear witness before the people, in our working lives, or in our relations with neighbours.

However, the Lord encourages us to be *living Gospels*. Let us remember his words: "Do not be afraid… What I say to you at night, proclaim in the full light of day; and what I whisper in your ear, shout from the rooftops." Let us go out into the street, convinced of the value of our witness. The Lord is with us. May everyone have a good week.

## Final Hymn and Dismissal

# Thirteenth Sunday

## 1. SETTING THE SCENE

### Poster with one of these texts:
- "God comes first"
- "The Cross brings dignity"
- "Jesus is radical"
- "Life is gained when it is given in devotion"

### Symbols:
- Portable baptismal font or water receptacle and shell.
- Lighted paschal candle.
- Rustic cross.

## 2. INTRODUCTORY RITES

### Introduction
In celebrating our faith, we also confess that we are members of the Church. With baptism, we began a journey encouraged by many witnesses. Today is a good occasion to put our following of Jesus into practice and to continue expressing the value of that commandment: first, you must love God above all things. Because we value the Christian vocation, we celebrate it in community.

### Hymn

### Greeting
Brothers and sisters, let us praise the Lord together, who looks on us with such favour.

### Penitential Rite
- Because we sometimes harden our hearts,
  *Lord, have mercy.*
- Because it is difficult for us to open them,
  *Christ, have mercy.*
- Because we are often overcome by selfishness,
  *Lord, have mercy.*

### Gloria

### Prayer
Father of goodness, who by means of your grace have made us sons and daughters of light; grant that we may live free from the darkness of error, and that we may remain always in the splendour of your truth. Through Christ…

## 3. LITURGY OF THE WORD

### Introduction to the Readings
To really understand the dynamics of baptism means adopting the destiny of Jesus: the vital and daring nature of his choices and the scale of his triumph at God's side. If we really want to be like Jesus, we have to take brave decisions and break with many habits that do not accord with the Gospel.

The Word of God today is clear and incisive: the principal duty of a Christian is to fulfil the will of God, following Jesus before any other loyalty. In obedience to God rests our greatest freedom and dignity.

### Readings
2 Kings 4:8-11.14-16a. *Psalm.* Rom. 6:3-4. 8-11. *Acclamation.* Mt. 10:37-42. *Brief silence.*

### Reflection
*(Encourage some parents and children beforehand to explain briefly how they understand the first sentences of the Gospel. They can communicate it, in the form of an interview, or after a brief explanation by the person co-ordinating.)*

Making radical choices is a characteristic of following Jesus that springs from baptism, whose underlying meaning is to die to sin, to live for God and enter a new life. This radicalism is in line with the old commandment to love God above all things, that is to say, above any other interest or loyalty. For a sensitive and true believer, God and Jesus come first. Nothing or nobody can influence this fundamental choice.

But one must not understand, by this, that the level of affection should be reduced in the family. Obeying God and putting the following of Jesus as the first priority does not have to create conflict with other loves, or to lessen our freedom. If affection is expressed in a good way, there need never be any rivalry between love for Jesus and family love. Choosing to follow Jesus has no adverse effects on one's life; on the contrary, it becomes balanced and strengthened. The real meaning of life is based on faithfulness to Jesus and to the Gospel, as much in regard to intimacy, as to relations with others. Nevertheless, if conflict arises, the solution must come through *obeying God before men*. Nothing or nobody should separate us from Jesus' love. Whoever tries to do so, sets out to deceive and is no respecter of liberty.

Today's message also leads us to this other consideration: how important the dynamism of baptism is, in preparing and educating people in a Christian way! We often educate people, so that they may rise up the ladder, earn money, be the first, become prominent… At other times, by contrast, we stress personal need, the desire to realise oneself; but we frequently forget the revolutionary content of the Gospel, such as taking up the cross, or gaining one's life by sacrificing it… The scale of values, which derives from the Gospel, does not accord with many others that are aired as being sensible. When Jesus invited that rich man to sell everything and give it to the poor, he was not inviting him to lose everything, but to gain it, because you gain a lot as a person, when you are detached, giving and sharing. Generosity is the best investment for the life of the spirit.

To sum up, Jesus is a hundred per cent merciful, but he is also totally radical. Gospel demands can make one a little afraid; but sooner or later, one comes to discover that deep down, they are what fulfil one most. (*Silence for internal reflection.*)

## Creed

## Prayer of the Faithful

- Let us pray for the Church, that it may live the adventure of Jesus devotedly, taking brave decisions and discarding what does not accord with the Gospel.
- Let us pray for all those whose attachments and encumbrances hinder them from fulfilling a serious commitment to the Gospel.
- Let us pray for all the servants of the Church, that they may inspire communities with the witness of their lives and their words.
- Let us pray for all Christians, that we may mature in the faith, being both responsible and active.
- And for our community, that it may bear witness to the supreme value of loving God, above all things.
- For these and for all our intentions, *let us pray to the Lord*.

## Offerings

- *Baptismal Register:* Lord, we were baptised, so that we might die to sin. May the redemption of Jesus penetrate our hearts, and may we know how to bring it closer to others by our witness of life.
- *Marriage Register:* When we got married, Lord, you were our principal witness. May you continue to bless our families.

## 4. RITE OF COMMUNION

## Introduction

Jesus is a pioneer in his radical love for God the Father and every person, whatever their condition. Let us learn from Jesus this devoted love for all around him.

## Hymn

## Prayer

Father, blessed is the community that knows how
to praise you
for the life of joy you give us every day.
All honour and power are yours.
Today, we rejoice with you
as we contemplate the character of Jesus,
such a wonderful example to us.
He was strict in his demands and clear in his doctrine:
"he who loves his father, or his mother, more than
me, is not worthy of me…;
he who does not take up his cross and follow me,
is not worthy of me…;
he who does not give up his life, will lose it".
We know, Father, that this is the way of your spirituality:
in Jesus, you have spoken your absolute word.
Now, you entrust us with your cause:
to spread humanity, taking the Gospel as a base.
Grant us strength, that we may follow in Jesus' example.
United in the same faith, we say to you: Our Father…

## Sign of Peace

## Distribution of Communion: Hymn

## Act of Thanksgiving

- ■ Good Father, we give you thanks for the radical gift of baptism and its power of constant conversion.
- ■ We give you thanks also, for the ideal of the new life, in the breath of the Spirit. With the spirituality that you offer us, we can leave a good example wherever we go.
- ■ Father, we are drawn to Jesus' example; but we are weak. May your Spirit help us to maintain our gospel commitment.

## 5. CONCLUDING RITE

## Resolution

To be open, receptive and giving.

## Blessing

## Conclusion

The following of Jesus is a great blessing in our lives. The love that we give to God and to Jesus remains in very good hands. They multiply it in a thousand acts of service and generosity. Let us return to everyday life, with the baptismal attitude of living the faith with commitment. Let it be clearly seen that we are filled with the love of God and a passion for the Gospel.

## Final Hymn and Dismissal

# Fourteenth Sunday

## 1. SETTING THE SCENE

### Poster with one of these texts:
- "The Spirit gives life"
- "The simple understand God"

## 2. INTRODUCTORY RITES

### Introduction
Brothers and sisters, a greeting of brotherhood and joy. The Gospel says that those who are simple understand the things of God. The truth is that God is not as complicated as some people say. It is enough to get on the spiritual wavelength, the wavelength of simplicity, in order to understand his revelation. Let us open our hearts to the message. There are words of encouragement, of profound doctrine and gratitude.

### Hymn

### Greeting
Brothers and sisters, let us bless the Lord with the sincerity and simplicity of our lives.

### Penitential Rite
- Because we trust in you, *Lord, have mercy.*
- Because you are our Saviour, *Christ, have mercy.*
- Because your forgiveness strengthens our hope, *Lord, have mercy.*

### Gloria

### Prayer
O God, who by means of your Son's humiliation, raised up a fallen world; grant that your faithful may experience holy joy, so that, free from the slavery of sin, they may rejoice in your presence now and for evermore. Through Christ…

## 3. LITURGY OF THE WORD

### Introduction to the Readings
When, in the New Testament, we find the expressions *spirit* and *flesh,* they frequently refer to concrete ways of life. *To live according to the flesh* is to allow oneself to be dragged along by selfishness, evil ambitions and negative tendencies. *To live according to the spirit* is to put into practice all the beautiful and positive aspirations that we feel. The Word urges us, today, to allow ourselves to be guided by the Spirit. Jesus' life was like that. The Gospel reminds us that this way of life can only be understood through simplicity.

### Readings
Zech. 9:9-10. *Psalm.* Rom. 8:9. 11-13. *Acclamation.* Mt. 11:25-30. *Brief silence.*

### Reflection
It is impossible to be a Christian without a certain level of spirituality. Furthermore, the sign of identity that one is a Christian is that one lives according to Jesus' Spirit. The letter to the Romans has expressed it radically: "he who does not have the Spirit of Christ, is not of Christ", that is to say, he is not a Christian, even though he brings his certificate of baptism. What defines and marks out a Christian is the stamp and aura of the Spirit.

Human beings have a spiritual nature and vocation. But one has to know how to get on the spiritual *wavelength,* to really find oneself and grasp God's message. Jesus, who was profoundly spiritual, because he allowed himself to be led by the Spirit, says that this *wavelength* is none other than personal simplicity and purity of heart. God has wished to reveal and communicate himself, but, surprisingly, only those who are simple understand him. The know-alls and the vainglorious do not understand; and they will not be able to understand, as long as they do not change their attitude.

Spirituality plays a decisive part in helping us to live. It is the mystical quality that gives specific tone to Christian identity. It creates the Gospel mentality. It facilitates the union between prayer and commitment. It stimulates a *life of devotion* in the believer.

There is nothing better than spirituality for relieving the burdens and cares that we carry in life. Those who suffer, as one of the Beatitudes says, will inherit the earth. If we choose to live according to the Spirit, our life will progress in harmony. If we do not choose spirituality, as an orientating and unifying attitude in life, we will be reduced to mediocrity, to materialism and to superficiality. Those who live according to the flesh, end up being worn down, fading away, and being ruined. (*Silence for internal reflection*.)

## Creed

## Prayer of the Faithful

- That all people may be educated in spiritual values, *let us pray to the Lord*.
- For those who are burdened by things that are not of their making, *let us pray to the Lord*.
- That we Christians may progress in knowledge and in faithfulness to the Spirit, *let us pray to the Lord*.
- That we may be witnesses wherever we are, *let us pray to the Lord*.
- For those who are on holiday, that they may enjoy a very happy holiday and return refreshed, *let us pray to the Lord*.
- For the intentions of each and every one of us, *let us pray to the Lord*.

## Offerings

- *Radio:* Father, you want to reveal yourself to everyone, but it is those who are simple that are on your wavelength.
- *Plant blooming with life:* Father, this plant symbolises what should be our natural state every day.
- *Withered plant:* But the truth is, Father, that we are a problem to ourselves: we live more according to the flesh than according to the spirit.

## Hymn

## Symbolic Action

*Someone goes up to the altar with fire (a flame) in a receptacle. He presents it to the assembly and says:* Without the Spirit of Jesus, we are not true Christians; we lack Someone essential. *He leaves the receptacle on the altar.*

## 4. RITE OF COMMUNION

## Introduction

We give thanks with Jesus to God, because he has revealed himself to us, and we pray that he will help us to maintain a simple and fraternal way of life.

## Hymn

## Prayer

Bountiful Father, praying together with Jesus, we say to you:
"Blessed are you, Lord of heaven and earth, because you have hidden these things from the wise and the clever
and you have revealed them to simple folk.
Yes, Father, for that is the way you are."
You have sent down the riverbed of life
a great torrent of salvation.
The human form of Jesus, overflowing with spirituality, is a great symbol for us that perfectly combines prayer and commitment.

You help us greatly, Father,
when we go deeply into the mystery of the faith.
Today, we celebrate your revelation and we thank
you for it.
With you, the burden of life becomes light.
Recognising that you love us,
we say to you in communion: Our Father…

## Sign of Peace

## Distribution of Communion: Hymn

## Act of Thanksgiving
- Father, it is our experience that the Spirit fills us with life. Through him, you touch the kernel of our being and purify our conscience.
- But it is not easy to be spiritual, Father. It is hard to follow your voice and the calls of our conscience.
- We know that faithfulness to the Spirit is so important. For that reason, continue to provoke us, and stir us to action.
- And thank you for wanting to dwell within us.

## 5. CONCLUDING RITE

### Resolution
To live attentive to the Spirit. To cultivate spirituality.

### Blessing

### Conclusion
Today's message has been especially deep and eloquent: on the one hand, it has reminded us of the value of living according to the Spirit; on the other, it has pointed out that the simple understand God's revelation, which brings relief to those who are weary and burdened with care. Re-clothed in the Gospel, which is every Christian's working outfit, let us set forth to a new week of labour. May the Lord be with us, so that we may know how to give to others what we have shared here.

### Final Hymn and Dismissal

# Fifteenth Sunday

## 1. SETTING THE SCENE

### Poster with one of these texts:
- "God does not speak in vain"
- "God sows his Word"
- "Seed… and good land"
- "He who has ears, let him hear"

### Symbols:
- Container of grain.
- Containers with different types of soil: good quality, stony, with weeds in it, hard earth.
- Hoe or trowel and jar of water.

## 2. INTRODUCTORY RITES

### Introduction
It is true that just as we need to feed the body, we need to feed the spirit also. These meetings are beneficial in this respect and they strengthen our Christian convictions.

God, in his revelation, has sown the seed of his Word. His plan is that we should go through life, each of us bearing fruit according to his or her own capacity. This is what today's message tells us.

### Hymn

### Greeting
Brothers and sisters, let us bless the Lord, who has sown his Word amongst us.

### Penitential Rite
- Because we are sometimes like hard soil, *Lord, have mercy.*
- Because you are the Word, who gives life to the world, *Christ, have mercy.*
- Because you have every reason to expect your seed to germinate in us, *Lord, have mercy.*

### Gloria

### Prayer
God, bountiful Father, you have made fertile the soil of human history with the Gospel of Jesus. He is both seed and good soil, at the same time. Grant that we may adopt his faithful way of life more and more each day, so that your seed is not wasted in us. Through Christ…

## 3. LITURGY OF THE WORD

### Introduction to the Readings
The Word of God is productive and fertile, like rain that makes the fields germinate and provides a harvest for the worker. In this way, God communicates and pledges his Word. It is not the way of God to speak in vain… What he says or promises, he fulfils. Thanks to his revelation, as people, we can grow in our humanity. God has sent down his Word like a seed, and he expects it to bear fruit. But this is not possible without our collaboration.

### Readings
Is. 55:10-11. *Psalm.* Rom. 8:18-23. *Acclamation.* Mt. 13:1-23. *Brief silence.*

### Reflection
Salvation in Christ is a generous gift from God, but it also has to be worked on. It is an aspiration that has taken root in our very depths: we cry out for and await the hour, when we will be fully the

children of God. This experience of redemption grows progressively, in the measure to which we accept the Word, and do not hinder its transforming power.

The Gospel speaks to us of sowing and the harvest. Jesus, the passionate missionary that he was, went about sowing the Word of God, letting its seed fall abundantly. If the harvest fails, you cannot blame the sower for being tight-fisted. He has been generous with all the land. To open oneself to the Word, preparing the land, so that the workings of God can take root, is the responsibility of every Christian. The Gospel does not bring profit to our purses, but it does bring humanity, courage, brotherhood, harmony, responsibility… basic and indispensable conditions for life.

But let us look at Jesus' own comments and interpretation of the parable: "If someone hears the Word of the Kingdom without understanding it, the Evil One comes and steals what has been sown in his heart. This means what has been sown by the wayside. What has been sown on stony ground means someone who hears the Word and accepts it joyfully at once; but he does not have any roots, is unreliable, and, as soon as any difficulty or persecution arises, he succumbs. The seed sown on thorny ground signifies someone, who listens to the Word, but the attractions of life and the allurement of riches choke it and it remains infertile. What has been sown on good land means someone who listens to the Word and understands it; in this case, it will bear fruit and will produce a yield of a hundred, sixty or thirty fold." (*Silence for internal reflection.*)

## Creed

## Prayer of the Faithful
- Let us pray, brothers and sisters, that the world may open itself to the revelation of God.
- Let us pray that we Christians may know how to proclaim the Word of God with joy.
- Let us pray especially for those who are not able to hear our good God, when he communicates himself…
- We also pray for those who refuse to face up to the Word of God.
- Let us intercede for each other, that our lives may be fertile with the fruits of the Gospel.
- Let us unite our own intentions with these. For all of which, *let us pray to the Lord.*

## Symbolic Action
*A person goes up to the table of symbols. As he turns the good soil over with the trowel, he says:* Lord, you look after us, you enrich us beyond measure. you sow your Word *(he drops a few grains)* and you water it with your Spirit *(he pours water from the jar).* What more can we ask of you?

## Hymn

## Offerings
- *Container used in the symbolic act (good soil):* Lord, we present to you this good soil, sown with your Word and watered by your Spirit. Bless us, so that we may bear fruit in abundance.
- *Cushion or prayer stool:* Lord, we present to you this symbol. It reminds us that praying also means sitting before the Master and listening.

## 4. RITE OF COMMUNION

## Introduction
Communion with Jesus should help us to have a fruitful life, in permanent commitment and blessed with witness of life.

## Hymn

## Prayer
We bless you, God of goodness, Lord of history. We know that you are in the world, in solidarity with us all,

as the greatest power that can inspire us:
a devoted God, converted into a seed,
into the Word that disquiets,
into wisdom that penetrates and questions…
God, how necessary and loving you are!
You continually sow your Word which is the Gospel:
it fills our lives with meaning,
guides us like a compass,
multiplies our aspirations,
it is pregnant with wisdom.
It germinates in all those who prepare their land…
Your Word, God, our Father,
does not return to you empty.
You have fulfilled your mission before:
to be revelation.
May your seed not fall in vain.
We open our hearts like a furrow
and we call out to you: Our Father…

## Sign of Peace

## Distribution of Communion: Hymn

## Act of Thanksgiving

- We give you thanks, good Father, because you scatter the seed of the Gospel over all the land. you want it to germinate and to grow to fullness a hundredfold. The harvest is not so plentiful, because we fall short of the ideal.
- Because of this, Father, accept this confession and increase our desire to measure up to your generosity. Free us from unhealthy counsel and bless us, so that we may convert your seed into a rich harvest.

## 5. CONCLUDING RITE

## Resolution
To prepare the "land" (conversion), so that the Word may bear fruit in abundance.

## Blessing

## Conclusion
All Christian people now have as a principal and vital commitment to sow the seed of the Gospel. It is not easy work. That is why we must carry it out with the greatest care.

It is for us to prepare the land and to sow… Then, God will come and he will foster growth. Let us do as much as we can and let us have confidence.

## Final Hymn and Dismissal

# Sixteenth Sunday

## 1. SETTING THE SCENE

### Poster with one of these texts:
- "God is not to blame for evil"
- "God sows good seed"
- "The Spirit helps us"

### Symbols:
- Bundle of tares or weeds and a sheaf of wheat.
- Yeast and flour.

## 2. INTRODUCTORY RITES

### Introduction
God only comes to save us. He offers forgiveness and waits patiently for the sinner to change his ways. He is convinced that this miracle can only be achieved by love, which is ever patient and all accepting. The parable in the Gospel of the wheat and the tares is a reflection of the mercy and tolerance we see in God. His way of acting is to faithfully present opportunities for repentance and conversion.

### Hymn

### Greeting
Brothers and sisters, let us praise the Lord together, who listens to those who call out to him.

### Penitential Rite
- You, Lord, are patient with everyone, *Lord, have mercy.*
- You, Lord, set us an example, *Christ, have mercy.*
- You, Lord, separate the wheat from the tares, *Lord, have mercy.*

### Gloria

### Prayer
Look favourably upon your children, Lord, and multiply the gifts of your grace in them, so that, inflamed by faith, hope and charity, they may faithfully persevere in your loving presence. Through Christ…

## 3. LITURGY OF THE WORD

### Introduction to the Readings
God is faithful and merciful towards the sinner. He does not condemn anybody; his way is only to save, infusing love and forgiveness into the religious experience of those who call upon him. The Spirit, who prays within us and for us, helps us greatly in our weakness.

Before a God who is so immeasurably understanding and gracious, there can be no other reaction from us, than that which sensitivity cries out for: let us stop being tares and put our heart and soul into the Kingdom of God.

### Readings
Wis. 12:13. 16-19. *Psalm.* Rom. 8:26-27. *Acclamation.* Mt. 13:24-43. *Brief silence.*

### Reflection
The wisdom of God comes down to us in a thousand ways. The Spirit is charged with bringing it into reality, so that we can understand it better. Notice the message that the second reading presents to us today. In a few words, it has just told us that praying is, above all, *allowing God to speak to us.* We have always heard that prayer is a dialogue. So, God's tongue is the Spirit who comes to help us in our weakness and to intercede for us, in a way

that is truly suited to us. Thus, the Spirit has a very important role in prayer. God speaks to us through the Spirit, and through him, he gives us his encouragement, opens up horizons for us, helps us to walk life's path, and to understand more clearly how to follow Jesus.

The Gospel has reminded us again, by means of parables, that the Kingdom of God involves many tasks. The world is like a field, full of good and bad plants, good people and mediocre people, people who live according to the flesh and people who strive to live according to the Spirit. Wheat and tares spring up together, and the way they grow makes it hard to separate them.

This parable of the wheat and tares can have different applications. For example, in oneself, there are wheat and tares, good and evil. The Church, bound together by people, is both holy and sinful. In this way, this parable criticises all of us. Sometimes we hear people say: "there are people who are so bad that they should be weeded out, got rid of, or, in the less severe cases, deprived of social life". This parable gives us a fantastic lesson: tolerance. Jesus says: "Let them grow together"; now is the time of mercy and conversion; at the end, the Son of Man will know how to proceed.

How great is God's wisdom! Wheat and tares are forced to live together. They have no choice. For that reason, on different occasions, Jesus warns his followers that they must be alert and vigilant, they must be as innocent as doves and as wise as serpents; and that it is necessary to pray, in order not to fall into temptation. He said this from experience: he also had to live alongside the tares. In the same vein, this great saying is attributed to Saint Paul: "conquer evil by the power of good". And Saint Francis of Assisi prayed in the following way: "Lord, where there is hate, may I bring love; where there is offence, may I bring forgiveness; where there is discord, may I bring unity."

To sum up, we have often been encouraged to be the leaven in the dough. This constructive presence of Christians, in the midst of communities, is like that of yeast and mustard seed; it points to that vitality and that mystical power, which derive from opening up to the Spirit and the living experience of the Gospel. (*Silence for internal reflection.*)

## Creed

## Prayer of the Faithful
- ■ Let us pray for the Church, that it may be a witness to the merciful love of God, who waits for everything and accepts everything.
- ■ Let us pray in gratitude for the presence of the Spirit, who comes to help us in our weakness and to intercede for us.
- ■ Let us pray that we Christians may be capable of loving and forgiving, according to the standards of the Gospel.
- ■ Let us pray that human justice may favour people's rehabilitation.
- ■ Let us unite all our intentions with these, *let us pray to the Lord.*

## Symbolic Action
*Someone goes up to the table of symbols, takes a bundle of weeds, raises it up and says:* If a person turns out badly, like a harmful weed, God is not to blame. Then, who is?

## 4. RITE OF COMMUNION

## Introduction
There is a great depth of goodness in everyone. It needs to be sought out and nurtured. Let us join ourselves with Jesus, so that we may live like him.

## Hymn

## Prayer

Our Father, you are great and you work wonders,
you breathe mercy and you pray within us
to give us what is best for us through your Spirit.
You reveal yourself as supremely human
and always on the side of freedom.
You scatter good seed in the field of history,
but your enemies, in their turn, try to stifle it.
You do not pull anyone out by the roots,
as our anger sometimes tempts us to do.
You prefer to wait until the end
because you never withdraw your offer of forgiveness.
What exemplary and instructive graciousness!
Blessed are you, our patient God,
who limit the sinner's opportunities
and await his conversion until the last moment.
We admire this wisdom, so loving and holy.
We give you thanks for the Spirit,
who comes to our aid,
so that our relationship with you is not lost.
Sometimes we feel like a vulnerable seed
among many temptations and threats.
But you know what is in our hearts.
You know that we are grateful for
your friendly presence.
Inspired by your grace, we say to you: Our Father…

## Sign of Peace

## Distribution of Communion: Hymn

## Act of Thanksgiving (*spontaneous*)


## 5. CONCLUDING RITE

## Resolution

To let the Spirit pray within us.

## Blessing

## Conclusion

By means of parables, Jesus has again communicated his passion and his preoccupation with the Kingdom of God. He has left us a lesson in patience, and tolerance, but also of encouragement to make use of the many resources that the Gospel offers. Let us be aware that frequently, without us knowing how, good plants and weeds grow side by side. Let us learn how to live together, without allowing ourselves to be corrupted.

## Final Hymn and Dismissal

# Seventeenth Sunday

## 1. SETTING THE SCENE

### Poster with one of these texts:
- "The Kingdom of God is the greatest treasure"
- "The Kingdom of God is the best investment"
- "More Gospel and less riches"

### Symbols:
- Gospel.
- Opened jewel chest.
- Cheque for large amount (photocopy).

## 2. INTRODUCTORY RITES

### Introduction
The number of times that we meet together in the name of the Lord has repercussions for our experience as believers and for the life of the Church. We meditate on the Word of God and we pray that we may follow the Christian ideal. We are still apprentices. There remains a lot for us to learn and a lot for us to put into practice. May this meeting encourage us to follow our vocation.

### Hymn

### Greeting
Brothers and sisters, let us bless the Lord, who has predestined us to be in the image of his Son.

### Penitential Rite
- Because we do not value your message enough, *Lord, have mercy.*
- Because we do not always take the Gospel seriously, *Christ, have mercy.*
- Because we are deceived by false values, *Lord, have mercy.*

### Gloria

### Prayer
O God, protector of those who wait for you; without you, nothing is strong or holy. Multiply the signs of your mercy within us, so that, under your provident guidance, we may so use the blessings of this passing world, as to cling to the blessings which are eternal. Through Christ…

## 3. LITURGY OF THE WORD

### Introduction to the Readings
The prayer of Solomon, from the first reading, is beautiful and evocative. What are our prayers like? What do we ask for when we pray? The second reading urges us to see everything through the filter of God's love. The Gospel reminds us that to follow Jesus and strive for the Kingdom of God involves choices and exclusions. Furthermore, the Kingdom of God is the choice for which it is worth investing everything.

### Readings
1 Kings 3:5. 7-12. *Psalm.* Rom. 8:28-30. *Acclamation.* Mt. 13:44-52. *Brief silence.*

### Reflection
Prayer is one of the most profound and healthy human experiences. It is essential, in order to maintain the attitudes and commitments associated with the Kingdom of God. The first reading tells us that young Solomon's prayer pleased God. It is expressed like this: "Lord, give your servant a humble heart to govern, so that he may distinguish between good and evil." His prayer was heard.

Sometimes, we hear complaints from Christians who say: I pray, but God does not listen to me. I wonder: do they pray well? Today, there is great diversity in the ways of understanding and expressing prayer. Are they all equally effective and valid? It is a good thing for each one of us to ask ourselves what our prayers are like.

Genuine prayers are not those that *involve periods of prayer* and are forgotten afterwards, but those which are (*as much as possible*) a *living communion with God*. In this case, prayer is like a way of living, it expresses a natural relationship with God, is attentive to the Spirit and interprets life like sons and daughters of light. The whole life of people who pray in this way is a liturgy for God. They experience, minute by minute, that God loves them. Prayer is like their *vital atmosphere*, the conscience and climate in which the totality of their lives unfolds.

The Gospel continues presenting parables to us about the Kingdom of God. This experience, that Jesus breathed at all times and that constitutes the central message of his preaching, is not always uppermost in the life of Christian communities, nor is it given priority. According to the parables of the treasure and the pearl, the Kingdom of God has such a unique and important alternative value that whoever has experienced it, does not hesitate in pledging everything for it. For whoever is aware of it, the Kingdom of God is supremely appealing, it makes life vibrant in a way that makes one more responsible. Throughout history and in the present day, there are eloquent examples of Christians, who place everything at the service of the Kingdom of God, even to the point of risking their own lives. Faith assures us that it is the greatest treasure. (*Silence for internal reflection.*)

## Creed

## Prayer of the Faithful
- That the Church may present the Kingdom of God as a task requiring priority, *let us pray to the Lord.*
- That the message of the parables may penetrate our lives and sink deep into our hearts, *let us pray to the Lord.*
- That governments may serve their people with discernment, respect and genuine attentiveness, *let us pray to the Lord.*
- That when we pray, we may only ask for that which brings good to people, *let us pray to the Lord.*
- For all our personal intentions, *let us pray to the Lord.*

## Symbolic Action
*Someone goes up to the table of symbols, raises the Gospel and says:* The Kingdom of God is the greatest treasure. *He puts down the Gospel, tears up the cheque and puts away the jewel chest.*

## 4. RITE OF COMMUNION

### Introduction
It is very important to understand the Gospel in one's innermost being. Then, we will be able to make great decisions. May communion with Jesus help us to receive his message more deeply within us.

### Hymn

### Prayer
We bless you, good Father,
because you direct the destiny of the
world with wisdom
and you look after all your creatures with love.
You have called us into existence
and you accompany us as a wonderful teacher.
You pray for us on our journey and make
clear our horizon of life.
You invite us to listen to Jesus' Word
and to remain steadfast in following him.

In him, you have seen the dream of
your Kingdom realised.
You have redeemed us in your great kindness,
you have made us your adopted children
and have given us all your treasures.
Whoever receives you, you bestow courage and
dignity upon them,
you surround them with tenderness and
offer them the opportunity
to be, like you, a beneficial presence.
Father, preserve in us a humble heart
and that set of values appropriate to your Kingdom.
Treat us kindly, on your part,
and support us with gestures and acts of humanity.
Inspire us with your Spirit and instil in us responsibility
so that we never avoid the truth of the Gospel.
In the family of the faith, we say to you: Our Father…

## Sign of Peace

## Distribution of Communion: Hymn

## Act of Thanksgiving

- Father, you are good and holy. We give you
  thanks for the enthusiasm with which you make
  us rejoice in your Kingdom.
- You want us to be simple, merciful, serving,
  united. you call us to share the faith in
  community, so that our commitment does not
  fade away.
- Father, pour forth your blessing upon everyone,
  so that we may live in the service of fraternal
  progress.

## 5. CONCLUDING RITE

### Resolution
To dedicate more interest and devote greater
energy towards the Kingdom of God.

### Blessing

## Conclusion
The Kingdom of God is the great treasure of the faith.
It is the centre around which the Gospel gravitates.
It is the point of view from which we Christians must
analyse what is happening, and it is the structure
that we are called upon to build. Let us renew our
option for God's Kingdom and bear great witness to
it. May we have a happy and positive week.

## Final Hymn and Dismissal

# Eighteenth Sunday

## 1. SETTING THE SCENE

### Poster with one of these texts:
- "Give them something to eat"
- "The Lord is good to all"
- "Generosity works miracles"

### Symbols:
- Five little loaves and two fishes.
- Large basket with various foods.

## 2. INTRODUCTORY RITES

### Introduction
Certainly, the word *solidarity* is one of the most widely used throughout history. In the Bible, it is like a backdrop. The Gospel is particularly explicit regarding this value. In general, everyone agrees that it is one of the most appropriate means of measuring the human qualities in a person. It is also a clear sign that we have understood Jesus and that we have grasped his message.

### Hymn

### Greeting
Brothers and sisters, let us bless the Lord, who was the first to love us.

### Penitential Rite
- Because we are often smug, *Lord, have mercy.*
- Because we are not sufficiently detached, *Christ, have mercy.*
- Because the faith influences us but little, deep down, *Lord, have mercy.*

### Gloria

### Prayer
God, bountiful Father, you promote brotherhood, encouraging in us acts of generosity and attentiveness to people. Stir up our feelings of loving solidarity and remind us of our daily duty to share. Through Christ…

## 3. LITURGY OF THE WORD

### Introduction to the Readings
The goods of the earth have a universal destiny. Taking care of basic needs takes precedence over private property. The prophet Isaiah criticised useless waste: "Why do you waste money on what is not bread?" Jesus invites us to share, in order to take care of the needs of those around us: "give them something to eat". Because we experience the love of Christ, we have a motive for living in solidarity.

### Readings
Is. 55:1-3. *Psalm.* Rom. 8:35. 37-39. *Acclamation.* Mt. 14:13-21. *Brief silence.*

### Reflection
There are many kinds of hunger and need: for food, work, company, shelter, personal dignity, for God… The readings that we have listened to question us about the way we use our wealth, and call to mind images, statistics and the geography of the world's poverty. The truth is that mother earth generates resources for everyone, but not all people enjoy them. Why?

Confronted by situations of need, we run the risk of acting like the disciples in the Gospel: avoiding the issue, "tell the people to go to the villages and buy some food", that is to say that each one should do the best he can for himself. Jesus, however, sees things a different way: there is no need to, he tells them. Resolve it yourselves. Give them something to eat. And he left behind this practical lesson in sharing.

When there is much and it is not shared well, hunger arises and needs of every kind are created. When we share in common the little that each of us has, resources multiply and many problems are resolved. When giving spreads, it increases solidarity. No one should renounce being generous, because to do so would be to impoverish oneself, throwing away God-given gifts and not enriching others.

We Christians have a special reason to be generous: the love of Christ that has penetrated deeply into our hearts and that no one can take away from us. Let us hear the reflections of an eastern thinker: "You give, but little, when you give your possessions. Because, what are your possessions, other than things that you preserve and keep out of fear that you may need them?… There are those who give a little of the quantity that they have, and they give it in exchange for recognition, and their hidden desire makes their gifts harmful. And there are those who have little and give everything. These are the ones who believe in life and in the generosity of life, and their coffers are never empty. There are those who give with joy, and that joy is their reward; and there are those who give in suffering, and that suffering is their baptism; and there are those who give, and do not know the pain of giving, nor do they seek joy in it, nor do it through desire to be virtuous: they give like the myrtle in the valley… Through such people, God speaks and smiles upon the land. It is good to give when we are asked; but it is better to give without being asked, out of kind understanding… And is there anything that you can hold on to? Everything that you possess will be given up one day. So therefore, give now, so that the time of giving is yours, and does not fall to your heirs. you often say: 'I would give; but only to those who deserve it'. The trees in your orchards do not speak thus, nor the flocks in your pastures. They give to be able to live, because to keep is to perish."* (*Silence for internal reflection.*)

## Creed

## Prayer of the Faithful

- ■ Let us pray as we listen and respond to the reproaches of so many needy people who ask for help.
- ■ Let us pray that a culture of solidarity may be progressively achieved in the world.
- ■ Let us pray that the Church may spread the witness of austerity and sharing that God desires.
- ■ Let us be grateful for the love that God has for us and pray that it will motivate us to be more generous.
- ■ Let us pray for each other, that we may be sensitive to the problems of our neighbours and collaborate in their solution.
- ■ Let us pray also for all our needs and intentions. *We beseech the Lord.*

## Symbolic Action

*If it is considered convenient, and after previous notice, a collection of food can be made. If not, a traditional collection for charity or for some local aid centre.*

## 4. RITE OF COMMUNION

## Introduction

Communion with Jesus is complemented by communion with our brothers and sisters. Christian love always has these two sides.

---

* K. Gibran, *The Prophet*, Buenos Aires 1974, pp.27-29

## Hymn

## Prayer

"Our Father, who art on earth,
whom I feel in the pine needle,
in the workman's blue overalled figure,
in the little girl next to him
with her arched back,
playing with the thread around her finger.
Our Father who art on earth,
in the furrow,
in the garden,
in the mine,
in the port,
in the cinema,
in the wine,
in the doctor's house.
Our Father who art on earth
where you have your glory and your hell
and your relaxation in the cafés
where the wealthy drink their refreshments.
Our Father who is at school for free
and in the greengrocer's,
and in the hungry,
and in the poet,
never in the usurer!
Our Father who art on earth,
in the cigarette, in the kiss,
in the ear of corn, in the breast,
in all those who are good.
Our Father who dwells everywhere.
God who penetrates every empty space.
You who take away anxiety, you who art on earth.
Our Father, you know that we see you": Our Father…
*(G. Fuertes)*

## Sign of Peace

## Distribution of Communion: Hymn

## Act of Thanksgiving

- Father, we have just recalled the importance of sharing. We give you thanks, because we are able to help and to live in solidarity.
- Make us into a community transformed. Reconfirm in us the commitment to solidarity, especially with the most needy.
- Thank you, because food arrives each day at our homes. Fill us deeply with the virtue of solidarity.
- With our warm-hearted Pope John XXIII, we say to you: Grant, Lord, bread to those who are hungry and hunger to those who have bread. Amen.

## 5. CONCLUDING RITE

## Resolution

Care and solidarity for the needy around us.

## Blessing

## Conclusion

We have spoken of generosity, of giving, of solidarity, of sharing… Now, we have the opportunity to translate into daily life what we have shared and to demonstrate it with practical gestures. Let us devote our best efforts to caring for others. May God bless us and go with us.

## Final Hymn and Dismissal

# Nineteenth Sunday

## 1. SETTING THE SCENE

### Poster with one of these texts:
- "Prayer nourishes faith"
- "Faith gives stability to life"
- "Faith takes away our fears"
- "Where do you find God?"

## 2. INTRODUCTORY RITES

### Introduction
The fact of being Christians does not free us from difficulties and problems. But what is not so Christian is when we are held back by fear from following Jesus and being faithful to the Gospel. The Lord continues to invite us to be courageous and committed, never on the defensive, always in the front line of action in the service of others, especially those who are less knowledgeable and who count for less in our society. With these sentiments, we begin our celebration today.

### Hymn

### Greeting
Brothers and sisters, let us praise the Lord, who blesses us with the gift of faith.

### Penitential Rite
- Through the love that you have for us, *Lord, have mercy.*
- Through the faith that you have given us, *Christ, have mercy.*
- Through the reconciliation that we need, *Lord, have mercy.*

### Gloria

### Prayer
Bountiful God, whom we dare to call Father, increase in our hearts the spirit of your sons and daughters, so that we may deserve to attain our promised inheritance. Through Christ…

## 3. LITURGY OF THE WORD

### Introduction to the Readings
The presence of God does not fail the believer. God has pledged his companionship and he reveals it to all those who open their hearts to him and are attentive to his still, small voice. God does not need to make any display, in order to reveal himself. Anyone who lives on the wavelength of faith, hears his voice and is strengthened by his encouragement.

### Readings
1 Kings 19:9a. 11-13a. Psalm. Rom. 9:1-5. *Acclamation.* Mt. 14:22-33. *Brief silence.*

### Reflection
*(If it is considered opportune, someone, who has been "given a shock" by life, may be asked to comment on the way God has helped him, or rather, through his experience of life, how he understands the saying: "God squeezes us, but he does not suffocate us".)*

God offers us a companionship that he never withdraws, on his part. People of a profound and exceptional faith communicate this happy experience to us: "in God we live, move and have our being" (Acts 17:28). But there are occasions when God gives us special signs. The prophet, Elijah, experiences that God is not in the earthquake or in the fire, but in the still, small voice and the silence, that is to say, that he is not in the kind of noise that causes commotion, frightens or upsets us. The presence of God is to be found in gentle, peaceful silence.

The confession of Saint Paul, ready to give his all for his brothers of the same race and blood, in the service of the Gospel, is interesting and noteworthy. He reaches the point where he says, at the height of generosity, that he would accept being excluded from the Kingdom of God, if it meant saving them. It is a graphic and eloquent way of showing the extent of someone's inner preoccupation with the redemption of others.

It is also surprising, in the Gospel, how Jesus sought particular and intense occasions for prayer. Although he leads a life of prayer and he understands that prayer must be a constant attitude (cf. Lk. 18:1; 21:36), it seems that he needs moment of greater intensity. On this occasion, he spent the night on the mountain, praying. In a fertile and creative silence, that allows him to get more deeply in tune with what is human and divine, he strengthens his life of faith and action. What a wide panorama can be viewed through prayer, in fact, if it is genuine! How aware we become of the needs of those around us, and what inspiration is found for commitment! In the silence of prayer, the different realities of life can be weighed up, with greater judgement, and personal growth can be suitably nurtured.

Through prayer, Jesus has a presentiment that his disciples are having problems. In the Bible, the sea is often a symbol of the forces of evil. Today, just as yesterday, the ship of the Church has to navigate in conditions which are sometimes particularly turbulent – an environment that favours religion and the following of Jesus but little, if at all. Shocks and insecurity sometimes come unexpectedly. And when problems become exacerbated, it is only human that doubts and fears should arise. The struggle for faith is difficult. On the voyage of faith, when difficulties are more menacing and crises persist, there are those who waver, who become very doubtful: is everything to do with Jesus some fantasy, a product of the imagination? There are those who tire of rowing, who feel almost helpless, who see their experience of faith become diminished and their confidence in God reduced. Then he turns to us again to reassure us of his presence: "Take heart, it is I, have no fear! Why do you doubt, you men of little faith?" In the ship of the Church, in spite of our sin, of our doubts and insecurities, we find Jesus and his Spirit who are light and strength. (*Silence for internal reflection.*)

## Creed

## Prayer
"Because, Lord, I have seen you and wish
to see you again,
I want to believe.
I saw you, for real, when I was a child
and I was baptised with water
and, free from past guilt, I could see
you without any veil between us.
I want to believe.
Give me back that pure,
clear breath of faith,
take me back to the days of childhood
and the eyes of yesterday.
I want to believe.
you who put dew on the flowers, and honey within,
let two fresh drops of faith fall on my dry eyes.
I want to believe.
Because, Lord, I have seen you and desire to see
you again,
I believe in you and I want to believe".
(*G. Diego*)

## Prayer of the Faithful
- That a culture of life, mutual understanding and solidarity may be promoted among all nations, *let us pray to the Lord.*
- That fear may never affect the commitment of Christians, *let us pray to the Lord.*

- That we Christians may be in the front line of service and true progress, *let us pray to the Lord*.
- That our community may be united and brave in its commitment to our people, *let us pray to the Lord*.
- That we may lead a life of prayer, *let us pray to the Lord*.
- For all our intentions, *let us pray to the Lord*.

## Offerings

- *Headphones:* Lord, you are not in the noise, nor in the bustle that distracts us. you come with a whisper. We want to hear your sound.
- *Crucifix, picture or poster of Jesus:* Father, we admire Jesus; we want to follow him. May our faith not falter.

## 4. RITE OF COMMUNION

### Introduction

Through faith, we feel that we are children of God and brothers and sisters of Jesus. Communion is a sign of our family life as believers. May Jesus nourish faith and unity among us all.

### Hymn

### Prayer

Blessed are you, Father, for so many wonders of creation
that reveal the gentleness of your presence:
for the air, the water, the mountains,
for the starry nights and the colour of the fields,
and for so many loving signs of your being
that, thanks to faith, we can admire and enjoy.
May you especially be blessed for all human beings,
made in your image and likeness,
capable of shaping the land, inventing, progressing…
redeemed and raised up to be your children,
forged and enriched in the fire of the Spirit.
Father, we have heard the quiet sound of your
voice and we know your presence.
We have found you in the mysterious depths of life,
where your Word re-echoes and the silence is filled.

We feel that you penetrate us like water in a sponge.
You know our history completely.
Following Jesus, we walk in faith.
He is the clearest sign that you are among us.
Jesus, more than anyone, urges us along
the path of faith,
held back sometimes by our doubts and lapses.
Jesus, more than anyone, gives us such an example
of fidelity: Our Father…

## Sign of Peace

## Distribution of Communion: Hymn

## Act of Thanksgiving (*spontaneous*)

## 5. CONCLUDING RITE

### Resolution

To strengthen faith. To nourish it with meditation on the Gospel and prayer.

### Blessing

### Conclusion

Prayer is more than a thermometer of the faith; it is the fountain from which the believer is nourished and where his mystical experience is deepened, so that he may withstand and overcome the traumas of life. Nothing is better than prayer for forging a brave and courageous soul, because it gathers all our energy and sheds light on the choices that we must make.

### Final Hymn and Dismissal

# Twentieth Sunday

## 1. SETTING THE SCENE

### Poster with one of these texts:
- ◼ "Faith reaches everything"
- ◼ "Faith breaks down barriers"

### Symbol:
- ◼ Round table with a tablecloth, half a loaf and some crumbs on the floor.

## 2. INTRODUCTORY RITES

### Introduction
We are at the height of summer and many people are on holiday. During this period, too, the faith calls Christians together. Furthermore, we have to be very aware that fundamental values cannot go on holiday; they need constant nurturing and attention. At all times and places, the Lord calls upon us to participate in Christian community and to develop the life that the Word of scripture teaches us. Let us celebrate this meeting in the spirit of faith that the Gospel is going to reveal.

### Hymn

### Greeting
Brothers and sisters, let us bless the Lord, who enlightens us and accompanies us with tenderness.

### Penitential Rite
- ◼ You, Lord, want everyone's salvation, *Lord, have mercy.*
- ◼ You, Lord, were a witness of forgiveness, *Christ, have mercy.*
- ◼ You, Lord, want us to be united, *Lord, have mercy.*

### Gloria

### Prayer
God, bountiful Father, you have prepared good things for those who love you; inspire us with love for you, so that, loving you in all things and above all things, we may live our lives more devotedly. Through Christ…

## 3. LITURGY OF THE WORD

### Introduction to the Readings
The salvation of God is not complete, if it does not reach all people. For this to happen, it has to cross the frontiers of the Jewish people. Jesus, God's missionary, has come to give life and to save every person, of every nationality.

### Readings
Is. 56:1.6-7. *Psalm.* Rom. 11:13-15. 29-32. *Acclamation.* Mt. 15:21-28. *Brief silence.*

### Reflection
Faith is a religious attitude. We could describe it as a gift from God, which brings vitality to the whole of one's personality. It is expressed through prayer, example, commitment… It is not so much a *credo* of truths that one must know so much as a personal attitude of acceptance of God and of obedience to the Gospel. It rests less on what other people say and do, and much more on religious experience itself. It is not conceived of in relation to personal security (gaining heaven), but in relation to an undertaking that one embarks upon, like Abraham, trusting purely in God… It cannot be reduced merely to something intimate, private or individual; it is also something communal and socially orientated: it places us right in the thick of people's problems.

The faith is a gift that God does not barter with, just as he does not barter with salvation. His heart is not mean, but generous. He is not indebted to any people, nor does he have any favourites. For that reason, the unfolding of his salvation must reach out to everyone; it is universal. This aspect is the one that is given special emphasis by the Gospel reading. Jesus' act of salvation is both for his countrymen and for foreigners. Matthew, the evangelist, who directs his Gospel to Jewish Christians, appears to be addressing them with this comment: How are we going to exclude pagans from Salvation, if Jesus himself accepted them?

The faith of the Canaanite woman is an example of the devotion and trust that pleases God and brings a healthy response from Jesus. Faith and prayer converge in this woman in an outstanding way. Sometimes we find in people, who are not of our community, a profound religious fervour and such an admirable faith that they serve as an example to Christians. (*Silence for internal reflection.*)

## Creed

### Prayer of the Faithful

- For the peoples most in need, that salvation and progress may reach them, *let us pray to the Lord.*
- That the strength of the faith may drive all Christians on to work for the benefit of those around them, *let us pray to the Lord.*
- For our community, that faith may strengthen our lives, *let us pray to the Lord.*
- For all those who are enjoying their holidays, that they may know a relaxation and a refreshment of spirit, *let us pray to the Lord.*
- For the needs and intentions of us all, *let us pray to the Lord.*

### Symbolic Action
*Someone, from a prominent place and with a passport in his hand, says to the assembly:* Faith opens frontiers, like a passport.

## 4. RITE OF COMMUNION

### Introduction
We approach communion through faith. And the communion nourishes faith. Let us be grateful for the gift of believing.

### Hymn

### Prayer
God, good Father, we unite our voices
to thank you for the gift of faith.
Believers from all peoples and cultures
recognise you as our common Father.
Faith is a language that we all understand:
it eliminates frontiers and fosters the experience of brotherhood.
Through Jesus, you spread salvation open-handedly.
Father, how lucky we are to have known you
and how lucky to have found ourselves among believers
who have communicated to us their faith of prayer and practice.
This community celebrates you and thanks you for being so human.
And it blesses you for your signs of faith and holiness
in so many holy people who are blessed.
Father, we see you in the mystery of each human being;
your goodness shines forth from so many.
With all those who sense you and call out to you
and with those who witness to you without knowing it,
we say to you: Our Father…

### Sign of Peace

### Distribution of Communion: Hymn

## Act of Thanksgiving

"Only God can give faith…
but you can give witness.

Only God can give hope…
but you can give it, in turn, back to your brother.

Only God can give love…
but you can teach how to love.

Only God can give peace…
but you can sow the seeds of unity.

Only God can give strength…
but you can give heart to the disheartened.

Only God is the way…
but you can point it out to others.

Only God is the light…
but you can make it shine in the eyes of everyone.

Only God is life…
but you can make the desire to live flourish.

Only God can do what seems impossible…
but you can do what is possible.

Only God is complete within himself…
but he prefers to rely on you."*

## 5. CONCLUDING RITE

### Resolution
To persevere in the faith.

### Blessing

### Conclusion
Faith invites us to look with eyes of purity at everything that happens. We must look with eyes of purity, above all, at other people, so that we may always respect their dignity and collaborate with everyone to develop a happy communal life.

May God bless us and accompany us throughout the week, so that we may live as true believers.

### Final Hymn and Dismissal

---

* Prayer of a group from Campinas, Brazil. In C. Floristán, **Celebrations of Community,** Santander, 1996, p.584.

# Twenty-First Sunday

## 1. SETTING THE SCENE

### Poster with one of these texts:
- "Who do you say that I am?"
- "God is our origin and goal"

### Symbols:
- Large stone.
- Large keys.

Carry out a survey beforehand on members of the community and neighbours with the questions: Who is Jesus for you? What can you say about Jesus? Present a summary of the results in the *reflection*.

## 2. INTRODUCTORY RITES

### Introduction

Brothers and sisters, we surely all have experience of the fact that God's plans and designs are always favourable to our personal and communal destiny. He has redeemed us in a wise and generous way. And he offers himself to us, according to our ability to respond. He is satisfied, if we take up his offer of salvation.

Let us make our faith stronger each day. Truly, our Father in heaven reveals himself to us in a thousand ways.

### Hymn

### Greeting

Brothers and sisters, let us bless God the Father for the gift of Jesus and of his Spirit.

### Penitential Rite

Recognising that God loves us and forgives us, we confess that we are sinners before God and before the community. (*Brief silence.*) I confess…

### Gloria

### Prayer

O God, you unite the hearts of your faithful with the same desire; inspire in your people, love for your precepts and hope in your promises, so that, in the midst of the world's troubles, our hearts may be steadfast in true joy. Through Christ…

## 3. LITURGY OF THE WORD

### Introduction to the Readings

The more we come to understand God, the more our admiration for him increases. But it matters to God less that we applaud him and more that we might be his witnesses. We will hear in the Gospel that direct question of his: "And you, who do you say that I am?" We could come up with some beautiful replies from the lips and writings of saints. But what matters today is that each one of us contributes his or her very own reply.

### Readings

Is. 22:19-23. *Psalm.* Rom. 11:33-36. *Acclamation.* Mt. 16:13-20. *Brief silence.*

### Reflection

In the second reading, we have heard a short text in which Saint Paul praises the generosity and wisdom of God effusively. In our normal situation, formed in his image and likeness, we are able to rake up a few of the traces of these divine attributes. But how difficult it is to understand and assume this generosity and wisdom of God, in situations of illness, unexpected death, conflict or decline. How difficult it is, then, for many people to make sense of events as a believer. We have to be very aware that God never tires of loving us.

The Gospel text revolves, to a great extent, around the figure of Peter. However, it raises some very important issues for everyone:

■ Jesus' direct questions are applicable to any moment in history and to any individual. It is appropriate, sometimes, to respond, in a personal and communal way, to the enquiry that Jesus wanted to make in his time: "Who do the people say that I am?" "And who do you say that I am?" Among people, there is a wide diversity of opinions, as varied as are their different ways of looking at life: for some, Jesus is a person who is *marketable, because he still sells…*; for others, he is a revolutionary and they do not go further than that; others consider him as the founder of the Church, nothing more; some notice his great message; and there are those, like Peter, who testify: "you are the Messiah, the Son of the living God". In fact, the Church has recognised Jesus' divine origin, from the beginning. The New Testament witnesses to this in many ways and Christian tradition recognises, in him, the human presence of God in the world, a new and singular presence. This is absolutely fundamental to Jesus' personality. In him, God has made himself like one of us, has fully shared in our humanity; he was a historical person. Understanding this human Jesus, no less human than ourselves, is crucial, if we are to value our life, from God's perspective.

■ Of the two questions in the Gospel's enquiry, the second is the more interesting and decisive, because it affects us directly. It will always be an open and challenging question, which involves the ideas, the living knowledge and witness that we give, both as a person and as a community.

■ Another very important aspect of this passage, in the Gospel, is that faith arises through God's intervention, as one of his gifts: "No one, of flesh and blood, has revealed this to you, except my Father who is in heaven." Profound, personal faith is not possible without God playing a great part.

■ Another point, reminiscent of our baptism, is that faith marks us, as if we were going through a new birth. Jesus gives Peter a new name and confers a mission upon him. We have also received a mission: now, we are the lips, the hands, the feet, the witnesses of Jesus.

■ It is a widespread fact that the figure of Jesus awakens admiration in many people, including those outside the Church, that is to say, those who are not among us Christians. We can understate his stature and diminish his radicalism. The logical thing, however, is that, through our testimony, he should penetrate more and more into people's inner being and their social life. (*Silence for internal reflection.*)

## Creed

## Prayer of the Faithful
■ For the conflicts that there are in the world at present, *let us pray to the Lord.*
■ For the Church, founded upon the faith of the apostles, *let us pray to the Lord.*
■ For all those who accept Jesus as their Saviour, *let us pray to the Lord.*
■ For those of us who form this community, *let us pray to the Lord.*
■ That we may increase our sensitivity to God's signs, *let us pray to the Lord.*
■ For those who are nearing the end of their holidays, that they may return happily to their homes, *let us pray to the Lord.*
■ For the intentions and desires of each and every one of us, *let us pray to the Lord.*

## Offerings

- *Forms from the survey:* Lord, we present to you an example of what Jesus means to us.
- *Photograph or poster of the Pope:* Lord, we present to you the figure of the Pope, as a sign of our openness and communion with the universal Church.

## 4. RITE OF COMMUNION

### Introduction

Through the gift and experience of the Holy Spirit, we, too, can say that Jesus is the Son of the living God. May communion with him uplift us, so that we continue to be his witnesses.

### Hymn

### Prayer

Our God, through the gift of faith
we can say that you are our origin and our goal;
but we can also confess that you are our Abba
and that you are acting in the midst of the Church.
We know you especially through Jesus,
because, in him, you have revealed yourself in a powerful way
and you have made your plans known to us,
those that we discuss and pray about and to the service of which the community is dedicated.
With Jesus, you have made us sharers in the Spirit.
In this way, we can penetrate into your mystery more deeply.
Father, we confess that faith is the most decisive experience that could happen to us,
that which produces in us the greatest vitality.
We carry the marks of our baptism deep within us.
Supported by Peter, as our foundation stone,
and by the faith of the apostles, we say to you:
Our Father…

### Sign of Peace

## Distribution of Communion: Hymn

### Act of Thanksgiving

- We give you thanks, Lord our God, for the experience of Jesus who helps us so much. In him, we find new light, new perspectives, new hopes and an unquenchable Spirit.
- We feel strongly drawn to him. He is the clearest sign of you and the best mirror for our conscience.
- Father, accept our thanks and our praise on account of Jesus.

## 5. CONCLUDING RITE

### Resolution

To bear witness to the faith, in a personal and communal way.

### Blessing

### Conclusion

We have shared our faith. We have stressed that God feels especially satisfied, if we recognise Jesus as Saviour and we are witnesses to the Gospel. Let us strengthen our resolution to communicate the faith. In this way, we give glory to God and build up his Kingdom. May everyone have a good week. Let us try to make those around us happy.

### Final Hymn and Dismissal

# Twenty-Second Sunday

## 1. SETTING THE SCENE

### Poster with one of these texts:
- "You seduced me, Lord"
- "Do not adapt yourself to this world"
- "Let no one cause you to stumble"
- "To think like God is a great ability"

### Symbols:
- Crucifix.
- Credit cards.

## 2. INTRODUCTORY RITES

### Introduction
Sometimes we act as if everything of any worth could be valued by the laws of the market place. Thank God, there are some values that do not have an economic measure. The Gospel reminds us of this: "What does it profit a man to gain the whole world, if he ruins his life?" Today's message is eloquent and bold. Following Jesus and worshipping God often brings suffering, but contentment too.

### Hymn

### Greeting
Brothers and sisters, let us bless God, who loves us passionately.

### Penitential Rite
- Because we sometimes do not want to think like you, *Lord, have mercy.*
- Because we have often not followed you, *Christ, have mercy.*
- Because we do not take sufficient care of life and the environment, *Lord, have mercy.*

### Gloria

### Prayer
God, bountiful Father, from whom all good gifts come, infuse in our hearts a love for your self, so that, in making our lives more religious, you may increase goodness in us and preserve it with loving affection. Through Christ…

## 3. LITURGY OF THE WORD

### Introduction to the Readings
The prophet Jeremiah understood that true freedom coincides with fulfilling the will of God. But obedience to God led him down a difficult path. In moments of particular stress, he reached a point where he began to curse the day he was born, succumbing to the temptation of despair. But he could not get away from God: his presence was consuming Jeremiah like a fire within…

On the same subject, Saint Paul invites us to worship God with our lives. For this, we often need to change our attitude and not be influenced by social fashion.

Jesus, in the same way as Jeremiah, emphasises obedience to God as the great virtue. Peter, who still had not changed his way of thinking, becomes Jesus' tempter. But the latter reprimands him sharply and exhorts him to think and to see life like God.

### Readings
Jer. 20:7-9. *Psalm.* Rom. 12:1-2. *Acclamation.* Mt. 16:21-27. *Brief silence.*

## Reflection

The grace of God, freedom and suffering are planes of experience that merge together in our life as believers. With what realism and what expressive power does the prophet Jeremiah state this. "You seduced me, Lord" is equivalent to what we understand by God's grace; "I allowed myself to be seduced" is equivalent to the human freedom that allows God to act through one, given that his actions are always beneficial. Suffering is a consequence of commitment. The believer does not need to seek the cross; people take it upon themselves to put one on one's back, anyway; sometimes, even, these people are one's own friends. Jeremiah reveals his mystical experience to us: "the Word was a burning fire within me"; but he also tells us of his painful experience of continuing with the prophetic mission that God has commanded, that is to say, not turning his back on his vocation.

Jesus' life was no different to Jeremiah's or ours. He was beset by difficulties on all sides. Even his close friend Peter wanted to deflect him from his destiny. But Jesus is forceful with everything that tempts him: "Get behind me, Satan… you think as men think, not as God thinks."

Perhaps because of this, Jesus insists so much on the importance of going through life in alertness and vigilance. Saint Paul said: "do not adapt yourselves to this world"; seek "the will of God, what is good, what pleases him, what is perfect". For Jesus, there is nothing more important than the fulfilment of God's will. That is why he does not tolerate people trying to deceive him in something so crucial and so sacred as the designs of his Father and his ideal.

To sum up, God entices. The Christian vocation is attractive, exciting, but it is not exempt from risks and sacrifices. Let us put this firmly in our minds: there is no true Christian following without the cross. But let us remember: "blessed are the persecuted… for theirs is the Kingdom of heaven". (*Silence for internal reflection.*)

## Creed

## Prayer of the Faithful

- That the Gospel values may be absorbed into people's way of thinking in the world, *let us pray to the Lord.*
- For our Church, that it may stand out in the world for its faith and devotion to life, *let us pray to the Lord.*
- For our town, that the Gospel way of life may influence it and contribute to the improvement of all, *let us pray to the Lord.*
- For the needy and sick of our town, *let us pray to the Lord.*
- For each one of us, that our life as Christians may be faithful to the will of God, *let us pray to the Lord.*
- For all our intentions, *let us pray to the Lord.*

## Offerings

- *Almanac:* Father, we present to you the holiness of each day as the thing that pleases you most.
- *Lighted candle and Gospel:* You seduced us, Lord, and we allowed you to seduce us; you enlightened us and we followed you.

## Hymn

## Symbolic Action

*Someone slowly displays a placard in front of the assembly with a question mark painted on it. Meanwhile, another person goes to the table of symbols. When the first person, with the placard, reaches the table, he keeps the placard raised. The second person takes the crucifix in one hand, the credit cards in the other, and says:* What use is it for someone to have everything, if he ruins his life?

## 4. RITE OF COMMUNION

### Introduction
The Christian spirituality of the cross is liberating. This was the nature of the worship that Jesus offered to the Father. In communing with him, let us confirm that we also want to worship the Father, leading a life according to his will.

### Hymn

### Prayer
Abba, Father, our God,
all our life should be a joyful hymn
to your loving and seductive goodness.
You attract us irresistibly
and we allow ourselves to be drawn to you.
Our soul sighs for you,
our body yearns for you;
nobody satisfies us like you.
We present to you the crude reality of life.
We know that offering up oneself,
in communion with Jesus,
brings together and concentrates the
worship that pleases you.
We renew our minds and hearts
so that we may think and feel like you.
We embrace the cross each day.
We re-clothe ourselves in Gospel spirituality
and we offer you our dedicated obedience
to the faith.
Father, you have made it very clear:
there is no greater honour than offering up one's life,
true freedom cannot be attained
without poverty of spirit,
there is no means surer than the power of the cross.
United in Jesus, we call upon you: Our Father…

### Sign of Peace

### Distribution of Communion: Hymn

### Act of Thanksgiving
■ Jesus, it is hard for us to assimilate the spirituality of the Gospel and the challenging language of the cross.
■ We often try to have it both ways. Like Peter, we say that we love you, but we cannot bear you being so daring, with yourself and with us.
■ It is clear: those who say they are our friends may tempt us, if they do not think and act like you.
■ Thank you, Jesus, for your example which is so complete; for being independent and critical of your friends also. And thank you, because you were steadfast to the end, drinking the cup of martyrdom.
■ We commit ourselves to God's way of thinking. We are with you: what use is it to have everything, if one has no direction or meaning in one's heart?

## 5. CONCLUDING RITE

### Resolution
To think and act like God: the new worship of Christians.

### Blessing

### Conclusion
Claiming that one can live the Gospel, without the presence of the cross and conflict, is almost a joke. To be like Jesus involves carrying the cross every day. Obeying God, and not allowing oneself to be swept along by the mentality of the world, carries with it that price. It is also the price of wholesome liberty and one that has to be paid to save one's life.

Let us make an effort to assimilate God's way of thinking and to fill our social life with human warmth. May God go with us and grant that our behaviour towards others may reflect the standards of Jesus.

### Final Hymn and Dismissal

# Twenty-Third Sunday

## 1. SETTING THE SCENE

### Poster with one of these texts:
- "He who loves does no harm to others"
- "If you correct someone, let it be with love"

## 2. INTRODUCTORY RITES

### Introduction
The holidays are over for most people and we are beginning to think about a new term. As a parish, we remember that we are the People of God. In this community, each person has their own name. We foster brotherhood through everyone's participation and collaboration. Let us celebrate with joy that God is the centre of our community. He wants us to be united and to live with a holy energy.

### Hymn

### Greeting
Brothers and sisters, let us bless the Lord, because he is our God and we his people.

### Penitential Rite
We have sinned. Sometimes, we have hardened our hearts. Let us ask for forgiveness personally and as a community. (*Brief silence.*) *I confess…*

### Gloria

### Prayer
God, our Father, you know that we admire you, because you are loving to everyone. Your mercy is greater than our weakness. We give you thanks for our belonging to this Christian community. Help us to live in love as disciples, so that we may advance in maturity and in holiness, in our service to this town. Through Christ…

## 3. LITURGY OF THE WORD

### Introduction to the Readings
God, you look into the depths of the human heart, you know very well the goodness that exists within us. For that reason, we ask you to trust in our capacity for conversion and in the gestures of humanity that we can all put into practice.

Today's readings remind us again that love goes a very long way. Love is so all embracing that, if it is exercised, all laws are superfluous. When someone loves, he does no harm to others. More than that, out of love, we should correct each other. This is an important and necessary way of helping one another.

### Readings
Ezek. 33:7-9. *Psalm.* Rom. 13:8-10. *Acclamation.* Mt. 18:15-20. *Brief silence.*

### Reflection
Saint Paul has left us a powerful motive for loving our neighbour. He quoted that old phrase *love your neighbour as yourself.* Jesus goes even further. Whoever truly loves is supremely free, he does not need any laws, he harms nobody, he fills those around him with a zest for life. All that is good in human beings is condensed in love. This aspiration, so deep rooted in everyone, is the only one that can achieve personal stability and peace of mind. For that reason, among Christians, it is an old and new commandment, it sums up all the ancient Law and is a testament to the new Gospel revelation.

The first Christians understood that, with Jesus, the *hour of love* had arrived and that this word should not be corrupted.

But history shows us every day another facet of reality. That is why we have reminded ourselves again that genuine love is not easy for anyone, whatever degree of maturity they may have attained. One has to train oneself very well to practise it and one must be aware that it is an *art*. The Christian God is an *artist* of love. Jesus, as a qualified witness, has shown that he is very well *trained*. The human sciences of our time have recently corroborated what Jesus had already proclaimed many years ago: there can be no personal equilibrium or stability, if we do not love others. This should make a deep impression on us, living as we are in this competitive and fragmented society.

Everything that we are and do has social repercussions, for good or for evil. When the ties of brotherhood weaken or break down, a solution has to be sought, as soon as possible, through reconciliation or exclusion, if the sinner rejects the attempts at correction by all his fellows. But first, all the possibilities have to be exhausted, with sensitivity and love. He who loves does not harm others, even when he is correcting them in a brotherly way. The Gospel suggests a way of proceeding in this: first of all, *alone*; secondly, in the presence of *another person or another two people*; finally, with *all the community* as a witness.

Not to practise correction and to leave one's brother in a state of error, is false respect and a lack of that genuine love, which seeks out what is good and dignified in another. We can surely confirm, from experience that the greatest joy we have experienced has been in situations of reconciliation, in a climate of love and brotherly concern. (*Silence for internal reflection.*)

## Creed

## Prayer of the Faithful

- That in our world, rivalries may be overcome and governments may serve their peoples, *let us pray to the Lord.*
- That the international community may find channels for exerting corrective pressure, regarding the dominance of powerful nations over those that are small and poor, *let us pray to the Lord.*
- That the institutions which remedy political, economic and social deviance and corruption, may perform effectively, *let us pray to the Lord.*
- That in the Church we may be receptive and grateful for fraternal correction, *let us pray to the Lord.*
- That in our town there may be an increasing practice of human values, such as love and mutual correction, *let us pray to the Lord.*
- For all our intentions and concerns, *let us pray to the Lord.*

## Symbolic Action
*Someone, in a suitable position, raises a Bible and says:* To love is to fulfil the whole Law.

## 4. RITE OF COMMUNION

### Introduction
True love springs from a sensitive heart, a clear conscience and a cultivated faith. May communion with Jesus strengthen our Christian life.

### Hymn

### Prayer
Father, how beautiful it is to live in the Christian family and to bless you in a community of brothers and sisters.
Is there any sight that bears greater testimony than a people united where neighbours are attentive to each other?
That is our ideal and our dream.
The cleansing and consuming love that emanates from you,

impels us to extend it, transforming
it into friendship,
respect, peaceful society.
Father, logic completely supports this view:
he who loves fulfils all the Commandments,
he is free and can do no harm to anyone.
But that is the ideal.
Sometimes, our life is so mediocre
that the correction that others bring
is very good for us.
That is why you recommend us to
be attentive to each other;
and you remind us that holiness is
both personal and communal.
Father, we open our soul to the Spirit
so that it may cleanse us and shape
us in full measure.
Re-clothed in the robes of conversion
we draw close to our brothers and sisters.
How beautiful is the community that
lives in reconciliation.
With all the redeemed, we say to you: Our Father…

## Sign of Peace

## Distribution of Communion: Hymn

## Act of Thanksgiving (*spontaneous*)

## 5. CONCLUDING RITE

### Resolution
To correct one another with love according
to the Gospel.

### Blessing

## Conclusion
All the means that we use in the interests of
brotherhood are important. Fraternal correction is
one of these. It is a very healthy thing, if we practise
it with love and with tact. Let us bring into our lives
the sentiments and suggestions, which have
inspired us in this meeting. May the Lord go with us
and help us to make them a reality.

## Final Hymn and Dismissal

# Twenty-Fourth Sunday

## 1. SETTING THE SCENE

### Poster with one of these texts:
- "The Lord is compassionate"
- "Forgiveness is a great value"
- "Forgive? Always!"

### Symbols:
- Some large bank notes (photocopies) on a tray.
- Some coins on another tray.
- Phrases on cardboard strips (*sign*).

## 2. INTRODUCTORY RITES

### Introduction
To be brothers and sisters is one of the basic values of the Christian community. But sometimes it is not achieved because of the lack of forgiveness and reconciliation. The Word of God today emphasises this value: it prompts us very directly to proceed with mercy in our hearts. In the same way that God forgives us, let us strengthen reconciliation and forgiveness among ourselves.

### Hymn

### Greeting
Brothers and sisters, let us bless the Lord for his loving mercy.

### Penitential Rite
- Because we need your forgiveness, *Lord, have mercy.*
- Because we lack sensitivity, *Christ, have mercy.*
- Because we find it hard to forgive, *Lord, have mercy.*

### Gloria

### Prayer
God, our Father, no one enlightens us better than you do. When we look back over our lives, we discover that our hearts are not always prepared to forgive. We value your message, but at times our conduct does not show this. It consoles us that you continue to be merciful. Strengthen our hearts, so that we may persevere in our following of Jesus. Amen.

## 3. LITURGY OF THE WORD

### Introduction to the Readings
Faith is a powerful reason to forgive. God himself demonstrates his love for us through forgiveness. If we live, overcoming anger and offence, and spreading forgiveness, we will be like God. Whoever does not forgive shows that he does not know God, he is living enclosed in his own darkness and he is harming himself as well as others.

### Readings
Eccl. 27:33-28:9. *Psalm.* Rom. 14:7-9. *Acclamation.* Mt. 18:21-35. *Brief silence.*

### Reflection
Forgiveness is a value of the highest quality. Whoever forgives is showing maturity, greatness of spirit, sensitivity and courage. It is the other way of expressing love.

Forgiveness is also a value given prominence in the Bible, above all, the forgiveness offered by our compassionate and merciful God. The parable in the Gospel is eloquent in itself. We sinful people are, before God, like that insolvent labourer, with such a great debt that it is impossible to pay back.

God, merciful to his very core, has compassion and forgives us completely.

God always forgives. Furthermore, as that other parable of the prodigal son expresses, he comes to meet us every day, full of affection and bearing forgiveness. He is never tired of forgiving. It is his great task, that keeps him busy day and night, and every day without exception. God forgives, because he is quite simply love and mercy.

But it is not easy to forgive. We know that for some people it is an extraordinary effort. Does Peter's question, concerning whether seven times a day is sufficient, tell us something? Jesus replies that one must not set any limits to forgiveness: "I say to you not seven times, but seventy times seven", that is to say, always. The logical and gracious response upon receiving forgiveness is to offer forgiveness. We have all been forgiven; but one does not know how to forgive, unless one experiences it deep within one's being.

Let us ask ourselves whether we are not a little grudging and stingy, when we should forgive. Sometimes we hear people say: "I am tired now of forgiving", "this is enough". If we were those being forgiven, would we say the same thing? At other times, we say: "I forgive, but they should give me an explanation, they should come and acknowledge it, my dignity will not be trampled on". Forgiveness with reservations is not true forgiveness. In the parable referred to, of the prodigal son, the father does not ask for any explanation.

In summary, forgiveness is a value of great human and evangelical quality. It must be an outstanding attribute of every Christian. Jesus gives us this parable from the abundance of mercy that he bears in his heart. In the Church, forgiveness is practised and celebrated in a sacrament: the sacrament of conversion and of reconciliation. (*Silence for internal reflection.*)

## Creed

## Prayer of the Faithful

- Let us pray for the so-called *poor countries,* burdened by external debt, which, like a millstone around their necks, impedes not only their development, but even their very survival.
- Let us pray for the so-called *rich countries,* that one day their economic empire, which oppresses a majority of the world, may be dismantled or collapse, in such a way that a system guided by mercy and sharing may be born.
- Let us pray also for peace, which is the fruit of a sense of community, of dialogue and forgiveness.
- Let us pray for the Church and for our community, so that we may be a meeting place, a centre of brotherhood and reconciliation.
- Let us pray that we may foster our commitment to educate our children in the values that we are considering now.
- Let us pray that we may practise forgiveness to those who cause us offence.
- For these and for all of our intentions, *let us pray to the Lord.*

## Symbolic Action

*Five people go up to a prominent place. Four of them bring various phrases on strips of cardboard. The fifth begins by saying:* In response to the offence or harm that others cause us, we have different reactions… *The other four people start saying the phrases slowly, with brief pauses between each one and raising the corresponding cardboard strip; they follow this order:*

- The one who did it to me, will pay.
- I cannot forgive.
- I forgive, but I do not forget.
- I forgive. God forgives me, too.

*The fifth person interjects again:* In which of these reactions do you see yourself reflected?

## 4. RITE OF COMMUNION

### Introduction
In his great mercy, God has made himself one of us and has redeemed us. Let us learn mercy and forgiveness from Jesus.

### Hymn

### Prayer

We bless you, Father, our companion on life's journey,
because you are always by our side
spreading love and compassion.
You do not treat us as our sins deserve
nor do you punish us according to our guilt.
Your heart goes out especially to the simple,
to those desirous of life and those in need of forgiveness,
because you are overflowing with mercy.
You accept the repentant sinner with loving tenderness.
You share the satisfaction of the merciful
who know how to understand and forgive.
You reject the pride of those who do not want to love,
but you keep your arms extended, full of patience,
always ready for the sincere embrace of conversion.
In no way can we be part of your people
if we do not forgive our brothers and sisters from our hearts.
Thank you, Father, for what we have learnt from Jesus.
Thank you, because in forgiving us, you teach us to forgive,
and in helping us so lovingly,
you prompt us to do the same for others.
In greater awareness, after such a worthy message,
we say to you: Our Father…

### Sign of Peace

### Distribution of Communion: Hymn

### Act of Thanksgiving (*spontaneous*)

## 5. CONCLUDING RITE

### Resolution
To forgive always, from the bottom of your heart.

### Blessing

### Conclusion
Forgiveness brings great joy, in the one who offers it and the one who receives it. To hold out the hand of forgiveness is to imitate the God of Jesus, who forgives us always. Let us be generous enough to forgive and humble enough to accept forgiveness. Brotherhood is not possible without forgiveness and reconciliation. Throughout the week, we have a good opportunity to put all this into practice. May the Lord help us.

### Final Hymn and Dismissal

# Twenty-Fifth Sunday

## 1. SETTING THE SCENE

### Poster with one of these texts:
- "My ways are higher than your ways"
- "God's justice is different"
- "God is different"
- "Go you, too, to my vineyard"

### Symbols:
- Pruning scissors, bunches of grapes and vine branches.
- Large clock.
- Stepladder (my ways are higher than your ways).

## 2. INTRODUCTORY RITES

### Introduction
Very often, our way of understanding life does not accord with God's. Because of that, we will hear today that: "My thoughts are not your thoughts, my ways are not your ways… My ways are more exalted than yours." God is right. He looks into and fathoms the very depths of people, whereas we often dwell on outward impressions of people and events. If only we could manage to understand life and human relations as God does.

### Hymn

### Greeting
Brothers and sisters, let us bless the Lord, who is good and just to everyone.

### Penitential Rite
- Purify us within: *Lord, have mercy.*
- Help us to live in solidarity: *Christ, have mercy.*
- Instil in us the mentality of the Gospel: *Lord, have mercy.*

### Gloria

### Prayer
O God, you have made the fulfilling of the Law reside in love for you and for one's neighbour; grant that we may fulfil your commandments, and so may reach eternal life. Through Christ…

## 3. LITURGY OF THE WORD

### Introduction to the Readings
God thinks of us with a sense of fundamental equality. For that reason, his thoughts are not like our thoughts. We soon create differences. And sometimes, we even wish that God were as ungenerous as we are. But he keeps his dignity and does not stop proposing the tender way of life of the Gospel to us.

Today's parable goes to the heart of life. It refers to the final salary of each person. God does not mind us knowing how he is going to proceed in the hour of our final reckoning. In relation to the parable, it is worth stressing the reaction of those who came first to being treated like the last. But the fact is that God's justice is not like ours. God looks with other eyes. And, besides, he is never prone to envy.

### Readings
Is. 55:6-9. *Psalm.* Phil. 1:20c-24. 27a. *Acclamation.* Mt. 20:1-16. *Brief silence.*

### Reflection
God is different. He has plans and marks out ways that often do not coincide with ours. But God does not want to be different, he has not got that obsession. Because of his desire to be like ourselves, he came down and has appeared in Jesus, like one

among so many. What he cannot permit himself, in becoming the same as us, is to abandon his standards and to proceed with our low and mean-minded thoughts, adapting himself to this world and allowing himself to be borne along, like *someone who follows the crowd*. He wants every one of us to understand his spirituality; but due to our blindness and hardness of heart, our ways do not coincide. Because he maintains his honour and his standards, he is distinct, while desiring to be the same.

In fact, God's plans and ways are higher, that is to say, they are more worthy and full of humanity. For that reason, once again, a parable from the Gospel can turn out to be disconcerting for us: its message undermines our ideas, breaks our moulds, dwarfs social justice and wounds our self-esteem. Is our God strange? What is noteworthy is that in the parable, there is no injustice. So, my friend, why are you envious that I am good, asks God.

Let us bear in mind that Jesus tells this parable to his disciples to teach them about what characterises the Kingdom of God. This Kingdom, which is also of this world, will always be an alternative. God's justice has different tables of measurement, other ways of evaluating; it is governed by a different scale of values: one is not paid according to efficiency, according to profitability, according to accumulated merit, nor is there any relation between categories and salaries. For God, other considerations and other needs come into play. His kindness is above all human justice. In his way of proceeding, there is not the faintest trace of privilege for anyone. His mercy embraces all.

Let us say, finally, that God offers his Kingdom at all stages in life. There are those who become aware of it early, those who need more invitations, those who catch up with it in adulthood, and it seems that some people do not discover it until an advanced age. What a pity! Because they have had less opportunity to enjoy and work for the Kingdom of God. To understand all this well, we certainly need a change of mentality, a conversion. Only in this way, as Saint Paul says, will we be able to "lead a life worthy of the Gospel". (*Silence for internal reflection.*)

## Creed

## Prayer of the Faithful

- Let us pray that God's plans may be understood and applied by all nations and governments.
- Let us pray that nobody may try to better his or her situation at the expense of others.
- Let us pray that the right to work may be a real possibility for all.
- Let us pray for our Church, that it may convey the thoughts and ways of God with clarity and example.
- Let us pray for our community, that we may know how to communicate the life that is worthy of the Gospel.
- For these and for all our intentions, *let us pray to the Lord.*

## Offerings

- *Employment contract:* Lord, work is a right and a duty. But now it is a scarce resource that not everyone can enjoy…
- *Basket with different products of work:* Lord, we present to you the fruits of our labour in solidarity, so that no one may lack the basic necessities of life.

## Hymn

## Symbolic Action

Collection for charity or to combat unemployment.

## 4. RITE OF COMMUNION

### Introduction
The greater our communion with Jesus, the more we will understand his Gospel message. Let us open our hearts and minds, so that we may receive the complete alternative way that his person represents.

### Hymn

### Prayer
O God, how different you are!
We do not tire of recognising
the affection that you have for everyone.
There is no room for privileged people in your heart.
You give yourself completely to all who accept you.
You are love without measure, generosity without limit
to all men and women. That is your justice.
Some discover you in the morning of life
and gratefully enjoy your presence.
Others, mysteriously, do not meet you
until the twilight of their lives.
But no one who feels you deep within them
is envious of others.
Only those become angry
who have not experienced you in their depths.
For them, you are more of an idea than a personal companion.
God, our Father, you have made us in your image.
But many of us have turned out to be a disappointment.
Your thoughts are not our thoughts;
your ways are not our ways;
we proceed in discord, with our false calculations
and thus, our accounts do not come out correctly.
Father, may your Spirit help us to understand the Gospel.
Grant us that degree of love
that generates freedom of spirit,
solidarity and justice beyond merit.

Because you are good to the point of overflowing we call upon you: Our Father…

### Sign of Peace

### Distribution of Communion: Hymn

### Act of Thanksgiving
- We give you thanks, Father, because your plans are more exalted, more just and more reasonable than ours. That is why they are an alternative.
- You analyse our situation with criteria of solidarity and you apply the measure of mercy, which is equality and justice as you understand them.
- Your thoughts astonish us, Father, but they are completely reasonable. If only we might understand that phrase in the Gospel, which says that the first shall be last and the last shall be first.

## 5. CONCLUDING RITE

### Resolution
To lead a life worthy of the Gospel.

### Blessing

### Conclusion
God's justice is in keeping with his holiness and mercy. For that reason, we remember that, for him, the last shall be first, because salvation is a gift. If we have accepted this message, let us get rid of the differences that hinder brotherhood. Have a happy week and may God go with us.

### Final Hymn and Dismissal

# Twenty-Sixth Sunday

## 1. SETTING THE SCENE

### Poster with one of these texts:
- "Faith is obedience to God"
- *"Saying yes* to faith gives it life"
- "Christ, always our example"

### Symbols:
- Gloves, boots, hat for working in the countryside.
- Poster of Jesus or crucifix.

## 2. INTRODUCTORY RITES

### Introduction
This Sunday's message presents basic aspects of spirituality, like responsibility, community, solidarity, humility… In life, as in the Gospel, there are some people who use beautiful words, but it is others who commit themselves and who fulfil the will of the Father. There is something fundamental about which we should never compromise: the intense nurturing of our inner and communal life, in order to live with feelings and attitudes similar to those of Christ.

### Hymn

### Greeting
Brothers and sisters, let us bless God; to him, all of us are important.

### Penitential Rite
- Lord, you desire our conversion, *Lord, have mercy.*
- Lord, you are an example for us all, *Christ, have mercy.*
- Lord, forgive our frailty, *Lord, have mercy.*

### Gloria

### Prayer
O God, you manifest your power especially through your forgiveness and mercy; pour down your grace upon us, so that, desiring what you promise, we may attain the blessings of redemption. Through Christ…

## 3. LITURGY OF THE WORD

### Introduction to the Readings
Personal responsibility is of decisive importance. Each one of us plays a crucial role in the direction of our lives. If we take a wrong turning, God leads us back on the right path. The ideal and the point of reference will always be Jesus.

The Gospel gives prominence to humility. We do not always obey, when, in the first instance, we say yes. The parable stresses that faith is obedience to God, because, sooner or later, we come to discover that God is always right.

### Readings
Ezek. 18:25-28. *Psalm.* Phil. 2:1-11. *Acclamation.* Mt. 21:28-32. *Brief silence.*

### Reflection
The second reading's content is packed with meaning and inferences. Besides recalling a hymn, in which the Philippians invoked and glorified Jesus, it offers us a rich incentive for the values of community: do not work through envy or through ostentation; let yourselves be guided by humility; always consider others superior to yourselves; do not become wrapped up in your private interests, but seek what is in the interest of others; keep

among yourselves the sentiments of Jesus Christ. In reality, it is a stupendous programme for the Christian community, equally valid for secular communities.

The other two readings also contain a motivation for living with graciousness and responsibility. Who has not, on some occasion, broken promises and commitments? Who has not gone back on his or her word? Both sons, in the Gospel parable, represent behaviour that is reprehensible, although one can be criticised more than the other. The second is a hypocrite, while the first one is protesting, he reacts instinctively, but later reflects upon it and goes to work. In reality, he is the one who fulfils the will of the Father; not the first one. The ideal, however, is to carry things through graciously, as much in the depth and content, as in the external details. We must obey God in a sincere and gracious way. And to obey God is, above all, to love, serve and make those people happy who are at our side. Let us not be surprised that Jesus says: there are people of bad reputation – publicans and prostitutes – who do better in this than religious people. The life of each person is a demonstration of whether he is building the Kingdom of God and fulfilling his will or if, on the contrary, he is a hypocrite, because he attends religious services, says that he prays, but afterwards, he is not seen to be pulling his weight in the work at the vineyard: the Kingdom of God. The people who seem to say *yes*, which in fact turns out to be a *no*, perhaps do it through superficiality, through a lack of understanding, or through failings in their Christian education, but that does not take away their share of personal responsibility. In which of the two sons do we see ourselves portrayed? (*Silence for internal reflection.*)

## Creed

## Prayer of the Faithful
- For the Church, that it may be a servant of the Gospel, *let us pray to the Lord.*

- So that service for the common good may be a priority in the work of those in government, *let us pray to the Lord.*
- So that we Christians may have feelings and attitudes similar to Jesus', *let us pray to the Lord.*
- So that each one of us may cultivate responsibility, *let us pray to the Lord.*
- For all our intentions, *let us pray to the Lord.*

## 4. RITE OF COMMUNION

### Introduction
The greatest sign that we are truly in union with Jesus is that we fulfil the will of God. Let us learn from the example that he gives us.

### Hymn

### Prayer
Blessed are you, Father,
you have enriched history with the gift of Jesus
leaving us in him a supreme example of personality
to be followed in every time and place.
With the Christians from Philippi, we say to you
with conviction:
there is no better achievement than to live like Jesus.
He, in spite of his divine state,
made no display of his Godly rank;
on the contrary, he stripped himself of his rank
and took upon himself a condition of slavery,
living as just one among so many.
And, being as others are,
He descended even to the point of submitting to death,
and a death on the cross.
For this, you raised him high above all things
and you granted him the *Name-above-all-names*,
so that on hearing Jesus' name, every knee shall bend
in heaven, on earth, and in the underworld
and every tongue proclaim: Jesus is the Lord!
Joining together our hands and our hearts,
and with Jesus among us (*people hold hands*),
we say to you: Our Father…

**Sign of Peace**

**Distribution of Communion: Hymn**

**Act of Thanksgiving (*spontaneous*)**

## 5. CONCLUDING RITE

### Resolution
To act with the sentiments and attitudes
appropriate to a life in Christ.

### Blessing

### Conclusion
Obedience to the Word of God and having
attitudes and sentiments like those of Jesus, is the
great message that this celebration leaves us with.
May our lives be re-clothed in the Gospel, within
and without, so that we may better serve our
people. May the Lord help us to succeed in this.

### Final Hymn and Dismissal

# Twenty-Seventh Sunday

## 1. SETTING THE SCENE

### Poster with one of these texts:
- "God loves you"
- "God is generous with you"

### Symbol:
- A vine stem in a big flowerpot.

## 2. INTRODUCTORY RITES

### Introduction
Brothers and sisters, we strengthen, in these meetings, our sense of continuing on this path together, as a spur, not only for the life of the community, but also for that of the town, because, as Christians, we must never lower our guard with respect to our commitment to transform our social surroundings. For this, nothing is better than to do it with a lively and resilient spirit, centred upon God the Father, upon Jesus and upon his Spirit. Without them, we men and women believers, Christian groups and communities lose our momentum and become useless.

### Hymn

### Greeting
Brothers and sisters, let us bless the Lord, who has called us to be members of his family.

### Penitential Rite
Let us purify ourselves as much as possible, asking forgiveness for our sins. (*Brief silence.*) *I confess…*

### Gloria

### Prayer
Our Father, in your generous love, you exceed the merits and desires of all who come to you in prayer; pour forth your mercy upon us, so as to free our conscience from all disquiet and grant us what we dare not even ask for. Through Christ…

## 3. LITURGY OF THE WORD

### Introduction to the Readings
The prophet Isaiah and the evangelist Matthew come together in presenting a beautiful and meaningful text for our consideration. We all represent what the Word of God calls the *vineyard of the Lord*. This vineyard is well planted and very well tended on God's part; however, the fruit is bitter, wild, and the tenants are irresponsible people.

### Readings
Is. 5:1-7. *Psalm.* Phil. 4:6-9. *Acclamation.* Mt. 21:33-43. *Brief silence.*

### Reflection
Parables are not exclusive to the Gospel. They are also to be found in the Old Testament. One of them is that of the vineyard. How well this parable describes the loving, delicate and attentive relationship of God with his people: "What more could I have done for my vineyard that I have not done? Why when I expected it to yield grapes, did it bring forth wild produce?" It is this people who rejected the prophets and, years later, vilely murdered Jesus.

Since the time of Jesus, we can now consider this vineyard to be the Church and, following from this, all people. Throughout history, we have been similarly enriched by new prophets, saints and witnesses of great quality. But it is enough to glance at history and at the present day, to observe that we have not made much progress in the care and in the administration of the vineyard. There are still struggles for power, messengers being snuffed out, abuses by some who want to dominate, as though they were the owners of the property… Why do we not bring forth the fruit that was duly expected of us? Do we not say that we ought to be the ferment of the Kingdom of God in the midst of society? Are we really in the service of genuine progress in our community and of the salvation which the Gospel brings?

We have been called upon to collaborate in the works of the vineyard and God expects nothing less of us than sensitive collaboration, in order to improve it. We have been charged with its care and administration. No one but God is the owner of the vineyard. So that we might perform our tasks well, he has left us the Gospel and the Spirit, and all our abilities, which are considerable; but we will not perform well, if we go our own way and not the way of the Spirit and the Gospel.

To conclude, we are left with a warning: that we should be worthy collaborators and responsible administrators of the Lord's vineyard. Human beings in general, and believers in particular, cannot assume any other function than that of co-responsibility in the vineyard's tenancy. For this, let us put into practice what is mentioned in the second reading: "all that is true, noble, just, pure, loveable, praiseworthy; all that is virtue… keep it in the forefront of your minds". (*Silence for internal reflection.*)

## Creed

## Prayer of the Faithful
- Let us pray for our world, for human rights and the rights of nations.
- Let us pray for the Church, that it may be of the Gospel and for the Gospel; that it may

demonstrate this with works of solidarity and with signs of hope.
- Let us pray for those who are the most poor and needy, for those who have less opportunity, so that they may be always the focus of our attention.
- Let us pray that among all of us, we may create a community that is fraternal, responsible and dynamic in the service of our people.
- For these and for all our intentions, *let us pray to the Lord.*

## Symbolic Action
*Place the names of people beside or inside the symbol: these are the servants who collaborate in the cultivation of the vineyard-community.*

## 4. RITE OF COMMUNION

## Conclusion
Communion unites us with Jesus and with each other. In this way, the stimulus to help each other is greater. God the Father wants us to be united and to strive for the good of our people.

## Hymn

## Prayer
God, loving Father,
you are the one Lord of the vineyard of this world.
With what care you have looked after us
and how well you have attended to our needs.
You accompany us silently
and you love us with the tenderness of young love.
How great has been your consideration and how many the opportunities you have offered us.
As for our freedom there is no more that
you could have done.
Father, today, we want to pray to
you concerning our Church,
which has beautiful qualities and
also brings shame upon itself.
That is why it is not the symbol

that many people expect.
In spite of everything, we love it like a mother;
it has many good aspects: it is a river of hope,
a channel of redemption, a seal of mercy;
in its best witnesses, it is critical and prophetic;
thanks to the Church, the faith has reached us
and through it, we have experienced
the courage of the Spirit.
But it needs to be converted.
That is why we say to you:
"Come back: look down from heaven, see,
come and visit your vineyard, the vine
planted by your right hand,
that you made vigorous…"
Surrounded by your love and desiring to be fruitful,
we call upon you: Our Father…

## Sign of Peace

## Distribution of Communion: Hymn

## Act of Thanksgiving (*spontaneous*)

## 5. CONCLUDING RITE

### Resolution
To be honest in life and to do good.

### Blessing

### Conclusion
As we end this celebration, let us remember the
message of the parable. God has fulfilled his
promise and continues to fulfil it. We know that this
community must be fruitful. We can all contribute
to this. Now, we have to continue to carry out our
responsibilities.

### Final Hymn and Dismissal

# Twenty-Eighth Sunday

## 1. SETTING THE SCENE

### Poster with one of these texts:
- "God invites us; many do not respond"
- "The poor respond better to God"
- "Few accept the Kingdom of God"
- "The Lord loves the humble"

### Symbol:
- Altar or table prepared for a banquet. Four people are sitting around it. There is a free seat with God's name on it. There are others that are unoccupied from which a card hangs saying "NO".

## 2. INTRODUCTORY RITES

### Introduction
We are all equal before God. He devotes himself to us with fatherly love and has an insistent obsession: to save us. However, it happens, that we often turn our backs on him; and we prefer our own interests to his invitation of salvation. We are going to remind ourselves of the importance of God's offer of salvation, to which the only response can be one which is free and gracious. God invites us. In his Kingdom, there is room for everyone, without exception.

That is why we have a table prepared for a banquet. Some people have accepted the invitation. God is the host. But there are other empty seats. Some people do not want to occupy them.

### Hymn

### Greeting
Brothers and sisters, let us bless the Lord, who wants us by his side, at his feast.

### Penitential Rite
- Because we have often not followed your promptings, *Lord, have mercy.*
- Because we offer you unreasonable excuses, *Christ, have mercy.*
- Because we have set a bad example, *Lord, have mercy.*

### Gloria

### Prayer
God, bountiful Father, you invite everyone to the feast of your Kingdom. you dream of a universal festivity. We, who are redeemed through Jesus, thank you for the Christian vocation that fills us with energy and opens our hearts to your bounty. you count on our presence and we thank you for your invitation. Amen.

## 3. LITURGY OF THE WORD

### Introduction to the Readings
Salvation is universal. God offers it to all who wish to receive it. It happens that the poor and underprivileged are the best at accepting it. The teaching of Jesus makes complete sense: it is only possible to understand God and his offers, if we are poor in spirit and pure in heart.

### Readings
Is. 25:6-10a. *Psalm.* Phil. 4:12-14.19-20. *Acclamation.* Mt. 22:1-14. *Brief silence.*

### Reflection
To invite someone to eat with you is a sign of cordiality, of a pleasant and festive celebration. At a gathering, there is communication, friendship,

interest in others, intimacy flourishes, confidence increases, etc. At a banquet, the guests are very important people.

So, there you have the parable of the Kingdom of God. The image that Isaiah presents to us is formidable: God, in his openness and generosity to all peoples, wants to have a celebration, because he desires that his abundant happiness should reach everyone; he does not want anyone to be sad. Thus, he organises the banquet for his great company with succulent dishes and vintage wines. What a surprise! God invites us, he wants us to be in his circle of friends, and, in addition to that, he acts as the cook, the waiter… Jesus has talked about this already: "I am among you, as one who serves" (Lk. 22:27). Can you imagine such a banquet of friendship and community?

Although God has arranged the feast for everyone, it is only attended by the genuinely poor, the simple and needy, those who are open to the newness of his message. Those who are closed to his concerns and his particular adventures are too *busy*. It is history repeating itself: the Lord offers us superior values, and many of us prefer inferior values, if not counter-values or vices that seem appealing.

How many people learn to enjoy spirituality, religion and the Gospel? We have seen that it does not involve an invitation to live a life of dullness; on the contrary, it is an invitation to a dazzling feast. Then why are there those who deny themselves and turn their back on it?

At the present time, we, too, are receiving a similar invitation. We know that attendance is open and without any charge. There is only one condition: to go in party clothes. But you do not have to buy them. It is a matter of going with a renewed heart, with a pure soul, with bright eyes. One cannot sit at the table as brothers and sisters in any state, but transformed, converted, as befits the children of God's family.

Are our meetings faithful signs of this great banquet of the Kingdom of God? (*Silence for internal reflection.*)

## Creed

## Prayer of the Faithful

- Let us pray for all the peoples of the earth, that they may progress towards unity and all discrimination may disappear.
- Let us pray for our Church, that it may appealingly express God's generous invitation of salvation in an attractive way.
- Let us pray for our community, that we may bear witness, among our neighbours, to the festive joy of the Kingdom of God.
- Let us pray for all those who collaborate for the good of the people and for those who make their neighbours' lives happier.
- Let us pray for each other. *Let us pray to the Lord.*

## Symbolic Action

*One of the guests, at the symbolic table, uncorks a bottle, raises it and says:* God invites us to his heaven. It is like a great banquet. There are some people who do not believe it, who take no notice. Why? *Brief pause.* Do you believe it? *Brief pause.* Do you accept the invitation?

## 4. RITE OF COMMUNION

## Introduction
Experiences that move us deeply, if they are festive, fill our hearts with joy and we need to celebrate them. Among them, the experience of communion stands out. Jesus invites us, he makes a covenant and offers himself as the feast.

## Hymn

## Prayer

We bless you, Father, because we love you.
A hymn of gratitude rises from our hearts
because you have invited us to the feast of life.
You want us to experience your covenant at all
costs.
You are so full of goodness
that you insist when someone does not keep the
engagement.
How much you love us, God,
and how much are they losing, those who refuse
your invitation.
If we allowed you to act, this world would be
delightful.
If we unite ourselves with your Spirit,
we are already tasting heaven on earth.
If we allow the Gospel to enlighten us,
life becomes an uplifting panorama.
Thank you, Father, for the benefits of the faith.
With all those who attend your family banquet
we sing to you and we say to you: Our Father…

## Sign of Peace

## Distribution of Communion: Hymn

## Act of Thanksgiving

- We give you thanks, Father, because you love everyone equally.
- You teach us how to live with dignity and to celebrate it fraternally.
- Your Kingdom is like a wedding banquet, a great gathering of shared tenderness, the thrill of hearts that rejoice.

## 5. CONCLUDING RITE

## Resolution

Not to give excuses, when we hear the call of the Gospel.

## Blessing

## Conclusion

God wants the best for us. For that reason, he already wants us to enjoy the salvation that he has given us, here and now. We have celebrated the faith. Let us be brothers and sisters in our lives and witnesses to the family love that we celebrate. The success that we may have is a sign that we are already part of the Kingdom of God.

## Final Hymn and Dismissal

# Twenty-Ninth Sunday

## 1. SETTING THE SCENE

### Poster with one of these texts:
- ◼ "Render to God what is God's"
- ◼ "It was difficult for Jesus"
- ◼ "There is no other Lord"

## 2. INTRODUCTORY RITES

### Introduction
We have come together, once more, to listen to the Word and to celebrate the faith. Jesus, in his admirable way, surprises us with the sharpness that he demonstrates, in uncovering other people's intentions. More than once, they tempted him, putting him in serious difficulties. But, thanks to the Spirit and to his alert way of life, he could always come up with a response and counter-arguments. Let us learn to live like him, with all our senses alert, so as not to fall into any temptation.

### Hymn

### Greeting
Brothers and sisters, let us praise God the Father together for the great gift of Jesus.

### Penitential Rite
- ◼ You, Lord, have compassion for us,
  *Lord, have mercy.*
- ◼ You, Lord, give us an example of authenticity,
  *Christ, have mercy.*
- ◼ You, Lord, want us to be free and sincere,
  *Lord, have mercy.*

### Gloria

### Prayer
Bountiful Father, you are our God. We do not want to compare you with anything or anybody, because you are unique and distinct. In Jesus, you have revealed to us the way to honour you: always to show concern for our neighbour. Grant that we may continue to devote ourselves in faithfulness to you and to our brothers and sisters, with sincere hearts. Through Christ…

## 3. LITURGY OF THE WORD

### Introduction to the Readings
Every man and woman can fulfil the will of God. Just as God has chosen us, in a free and friendly manner, he has given us the same ability to respond freely to him. God sees in each human being a deep fund of goodness. Let us also see it.

### Readings
Is. 45:1. 4-6. *Psalm.* 1 Thess. 1:1-5b. *Acclamation.* Mt. 22:15-21. *Brief silence.*

### Reflection
With what simplicity and precision does the second reading describe the mission of evangelising: "when the Gospel was proclaimed amongst you, there were not only words, but also the power of the Holy Spirit and deep conviction". To evangelise effectively, nothing is better than to be brimming over with spirituality. Missionaries, here and there, are witnesses who speak from the abundant grace that they bear in their hearts.

The Gospel passage has, as its background, the issue of nationalism that existed in Jesus' time. Some Pharisees consider that this is an opportune question with which to put Jesus in a tight spot: so that he has to define himself politically, in favour of the established regime, or in favour of resistance against the invader.

Let us say in passing, that in all times and places, there have been deceitful people. Jesus experienced it repeatedly. They often wanted to catch him out, in order to compromise him. The question of the tribute to Caesar is another example. He, however, was always alert, vigilant and aware. For that reason, they never caught him off guard, or unawares. Moreover, he knew very well when someone was approaching with good or evil intent.

Those who came to *ensnare* him cynically smooth over the question, by praising his honesty: "we know that you are sincere and that you preach the way of God, in all honesty, and that you are not afraid of anyone because you are not concerned with appearances. Tell us, then, what you think." Jesus, who is alert, unmasks their intentions: "Hypocrites! Why do you tempt me?", and he answers them in a way they do not expect. He had objectives superior to those that were merely political. His priorities were aimed much higher. With poise and authority, he shifts the political question to the religious sphere: God is infinitely greater than Caesar. This is what the first reading points out: "I am the Lord and there is no other". For that reason, render to Caesar what is Caesar's, and to God what is God's.

In summary, let us learn from Jesus to be citizens with discernment, alert and critical, and to live with such a rich inner life that we have sufficient resources to deal with anyone who attempts to harass us. (*Silence for internal reflection.*)

## Creed

## Prayer of the Faithful
- ■ That respect and collaboration may grow among people, *let us pray to the Lord.*
- ■ That we may live with the sincerity and awareness of Jesus, *let us pray to the Lord.*
- ■ Let us pray for the young Churches of the Third and Fourth Worlds, that they may be strengthened and may set an example as a new Church, *let us pray to the Lord.*
- ■ That prayer may help us to lead a sober, simple life, and keep us from all temptation, *let us pray to the Lord.*
- ■ Let us pray for each other, that we may live the faith with joy and that we may be missionaries in our neighbourhoods, *let us pray to the Lord.*

## Symbolic Action
*Someone presents an icon, image or picture of Jesus to the assembly and says:* Out of love for God, we Christians want the life of society to reflect your Kingdom.

## 4. RITE OF COMMUNION

### Introduction
We are neighbours in this town and citizens of the people of God. We have civic and religious duties. In communion with Jesus, we find our point of equilibrium.

### Hymn

### Prayer
In the brotherhood and protection of the Spirit
we praise you, our Father.
We recognise with deep conviction
that you alone are God.
Only you deserve adoration and glory.
You have revealed yourself, rich in tenderness,
you have freed us from many idols
and from people who have wanted to give themselves airs,
falsely bolstering up their personality

and seeking applause and deference.
Father, we want to look at history
with the critical eyes of faith.
We want the Gospel to permeate social life.
As citizens and believers,
we are drawn to the independence of Jesus.
He knew how to distinguish: to render to Caesar,
what is Caesar's
and to God, what is God's.
Father, we are convinced by the way of the Gospel:
nobody higher than anyone else, nobody lower
than anyone else.
In solidarity and communion, we say to you:
Our Father…

## Sign of Peace

## Distribution of Communion: Hymn

## Act of Thanksgiving

- Father, we admire Jesus, full of inner light, who knows how to read the thoughts of people who approach him.
- We admire Jesus, lucid and critical, who disarms the hypocrites who challenge him with deceitful intentions.
- We are attracted to Jesus, who knows how to conduct himself as the Son of Light, who is as wise as a serpent and as gentle as a dove.
- Father, then as now, temptations appear all the time. We give you thanks for Jesus' exemplary conduct. Help us to live with similar dignity.

## 5. CONCLUDING RITE

## Resolution

To get rid of hypocrisy and to be always alert, so that we may overcome any temptation.

## Blessing

## Conclusion

This shared celebration has energised our sense of being Christian. Let us go out into the world, with all our faculties alert, so that we may be good neighbours; but also, so that we may be astute and not allow ourselves to be deceived by anyone who tries to tempt us. Let us remember that phrase from the Gospel: "render to Caesar, what is Caesar's; and to God, what is God's".

## Final Hymn and Dismissal

# Thirtieth Sunday

## 1. SETTING THE SCENE

### Poster with one of these texts:
- ◼ "The most important thing is to love"
- ◼ "Everything comes down to love"
- ◼ "Love God and your neighbour"

### Symbols:
- ◼ Bible.
- ◼ Placard with these phrases:
- ◼ Love God.
- ◼ Love your neighbour.

## 2. INTRODUCTORY RITES

### Introduction
Friends, we celebrate God's love, which brings us together, and our mutual love inspired by faith. The word of scripture will tell us today that everything is summed up by love. Love is what saves us.

Loving God and loving one's neighbour are not the same, but they are inseparable for a Christian: they are tried and proven together and make mutual demands. The absence, or negation of one of them, excludes the other. We cannot say: "I love God", if we do not demonstrate it through love to our friends.

Inspired by our best experiences of love, let us celebrate God, who was the first to love us, and let us bless Jesus, who shows us with his own life how far the powerful force of human love can reach.

### Hymn

### Greeting
Brothers and sisters, let us praise the Lord together, who was the first to love us.

### Penitential Rite
- ◼ Because we do not love you with all our heart and soul, *Lord, have mercy.*
- ◼ Because we are not generous enough, *Christ, have mercy.*
- ◼ Because we easily forget the commandment to love, *Lord, have mercy.*

### Prayer
God, bountiful Father, all your revelation is summed up and culminates in love for you and for one's neighbour. This is our vocation and our principal commitment. Lord, who were the first to love us, nurture in us this great experience of faith. Through Christ…

## 3. LITURGY OF THE WORD

### Introduction to the Readings
To help others to fulfil themselves as people is an excellent way of understanding God's love. Jesus makes it clear that everything comes down to one single love, but it has two facets: God and one's neighbour. This is what he gave certain Pharisees to understand, when they asked him a deceitful question.

### Readings
Exod. 22:20-26. *Psalm.* 1 Thess. 1:5c-10. *Acclamation.* Mt. 22:34-40. *Brief silence.*

### Reflection
On a number of occasions, we have heard slogans or sayings that go like this: affection is what is effective, good conquers evil. It is clear that there is

no better energy for the human spirit and for peaceful society, than the power of love. With love and friendship, any difficulty can be bravely confronted.

The Israelite people had suffered severe oppression during their long stay in Egypt. The experience teaches them not to repeat the same mistakes. Their future story must be different. From God's love that has liberated them, spring forth various norms that embody an ideal: the love of God and the love of one's neighbour. "Thus, says the Lord: you will not oppress, nor vex the stranger, you will not exploit widows and orphans, you will not be a usurer…"

Jewish law, in Jesus' time, contained 613 commandments; for the Jews, they were all important, although, logically, some carried more weight than others. On one occasion, some Pharisees with devious intentions ask Jesus what is the most important commandment. Jesus restates the great tradition and gives an excellent summary. Love for God cannot be conceived of, without love for one's neighbour. For that reason, the principal commandment, and definitely the most important one, is double-edged, because love for God is inseparable from love for one's neighbour.

As many of us have been taught, virtue is demonstrated by keeping the commandments. At the present time, we believe that the Beatitudes complement them and, moreover, go much further. In any case, for us, the most important and crucial thing is to fulfil the sum of all the commandments: to love God with all of one's being, and one's neighbour with the same intensity. This value is the highest form of example in a Christian community. It is what gives it consistency. What is not love causes disharmony and degrades it.

In some communities, love for one's neighbour is emphasised more than love for God. For Jesus, the first and most important thing is to love God with all one's heart, with all one's soul and with all one's being. There is no doubt that this guarantees love for one's neighbour, whereas the reverse is not always so certain. It happens, with relative frequency, that without love for God, we end up loving nobody. (*Silence for internal reflection.*)

## Creed

## Prayer of the Faithful
- ■ Let us pray for the men and women of our time, that we may live our vocation of love with fervour.
- ■ Let us pray for our Church, that it may be a steadfast witness to the love of God and of Jesus.
- ■ Let us pray for those most in need of love and acceptance.
- ■ Let us pray for our community, that we may exercise a healthy influence upon our town, by means of a generous love.
- ■ Let us pray for the unity of our town and for the intentions that concern us. *Let us pray to the Lord.*

## Symbolic Action
*Someone goes up to the place of symbols. Raising the Bible, he says:* This book, with so many pages and with such a great message, can be summed up in these two sentences. *He puts down the Bible and raises the placard.*

## 4. RITE OF COMMUNION

## Introduction
To love is more than a commandment or counsel; it is a vital necessity fostered by faith. May communion with Jesus strengthen in us our love for God and for others.

## Hymn

## Prayer

God, good Father,
if only we knew how to sing with our whole life
the song of love that you deserve.
We have learnt from our Mother, the Church,
that love is born in you and culminates in you.
You made us, so that we might love,
and we hope one day
that such a high ideal may be fulfilled completely.
While life flows on, we give you thanks
for the kiss, the caress, for friendship,
and for your tender presence.
What happiness when love
strengthens our relationships.
Father, all was sown in the seed of your first love:
there are expressions of warmth in our homes,
gestures in the streets, in the parks and gardens
because we need to be in loving communication.
Good Father, help us to impregnate with Christian love
everything that we say or do.
Nourish us with your spirituality,
so that we may be signs
of Gospel love among our people.
Celebrating the brotherhood that unites us,
we say to you: Our Father…

## Sign of Peace

## Distribution of Communion: Hymn

## Act of Thanksgiving

"My God, in my love for you, I am not moved
by the heaven that you have promised me,
nor does hell, which is so feared, move me
to stop offending you, because of such a fear.
You move me, Lord; it moves me to see you
nailed to the cross and mocked,
it moves me to see your body so wounded,
the affront you suffered and your death move me.
Finally, it is your love that moves me, and in such a way
that even were there no heaven, I would still love you,
and even if there were no hell, I would fear you still.
You do not have to give to me, because I love you,
since, however much I hope,
I could not hope to love you,
in the same way that you love me".
(*Anonymous*)

## 5. RITE OF CONCLUSION

### Resolution

To love God and our neighbour.

### Blessing

### Conclusion

It often seems to us that love is beautiful and easy,
as though it were like a dream. And we do dream…
But other times, we do not understand why our love
is so feeble and becomes exhausted so quickly…

Friends, God is love. He has made us in his image.
For that reason, to love is our vocation and our best
road to freedom: love and do as you will.

### Final Hymn and Dismissal

# Thirty-First Sunday

## 1. SETTING THE SCENE

### Poster with one of these texts:
- "Example? Always in the forefront"
- "To be brothers and sisters, is the priority"
- "The humble person is valued"
- "The one who serves shall be first"

### Symbols:
- Mop, sweeping brush and floor cloth.
- Alb.

## 2. INTRODUCTORY RITES

### Introduction
In the Church, the title of brother and sister is fundamental. It is appropriate for all of us, who are baptised, that we should share the same bread and the same Word of salvation. Within the Church, there is only one common Father and, through him, brother and sister relationships are fostered. With Christians, other titles are secondary. The Gospel presents us today with the fundamental values that should characterise us.

### Hymn

### Greeting
Brothers and sisters, let us bless God, our one and only Lord and Father.

### Penitential Rite
- You, Lord, have loved us from the beginning, *Lord, have mercy.*
- You, Lord, gave up your life for all, *Christ, have mercy.*
- You, Lord, have always fulfilled your promises to us, *Lord, have mercy.*

### Gloria

### Prayer
God of mercy, in your kindness you have made the service of your faithful followers worthy and pleasant; grant that we may proceed, without stumbling, towards the good things that you promise us. Through Christ…

## 3. LITURGY OF THE WORD

### Introduction to the Readings
Hypocrisy and doing things out of self-interest, or through pride, do not go with the Christian way of life. Nor does the preoccupation with being comfortable, or the cult of image. In reality, these attitudes do not work, nor are they credible, and for that reason, in the end, they get no results.

In Christianity, brotherhood, humility and service are values of the first order. As a consequence, they should characterise our style of community life that seeks to constitute and to promote the Kingdom of God.

### Readings
Mal. 1:14b-2:2b. 8-10. *Psalm.* 1 Thess. 2:7b-9. 13. *Acclamation.* Mt. 23:1-12. *Brief silence.*

### Symbolic Action
Today, the Gospel is proclaimed from any pew in the church, not from the ambo, so as to bring out that we are all at the same level, in the community, all equal, all brothers and sisters. The same goes for the Reflection.

## Reflection

Jesus' teaching and example will always be shocking and alternative. We know that he had many debates with the influential people of his time, above all, religious people, like the Pharisees. Many of these had a way of understanding religion and life, in general, that was opposed to Jesus'. For that reason, conflicts abound. Jesus understood clearly, like any sensible person, that example is what convinces people and persuades them. An example is often worth a thousand words. Nevertheless, Jesus does not completely rule out those who do not act on their words, because what they say may be valid: "Do what they tell you; but do not act as they do, because they do not practise what they preach."

Jesus has no time for duplicity, inconsistency or hypocrisy. Not to practise what one preaches appears unseemly to him. He proceeds by example. Besides that, he is independent, critical, he wants to open people's eyes, he encourages them to go through life with eyes wide open… That is why he is so clear and direct.

Fundamentally, what is being debated in today's message is a way of being and of building up community. The first reading and the Gospel rule out religious practice that is hollow, merely a façade, tainted by vanity and ostentation, whereas Jesus proposes a fraternal community, in which nobody, other than God, ranks above others and where humility and service must be cultivated carefully.

And so it was, at the beginning of Christianity. Jesus' followers designed the Christian community along very different lines to Jewish communities. They rejected all ambition for power, exhibitionist behaviour and opted for simplicity, equality, the spirit of service, brotherhood; always with constant reference to Jesus' example and teaching.

This clear warning of what should not be done, and the criticism of the way that runs contrary to example, which at times can shamefully be seen among those who guide the People of God, continue to be relevant for the Church. After two thousand years of Christian reflection, we are still a long way from the model that Jesus presented to us. The psalm has insisted on the spirituality that should motivate us: "Lord, my heart is not ambitious, nor haughty mine eyes; I do not pretend to grandeur…" The Christian quality must always be that of coherent, humble example and service. (*Silence for internal reflection.*)

## Creed

## Prayer of the Faithful

- Let us pray that the values, which the Gospel proclaims today, may permeate society.
- Let us pray for the Church, that its necessary organisation does not hamper, but rather promotes the workings of the Spirit through itself.
- Let us pray for parents and children, that there may be dialogue and readiness to listen to each other.
- Let us pray for the young, that they may draw on the good human experience of older people and that they may be a driving force in the life of society and the Church with their own dynamism.
- Let us pray for our community, that it may be strengthened in brotherhood, in service and in the other values of the Christian alternative way of life.
- Let us pray for all of us, that we may live the faith coherently.
- For these and for all our intentions, *let us pray to the Lord.*

## 4. RITE OF COMMUNION

### Introduction

Holy Communion is a great sign of love and of mutual service. Jesus has instilled these values in us and has gone ahead, leading by example.

## Hymn

## Prayer

God of all goodness, our spirit leaps for joy
on celebrating you as our one and only Abba.
You are the centre of our admiration
and the reason for our meeting.
This community has grown up in your shadow,
we, who want to be fraternal,
humble and ready to serve.
We bless you in this Church, the cradle of our faith.
It brought us the first Gospel message
and entrusted us with the mission of evangelising.
With what skill it helped us grow up as Christians.
Now, we all praise you for the great example of Jesus.
He chose to be poor, simple and like a servant;
he left us that profound example of
washing the disciples' feet
and his permanent choice to be just one of us.
He did not want to stand out in any way,
except in fulfilling your will.
That is why, good Father, we say to you,
together with the psalmist:
"my heart is not ambitious, nor mine eyes haughty;
I do not pretend to grandeur beyond my capacity;
but rather, I pacify and moderate my desires,
like a child in his mother's arms".
With all who listen to the Word and fulfil it,
we say to you in joyful communion (*with joined hands*):
Our Father…

## Sign of Peace

## Distribution of Communion: Hymn

## Act of Thanksgiving

"Where there is a tree to plant, plant it.
Where there is a wrong to right, put it right.
Where an effort is needed, but everyone shies
away, take it upon yourself.
Be the one who took the stone from the road,
the hate from men's hearts
and the difficulty out of the problem.

There is the joy of being wholesome and just,
but there is, above all, the immense joy of serving.
How sad the world would be, if everything in it
was already complete. If there were no rose tree
to plant, no enterprise to undertake.
Do not fall into the error of only awarding
merit to great works.
There are little acts of service: laying the table,
putting the books in order, combing the little girl's hair.
Serving is not a task for inferior beings.
God, who is the fruit and the Light, serves us.
And he asks you each day: Did you serve today?"
(*G. Fuertes*)

## 5. CONCLUDING RITE

## Resolution

Simplicity, service, consistency with the Gospel.

## Blessing

## Conclusion

Friends, the values which we have considered today
lead to that social way of life, which we Christians
call the Kingdom of God. The alternatives, sooner or
later, lead to disaster and misfortune. Therefore, let
us express in our lives what Jesus teaches us with
his Word and his example: he did not come to be
served, but to serve in a simple way, without
ostentation. Let us promote these values among our
neighbours, above all, by means of our relationships
and our example.

## Final Hymn and Dismissal

# Thirty-Second Sunday

## 1. SETTING THE SCENE

### Poster with one of these texts:
- "It is for the wise to live in alertness"

### Symbol:
- Oil lamps or lighted candles.

## 2. INTRODUCTORY RITES

### Introduction
If by wisdom we understand profound humanity and experience of God, that is more or less a summary of what is to be communicated to us today. The Word of God reminds us that one cannot live on borrowed experience. Profound wisdom, which enriches us as people, cannot be improvised or purchased; it is acquired through attentive and daily cultivation of one's personality. This is our responsibility.

### Hymn

### Greeting
Brothers and sisters, let us bless the Lord, who loves us as *sons and daughters of the light*.

### Penitential Rite
- Because you know us from within, *Lord, have mercy.*
- Because we need your light, *Christ, have mercy.*
- Because your forgiveness gives us heart, *Lord, have mercy.*

### Gloria

### Prayer
Bountiful Father, keep us from all evil, so that, with our bodies and minds well disposed, we may freely fulfil your will. Through Christ…

## 3. LITURGY OF THE WORD

### Introduction to the Readings
To perceive God's wisdom in what is profound and in life's daily details is very important. This wisdom goes much further than the scope of human knowledge. It is a gift that illumines our path, breathing life into our faith and hope.

The Gospel parable reminds us of the crucial importance of personal responsibility. Without oil or light, our life, like that of any motor, breaks down and is of no use.

### Readings
Wis. 6:13-17. *Psalm.* 1 Thess. 4:13-18. *Acclamation.* Mt. 25:1-13. *Brief silence.*

### Symbolic Action
During the proclamation of the Gospel, a tray is brought up with four lighted candles. Two of them are put out, when mention is made of the foolish virgins who have no oil.

### Reflection
The Wisdom books of the Old Testament sing to that integral wisdom, which offers people great help in leading their lives. Whoever looks for it with genuine desire and good intentions, will find it, "since he will find it sitting at his door". It seeks us out by itself, if we are found to be worthy, and it is kind to us, as the first reading affirms.

In fact, if we open ourselves to this biblical wisdom, we will have many resources at our disposal to lead a life of quality. Moreover, we will know how to await death and look it in the face, for what it really is, according to the faith: a loving encounter with God, to whom all our being aspires: "my soul is thirsting for you; my flesh is yearning for you". Have we not dreamt of death as a communion with God, who awaits us with outstretched arms?

There is no doubt that this loving encounter will arise, if we live with our lamps alight. There we find an indication of the wisdom that the Gospel parable reveals. It tells us of people who are attentive and those who are careless. Only the attentive ones are abreast of events, maintain a level of holiness, and bring real quality into the concrete moments of daily life. The people who are careless and inattentive are defeated by problems. And then come the complaints: "Lord, Lord, open up for us…"

We all run the risk of giving up, when our hopes are flagging. The easiest thing is to doze off and not bother about anything. But is that not the recipe of mediocre people? Every generation has received good advice regarding constancy, patience, attentiveness, responsibility… so that we do not miss the train of life. If opportunities pass us by, it is due, in no small part, to our carelessness and lack of responsibility.

It is surprising in the parable that some of the virgins did not want to share the oil with the others. It has to be said that the question of sharing is not what the parable wishes to bring out. What Jesus intends is that we should focus on values of a personal kind, which depend exclusively on us: either one is attentive or careless; either one works for holiness in one's life, or does not bother about it. Nobody can take our place where this responsibility is concerned. Therefore, it is not proper for a Christian to go through life in a muddled or dreamy state. A Christian must always be a son, a daughter of the light. With this, the parable finishes, insisting on vigilance and a life of attentiveness. (*Silence for internal reflection.*)

## Creed

## Prayer of the Faithful

- That God's wisdom may be respected by all peoples, *let us pray to the Lord.*
- For the Church, that it may always manifest itself as the defender of human dignity and the wisdom that ennobles, *let us pray to the Lord.*
- For our community, that it may enlighten Christian people to know how to walk in their own light, *let us pray to the Lord.*
- For those who are frail in health or in enthusiasm, that their hope may not be completely dampened, *let us pray to the Lord.*
- For all of us and for our intentions, *let us pray to the Lord.*

## 4. RITE OF COMMUNION

## Introduction
Jesus asks us to be the light of the world, signs of God's goodness. Communion with him helps us to remain vigilant, strong and full of hope.

## Hymn

## Prayer
Blessed are you, our God and Father,
for the teaching that you practise amongst us.
With what sensitivity you exhort us to be attentive,
to become responsible for the gifts we have received;
and with what patience you persevere with us in our acts of carelessness.
We live at an interesting moment in history plagued with inventions and movement.
Everything speaks to us of change, of creative imagination.
How can people go about without

direction, without a guide,
unmotivated, lacking meaning and morale?
Your message rings out today like the tolling of a bell
that awakes us and commits us to live with sensitivity.
Accept, then, that scale of values, born of the Gospel,
which channels our responsibility.
Let us not be perturbed by the
disenchantment of pessimists,
nor be assailed by doubt or disillusion.
Help us to live with meaning and honour.
Because we do not want to fail as people,
we light the lamp of faith each day.
And with the encouragement of the community,
we say to you: Our Father…

## Sign of Peace

## Distribution of Communion: Hymn

## Act of Thanksgiving (*spontaneous*)


## 5. CONCLUDING RITE

### Resolution
To be alert, fully awake, and to live attentively.

### Blessing

### Conclusion
The Christian faith is a powerful reason for living.
Let us walk with our lamps burning, as is fitting for
those who live in attentiveness and do not allow
themselves to be deceived. God accompanies us,
endowing our consciousness with a practical
wisdom, which helps us to be courageous and
balanced. Let us also encourage our neighbours to
walk in dignity.

### Final Hymn and Dismissal

# Thirty-Third Sunday

## 1. SETTING THE SCENE

### Poster with one of these texts:
- "Make your gifts bear fruit"
- "We are all worthy to make a contribution"
- "We all have qualities"

## 2. INTRODUCTORY RITES

### Introduction
On previous Sundays, we have been invited to evaluate our journey as Christians in the light of the Kingdom of God. Today, we are told that life is like those talents in the Gospel, which are granted to us to invest fruitfully by taking risks… The lazy and tight-fisted attitude is not acceptable.

### Hymn

### Greeting
Brothers and sisters, let us bless the Lord with our gifts and abilities.

### Penitential Rite
Let us make an examination of our conscience and see what we are doing with the gifts that have been given to us. (*Brief silence.*) Let us ask for forgiveness, if we have found good cause: *I confess…*

### Gloria

### Prayer
Lord, our God, grant that we may always live happily in your service, because in serving you, the creator of all goodness, lies our true and lasting joy. Through Christ…

## 3. LITURGY OF THE WORD

### Introduction to the Readings
In the first reading, the woman is praised, more for her virtues and qualities, than for her beauty. In the second reading, we are again recommended to be attentive and vigilant, as the characteristic attitude of the Christian way of life. Faith is able to cast light on the destiny of every person.

The Gospel presents to us the parable of the talents. It invites us to develop the gifts and qualities that we have received, and to make them bear fruit. An attitude of laziness is similar to being unfaithful.

### Readings
Prov. 31:10-13. 19-20. 30-31. *Psalm.* 1 Thess. 5:1-6. *Acclamation.* Mt. 25:14-30. *Brief silence.*

### Reflection
The song of biblical wisdom to women is in contrast to other songs from modern and post-modern life. The values that it brings out are those which, in truth, make people beautiful. This first reading, and also the Gospel, give particular emphasis to hard work, ability, responsibility with the gifts one has received; specifically, putting one's life to the service of God and one's neighbour.

The Gospel parable focuses on two attitudes: that of those who make their qualities and personal attributes productive in the service of the common good, and that of those who bury and make sterile what the Lord has given them. I have always liked the testimony that the founder of the Scout movement, Baden-Powell, left for his followers: "I believe that God has placed us in this enchanting world, so that we may be happy and enjoy life. But, happiness does not come from riches, or from having success, or from self-gratification… The way to achieve happiness is by making others happy… Try to leave the world in a better state than it was when you came into it. In this way, when the moment of death arrives, you will be able to accept it happily, because at least you did not waste your time and you did as much good as possible."

In truth, life is the greatest of gifts and the greatest risk of all. It is the primordial gift with the capacity to generate many other talents. To develop it, make it fertile, is the great mission and the prime responsibility of a Christian. Life itself demands that we are industrious, while we await the *Day of the Lord*, as the second reading indicates. Through experience and through faith, we know that life is gained through sacrifice, that it grows by making use of its opportunities, that its scope is joyfully expanded when we invest it for the benefit of others. Whoever keeps it to himself and smothers it, so much so that it bears no fruit, makes it wither away, and he ends up by ruining it.

There are no credible reasons that can justify neglect or idleness. There is no reason for one's personal life to end in disappointment or fruitlessness. No, there is no excuse for the sin of omission, a more common sin than we believe. Perhaps we may attach no importance to it. However, its ill-fated consequences and its seriousness are plainly evident in many people's deterioration and the dwindling of social life. The Gospel forcefully rules out the cringing, cowardly and mean attitude of anyone who has not tried to put his talents to good use: he has not been faithful and trustworthy, he has not carefully husbanded what he received as a gift. Who among us cannot see themselves reflected in this image, to some extent?

God's plan and his glory depend on us living our life bearing fruit in abundance and consistently (Jn 15:8. 16). The key to success is in being "faithful and trustworthy", as the parable repeats. Therefore, in the Church, there

should be no one useless, that is to say, no one must say: "I do not know, I am worthless, I am not able…" It is a senseless and reprehensible act to bury one's qualities and talents. We all have knowledge, have our own worth and are able to do something. Neither should we go through life being content with the minimum, reducing our commitment, living comfortably. That is a way of burying our gifts, which have been given us for another purpose: the common good and the Kingdom of God. May we never feel in the depths of our conscience the parable's reproach, but rather congratulation for having made our talents bear fruit: "since you have been faithful with little… you may attend your Lord's banquet". (*Silence for internal reflection.*)

## Creed

## Prayer of the Faithful

- For people most in need, that they may obtain what they need, *let us pray to the Lord.*
- For the Church, that it may be the bearer of encouragement and hope in the midst of society, *let us pray to the Lord.*
- For those who are collaborating actively in this diocese, that they may continue to act with generosity, *let us pray to the Lord.*
- For those who give a dedicated service to our community, that they will not lack our support and gratitude, *let us pray to the Lord.*
- That we may place our talents at the service of others, *let us pray to the Lord.*
- For all of us, so that, united in the same faith, we may strive to promote the welfare of our town, *let us pray to the Lord.*

## Offerings

- *Lighted candle and Gospel:* We present to you, Father, the illuminating example of Jesus. He was truly faithful and trustworthy.
- *Dish half full of fruit:* We present to you this dish, half full or half empty. You can see that we have done something; but we have to do more, if we are to present to you the full dish, as you expect of us.

## Hymn

## Symbolic Action

*An adult goes out to the centre with a child less than a year old and another older child (11-16 years). Presenting both of them to the assembly, he says:*
Brothers and sisters, life is a great gift, a present from God and from our parents. What have we done with it? What can we still do?

## 4. RITE OF COMMUNION

### Introduction

Jesus' existence was fruitful. God the Father is proud of him. May this communion strengthen in us our responsibility for what he has given us.

### Hymn

### Prayer

Our Father, heart of the world,
God of the earth and Lord of the universe,
may creation sing out to you for the wonders you have worked.
You have left your touch upon the flowers and upon our bodies,
in the fountain, in our work, in our skills, in the happenings of life…
May our lives also praise you
with words and gestures;
with timely responsibility
and sincere witness;
with daily fidelity and the joy of growth.
May all our history be a landscape for your recreation.
Father, you have heaped us with gifts;
we add ourselves to those that further your Kingdom.
Thank you for the project that you entrusted to us, enriching us with the Gospel.
We wish to fulfil your will;
that is why we say to you: Our Father…

## Sign of Peace

## Distribution of Communion: Hymn

## Act of Thanksgiving

- We give you thanks, Father, for the great gift of life. It is sown with talents and opportunities, and, in our case, you have enriched it with faith.
- We give you thanks for the qualities and possibilities that there are in each of us, because we are worth something and we are capable of many things.
- We recognise that we have sinned greatly through omission, that we do not develop our abilities as much as we should, that we are complacent and we do not work enough for your Kingdom.
- Blessed are you, good and gracious God, when you remonstrate with us and demand our attention, because, in that way, we realise that we have to be more faithful and responsible.

## 5. CONCLUDING RITE

### Resolution

To be faithful and trustworthy, in relation to the gifts and talents that we have received.

### Blessing

### Conclusion

This celebration should have encouraged us to make use of the gifts that we have. We do not want our lives to be squandered uselessly. Let us bear fruit, then, putting ourselves in the service of the designs of God and collaborating with the Church. May our activities bring results, at every level, throughout the week.

### Final Hymn and Dismissal

# Thirty-Fourth Sunday
## Christ the King

## 1. SETTING THE SCENE

### Poster with one of these texts:
- "Jesus, a King of a different kind"
- "Jesus, the Lord through service"
- "Jesus, the love that triumphs"

### Symbols:
- Cross and stole.
- Map of the world.

## 2. INTRODUCTORY RITES

### Introduction
The liturgical year finishes with the feast of Christ the King. This feast represents a deserved and warm homage to Jesus, the great witness to God and to life. We have nothing against this title. However, let us remember that he reigns from the cross. That is his throne of honour.

For us, Jesus must be the only Lord. We celebrate this meeting in his memory and we give thanks, in his memory, to the Father, reaffirming that we want to follow him.

### Hymn

### Greeting
Brothers and sisters, let us bless the Lord, who has made us in his image.

### Penitential Rite
- You, Lord, are the salvation of all people, *Lord, have mercy.*
- You, Lord, are a model for all the generations, *Christ, have mercy.*
- You, Lord, attract us through your goodness, *Lord, have mercy.*

### Gloria

### Prayer
God, holy Father, you want to restore all things in your beloved Son, King of the universe. May the whole of creation, freed from sin, serve you and glorify you for ever. Through Christ…

## 3. LITURGY OF THE WORD

### Introduction to the Readings
The message of the first reading is dramatic: a people can be deceived by the conduct of their pastors and leaders; but God himself promises to be their shepherd.

The second reading speaks of Christ as the vanguard of life, the shepherd who leads us to eternal life, the first to arise from the dead.

The Gospel reveals the valid way that Jesus has of judging life and behaviour: in the end, what matters, above all, is to love one's neighbour.

### Readings
Ezek. 34:11-12. 15-17. *Psalm.* 1 Cor. 15:20-26a. 28. *Acclamation.* Mt. 25:31-46. *Brief silence.*

## Reflection

It is a great achievement to end the liturgical year celebrating Christ the King. It is a title that the Church has given him, which Jesus deserves and which we Christians give importance to with wholesome pride. But, with nearly everything to do with Jesus being different and dramatic, it is certain that he did not live like a king, but as a servant; his choice was not for power, but humility and detachment; his throne was the cross; and his crown, one of thorns. Therein lies his *attraction*… That is how his example shines out.

In fact, Jesus distances himself from human reigns and dominions. Although his "Kingdom will have no end" (Lk. 1:33), he does not claim to be like those of this world; he has other ideas and other frames of reference: "you know that those who are recognised as the rulers of nations tyrannise people, and powerful people oppress them. That is not to be the way with you: he who wants to be great, let him be your servant; and he who wants to be first, let him be everyone's slave. Because the Son of Man has not come to be served, but to serve and to give his as a ransom for many" (Mk 10:42-45). Jesus is recognised as King and Lord, because he has served humanity like no other, and because his example is an exhortation to sacrifice oneself in mercy, solidarity and service, even unto martyrdom. What a blessing it would be for history, if we Christians were true witnesses of this King, if we were to look upon others through his eyes and to establish relations motivated by the faith.

Let us note that the readings present Jesus as pastor and judge. The Gospel parable places him in judgement over "all nations". The judgement rests on one single question: love for others. For Jesus, a person's quality of life is shown by whether they love or not. When sentence is passed, those to the right, as much as those to the left, are surprised: "Lord, when did we see you hungry, or thirsty, or homeless, or without clothing, or sick, or in prison, and…?" Jesus identified with all people down on their luck. He who loves fulfils the entire Law (cf. Mt. 22:40; Rom. 13:10). Thus, what saves us are not desires or words, but rather works of love and mercy. What God expects of us, above all, is loving solidarity, like that shown by Jesus. (*Silence for internal reflection.*)

## Creed

## Prayer of the Faithful

- For the peoples of the earth, that they may progress along the lines revealed by the Gospel, *let us pray to the Lord.*
- For the Church, that it may be a witness to the Kingdom of God, serving tirelessly and faithfully, *let us pray to the Lord.*
- For the servants of the Church, that they may trust in the power of the Spirit above everything, *let us pray to the Lord.*
- For our community, that it may be firmly established in Jesus and keep his memory alive, *let us pray to the Lord.*
- For all of us, that we may nurture Christian life in our town, *let us pray to the Lord.*

## Symbolic Action

*A person, dressed in an alb, appears in the midst of the assembly. He carries out the "final examination", going up to various people, and questioning them with phrases like these:* Are you living in loving solidarity?… No, do not answer now. Think about it!

## 4. RITE OF COMMUNION

## Introduction

Let us receive Jesus in communion and reaffirm our desire that his love should be in us and among us. Jesus only insists on one thing: that we should love one another.

## Hymn

## Prayer

Lord, our God, gathered together in your name,
we remember the old story
that we have been telling over the centuries:
the story of Jesus of Nazareth,
a man who dared to call you Abba, Father,
and who taught us to repeat that name.
God, our Father,
we give you thanks for that man
who transformed the face of our earth,
unveiling a tremendous vision:
the Kingdom that one day will come, a Kingdom of freedom,
of love and peace, your Kingdom, the fullness of your creation.
We remember, Lord, that where Jesus passed
people discovered his humanity,
were filled with a new richness
and, with their souls renewed,
they devoted themselves to the service of their neighbours.
We remember how he spoke of a lost sheep,
of a prodigal son, of those gone astray, who count for nothing
and of the poor, without freedom, without a name
and without affection.
We remember that he went in search of them,
that he always took their side
without forgetting others.
That cost him his life,
because the powerful of the earth would not tolerate it.
But you restored him to life
and confirmed him in your love.
Thus, he is united with you for ever
and is for us the Gospel and Redeemer.
With Jesus, blessed and glorified,
we say to you: Our Father…

## Sign of Peace

## Distribution of Communion: Hymn

## Act of Thanksgiving (*spontaneous*)

## 5. CONCLUDING RITE

### Resolution
To love, to serve, to create the family of Christ.

### Blessing

### Conclusion
We Christians believe in a Lord who reigns from the cross, who identifies with the most needy, and who expects from us less applause and more commitment. He attained this title not through gaining points, but by losing; not by triumphing, but through death; not through receiving or accumulating, but by giving. Let us acclaim the majesty of Jesus in the streets. We know through experience that this is the only truth that saves.

### Final Hymn and Dismissal

# OTHER FEASTS

# Saint Joseph, Husband Of Mary

## 1. SETTING THE SCENE

- *Poster* with this text: "Saint Joseph, faithful and just".
- Table for the symbols.

## 2. INTRODUCTORY RITES

### Introduction

Today we celebrate the feast of Saint Joseph. We are interested in Saint Joseph as a believer, as a good and faithful person who fulfilled a very special mission in relation to Mary and Jesus: he collaborated in the fulfilment of God's plan of salvation. The universal Church recognises him as an example of faith and human integrity. For that reason, he is worthy of our imitation.

- We present the *symbols* that set the scene for this celebration:
- *Tools:* They remind us of Saint Joseph's simple working life.
- *Colourful plant:* The saints give us an example of vigorous life.

### Hymn

### Greeting

Brothers and sisters, let us bless the Lord, who glorifies the saints.

### Penitential Rite

The example of the saints reminds us of our common calling to holiness. Let us ask forgiveness for our own sins and for the sins of others. (*Brief silence.*) I confess…

### Gloria

### Prayer

Holy Father, you entrusted the first mysteries of man's salvation to the faithful custody of Saint Joseph; through his intercession, may the Church faithfully observe those mysteries and bring them to completion in its mission of salvation. Through Christ…

## 3. LITURGY OF THE WORD

### Introduction to the Readings

God wants to be present in man's life, on his own initiative. This can be seen in many ways. That is why we are able to say that all is *Thanksgiving*. Believers trust in God and obey him, allow him to act, in spite of the difficulties and doubts that arise in life. Saint Joseph did likewise.

### Readings

2 Sam. 7:4-5a. 12-14a. 16. *Psalm.* Rom. 4:13. 16-18. 22. *Acclamation.* Lk. 2:41-51a. *Brief silence.*

### Reflection

Saint Joseph is mentioned very little in the Gospels. Saint Matthew says, in passing that he was a good and just person (Mt. 1:19). As a believer, he lived in religious silence, through the unexpected events that happened to Mary, and which gave him cause for surprise.

As well as being a profound believer, he was also a man of prayer. It is through prayer that his doubts are dispelled and his collaboration in the service of God's plans is forged, along with Mary.

Joseph was just another human being, a carpenter among other workers. He came from a simple background. When they went to the temple to present their offering, on the occasion of Mary's purification, they offered up a pair of turtle doves, the offering of the poor.

At his and Mary's side, Jesus "grew in wisdom, in stature and in favour before God and before men" (Lk. 2:52). (*Silence for internal reflection.*)

## Creed

## Prayer of the Faithful

- That those in government may be sensitive to the silence of the poor and marginalised, *let us pray to the Lord.*
- That we believers may heed the Gospel and live by faith, with missionary spirit, *let us pray to the Lord.*
- That we Christians may listen to the Word of God and apply it in our lives, *let us pray to the Lord.*
- For families, that they may live through their times of joy and sadness in true union, *let us pray to the Lord.*
- For fathers, that they may help their children to grow up in freedom and responsibility, *let us pray to the Lord.*
- For our community, that we may be a true family, open to the needs of the Church and of society, *let us pray to the Lord.*

## 4. RITE OF COMMUNION

## Introduction

The same vocation unites us all. The same Gospel inspires us. We have the same mission. Jesus is our nourishment.

## Hymn

## Prayer

Blessed are you, good Father.
Our hearts are glowing with gratitude
because you have redeemed us through Jesus,
entrusted to the care of Joseph
of Nazareth, the carpenter.
Through Jesus, you have opened
the gates of your Kingdom
to all the men and women of this world,
if we are understanding towards the weakness of others,
if we are lovers of justice and peace,
if we cultivate mercy and forgiveness,
if we are long-suffering, generous, pure in heart…
Yes, Father, you desire that your salvation should extend
over the length and breadth of history,
because you are brimming over with holiness.
Today, celebrating Saint Joseph, we give you thanks
for all the good people
who have lived and live upon our earth.
Many of them, witnesses to the Christian faith,
are the best mirrors of the Spirit
and great collaborators in the work of salvation.
Feeling that we are part of this great fraternity,
we say to you, together with the saints of every
age: Our Father…

## Sign of Peace

## Distribution of Communion: Hymn

## Act of Thanksgiving

- We give you thanks, Father, for your great initiatives in the history of salvation. Today, like yesterday, you continue to call on us to collaborate in spreading the Word. Inspire us with opportune and effective ways for bringing the Gospel closer to our people.
- We give you thanks for the saints, true bright stars, with their own light, in the Church and in society. Through them, your goodness, tenderness, forgiveness and holiness shine forth on us.

- You, who know us through and through, know what we feel for you. Help us to be the word and sign of your presence, so that all may give you the glory that you deserve.

## 5. CONCLUDING RITE

### Resolution
Like Saint Joseph, to look at our own life and that of the people around us with the eyes of a believer.

### Blessing

### Conclusion
We have reflected on the person of Saint Joseph. We have valued his silent faith and his collaboration with God's plans. May his example encourage us to live with the Christian spirit of the Beatitudes, taking up the standard of so many good people who have gone before us.

### Final Hymn and Dismissal

# Assumption of the Blessed Virgin Mary

## 1. SETTING THE SCENE

Poster with this text: "Blessed are those who fulfil their mission".

## 2. INTRODUCTORY RITES

### Introduction
Today we celebrate the Assumption of Mary, a symbol of completeness for all those who live in simplicity, and of human hope, in the face of all despair. In Mary's assumption to heaven, we celebrate the triumph of life over death, the victory of good over the powers of evil, and the vigorous force of Christian life. In Mary, we also see our own destiny, because, like her, we are children of God.

### Hymn

### Greeting
Brothers and sisters, let us bless the Lord, who calls us to life in all its fullness.

### Penitential Rite
■ You, Lord, called us to life, *Lord, have mercy.*
■ You, Lord, are our brother and friend for ever, *Christ, have mercy.*
■ You, Lord, dwell and pray within us, *Lord, have mercy.*

### Gloria

### Prayer
Because you were well pleased, Lord, with the humility of your servant, the Virgin Mary, you wished to raise her to the dignity of being Mother of your Son, and have crowned her with glory and splendour; through her intercession, we pray that we, who have been saved by the mystery of redemption, may also, receive the reward of your glory. Through Christ…

## 3. LITURGY OF THE WORD

### Introduction to the Readings
Jesus is the prime example of glory. He is the first to have conquered death, the first to be raised to life. It was he who finally opened the gates of salvation and, through this gesture of solidarity, enabled all of us to attain the glory of heaven.

Mary also embodied that reality of which Jesus was the prime example. The Gospel recounts her song to God's mercy and liberation.

### Readings
Rev. 11:19; 12:1-6. 10. *Psalm.* 1 Cor. 15:20-26. *Acclamation.* Lk. 1:39-56. *Brief silence.*

### Reflection
The Assumption of the Virgin Mary to heaven is a truth, officially recognised by the Church, since 1 November 1950. It is the last proclaimed teaching, in which Mary's glory next to God is proclaimed.

Just as Jesus triumphed over death, Mary exemplifies the victory of faith. She anticipates the blessing and the destiny of all believers: we live in this world with yearnings for life, with our eyes fixed upon resurrection.

In venerating Mary, assumed into heaven, we reaffirm that we are created for life, to care for and nurture everything that helps us to live. The last step is immortality. For that reason, today should be an appropriate day, for Christians, to reaffirm all their commitments in the face of one-dimensional cultures that deny transcendence, and in relation to trends and ways of thinking, which do not elevate human dignity.

The Assumption of Mary is like an act of homage to the simplicity and fidelity that she represents. It is like that praise for the human ideal that Mary proclaims in her canticle of praise: God "raises the lowly". Mary is encumbered, because she chose the simple way of faithful poverty. That was the nature of her spirituality, which pleased God and led to him choosing her as the Mother of the Saviour.

Mary dedicated her life totally to Jesus. She suffered as a co-redeemer, but she was also exalted as a first witness to the resurrection by the Church. That is why the Assumption of Mary is a tremendous sign, endorsing and encouraging our faith. (*Silence for internal reflection.*)

## Creed

## Prayer of the Faithful
- For our Church, that it may be faithful to the Gospel, *let us pray to the Lord*.
- For those who have social responsibilities, that they may concern themselves with the common good, *let us pray to the Lord*.
- For all those who place their lives at the service of a beautiful ideal, that they may see it culminating with Mary, *let us pray to the Lord*.

- For women who suffer affronts to their dignity, that they may find in Mary an example and stimulus for their liberation, *let us pray to the Lord*.
- For all of us, that our faith and our testimony may be of benefit to our town, *let us pray to the Lord*.

## Offerings
*Heart (cardboard):* Lord, we are of clay, it is hard for us to be faithful; sometimes, we end up like abandoned scraps of potter's clay; but it can be kneaded together and transformed into the human heart, that feels and loves.

*House:* As a mother, Mary is familiar with household problems. May she intercede for all our families, so that they may become a school for humanity.

## 4. RITE OF COMMUNION

### Introduction
Communion with Jesus is always a spur for renewing our lives. Approaching communion today encourages us to seek and hope for the glory that others have already attained.

### Hymn

### Prayer
Good and gracious God, we give you thanks for Mary of Nazareth,
a simple mother, who lived deeply in you
and humbly followed the plans you laid out for her.
She was a believer and a generous mother.
From the outset of her conscious vocation
she adopted an attitude of obedience and readiness:
a gracious trustworthy response,
which touched your heart.
We celebrate her as the woman of the world:
an ideal for generations,
overflowing with humanity.
We admire her feminine quality,
infused with mystery,

so constant and so faithful: an affirmation of
unconditional love.
We recall her openness to the Spirit,
her revealing of the Gospel,
as the bearer of the truth.
For the wholeness that her *Magnificat* reflects
we also applaud her
and say: "blessed are you who has believed!"
God of all goodness, we celebrate the wonders
that you bring about, through so many believers.
Thank you for blessed Mary,
fruitful in redemption.
She is an example to us.
In communion with her, the Mother of the Church,
we say to you: Our Father…

## Sign of Peace

## Distribution of Communion: Hymn

## Act of Thanksgiving
Our Father, we thank you for Mary,
the Virgin Mother, simple and poor,
original and bold in her mission.
A devoted disciple and fertile sacrament,
she has planted the fruit of her womb
in the furrow of history:
the absolute Word of love and salvation.
Like her, we wish to be worthy of your covenant
and march onward through life, in hope,
and in solidarity towards the Promised Land.

## 5. CONCLUDING RITE

## Resolution
To review the progress of the Christian life that we
have undertaken.

## Blessing

## Conclusion
With Jesus' triumph and Mary's complete
faithfulness, God wishes to encourage our dignity
and stimulate our hope. What we have celebrated
in Mary is the destiny that God has envisaged for all
human beings. That is why we admire God's
goodness so much. Let us go out from this
meeting, with our spirits uplifted. Let us
communicate the value of life to others, open to
the fullness of the resurrection.

## Final Hymn and Dismissal

# All Saints

## 1. SETTING THE SCENE

### Poster with one of these texts:
- "Blessed are the saints"
- "Sainthood is of great value"

### Symbols:
- Give as much prominence as possible to the images of saints that there may be in the church.
- Distribute posters or pictures of different saints around the place of worship.

## 2. INTRODUCTORY RITES

### Introduction
The celebration of All Saints brings us Christians within sight of our greatest hope: to live for eternity in communion with the God who loves us. At the same time, it shows us that the ideal of holiness is attainable for all, because saints neither were, nor are, cast in a different mould to us.

We remember with satisfaction the considerable number of our brothers and sisters, who have striven to live honourably, fulfilling the will of God. They give us heart on our daily journey and are a reason for healthy pride within the Church.

We are all called to holiness. We must all be worthy children of a Father, who is good to all creatures.

### Hymn

### Greeting
Brothers and sisters, let us bless the Lord, the Saint among all saints.

### Penitential Rite
- You, Lord, are holy, *Lord, have mercy.*
- You, Lord, are the Redeemer and Reconciler, *Christ, have mercy.*
- You, Lord, intercede for us, *Lord, have mercy.*

### Gloria

### Prayer
Our Father, it is your wish that we should celebrate the merits and graces of all the saints in the same feast; grant us, through the intercession of that multitude, the abundance of your mercy and forgiveness. Through Christ…

## 3. LITURGY OF THE WORD

### Introduction to the Readings
The most moving image of the People of God that one can imagine is a multitude of brothers and sisters, in the peace and grace of God, full of life and celebrating their love. This is the vision that the word of scripture offers us today.

God calls us to be his children and welcomes us, although we have fallen into error and sin, because he is merciful and wants to save us.

The Gospel offers us the message of the Beatitudes, as an ideal and as a daily programme to make us more human. This applies to us all.

### Readings
Rev. 7:2-4. 9-14. *Psalm.* 1 Jn 3:1-3. *Acclamation.* Mt. 5:1-12a. *Brief silence.*

## Reflection

The saints are the best exponents of our Church: it is they who give it colour and make it credible, they who reveal and bring the Christian ideal closer.

Holiness is a special and necessary aspect of God's being and it is also the quality that he envisaged as appropriate to humans "before the creation of the world". God's choices are right (how could one doubt it!), but we do not always give them our support; that is when they are transformed into challenges.

In the Church, as the Council reminds us, we are all called to sainthood (*Lumen gentium V*). It is one of Jesus' basic commands and a gift of the Spirit: "be, therefore, perfect, as your heavenly Father is perfect" (Mt. 5:48). This command is found throughout the New Testament (cf. 1 Thess. 4:3; Eph. 5:3; Col. 3:12…). The path to Christian holiness is marked out for us in the Beatitudes.

Some years ago, the word *holiness* was not regarded favourably; for many people, it was a devalued expression, because they had not discovered its true meaning, or because they had come across unsatisfactory examples; for others, however, it was and continues to be a force of life, thrilling energy and an embodiment of personal value.

It is the saints who incarnate and reveal this value, instead of it becoming lost in abstraction. A saint is a fully realised person, whose existence dazzles and radiates magnetism; a happy person, with an energetic inner life, but who acts with sensitivity and even with a sense of humour, a mixture of personal balance and being secure within himself. A saint is a person who has an art and genius for living, not necessarily a hero or a martyr, but very much a passionate witness of the truth, with the freshness of spring in his heart. A saint is, in a nutshell, someone who knows how to live. In this way, he has the ability and boldness to achieve what is, for the rest of us, almost beyond our imagining. (*Silence for internal reflection.*)

## Creed

## Prayer of the Faithful

- Let us pray for those who are building the Kingdom of God in faithfulness to their principles, promoting honour and developing social energy.
- Let us pray for our Church, that it may be true to the Beatitudes and convey this message with passion.
- Let us pray for all people who strive to be faithful to their calling.
- Let us pray that whoever seeks God with sincerity, may find him.
- And for all and each one of us, that we may unfold the gifts we have received to the utmost. *Let us pray to the Lord.*

## 4. RITE OF COMMUNION

### Introduction

When the Kingdom of God reaches its fullness, we will celebrate the great feast of the blessed, all together. In the meantime, the communion is a nourishment and incentive for us.

### Hymn

### Prayer

We know, good and loving Father,
that the time of the saints is not over.
Of flesh and blood, like us,
they are the incarnation of the ideal
that you have revealed to us.
Young in spirit and sensitive to history,
they have broken moulds and frontiers
with the naturalness of him who breathes honesty
and is the Servant of Truth.
They, like Jesus, are the messengers of the New Life.
They achieve what is most difficult,
that to the rest of us
seems almost impossible.
Blessed are you, Father,

because the saints are a mirror of your originality.
They are in the world, without being of the world.
Their surroundings could not tame them.
They have not allowed themselves to be infected
by the fashions that create mass conformity.
They are the evident fruit of the freedom of the Spirit,
the human fulfilment of the Christian vocation.
We thank you for the example of
so many brothers and sisters.
Uplifted by their example, we say to you:
Our Father…

## Sign of Peace

## Distribution of Communion: Hymn

## Act of Thanksgiving
- We give you thanks, Father, for our belonging to this community in which we feel like your brothers and sisters and your children.
- We give you thanks, because you help us to see the deeper meaning of life.
- We feel you on our side. We commit ourselves to love with all our hearts, to be peaceful, simple, merciful; to spread life and to share, based on the values that we have received.

## 5. RITE OF CONCLUSION

## Resolution
To be holy, putting the values of the Beatitudes into practice.

## Blessing

## Conclusion
Between our most cherished dreams and the hard reality, in which we often find ourselves, there is the longed-for aspiration for the values of the Beatitudes. Let us do everything possible to bring them into our surroundings. The saints, of flesh and blood like us, assure us that it is possible to do this. They succeeded.

## Final Hymn and Dismissal

# Immaculate Conception of the Blessed Virgin Mary

## 1. SETTING THE SCENE

### Poster with one of these texts:
- "Mary, full of grace".
- "Mary, wholesome to her very core".
- "Without sin, like Mary".

### Symbol:
- Image of the Virgin in a prominent place.

## 2. INTRODUCTORY RITES

### Introduction
The Christian motive for which we congregate today is to venerate Mary, immaculate and wholesome to her very core, a great example of faith and co-operation with the designs of God.

She has come to be a unique figure in the life of the Church. Today we emphasise her beauty and purity of spirit, together with her attitude of great freedom in the face of sin. Mary's personality was of the highest quality.

Let us take advantage of this celebration to reaffirm our decision to take steps along the path marked out for us by Mary, a wholesome, faithful and simple woman.

### Hymn

### Greeting
Brothers and sisters, let us bless the Lord,
who chose Mary.

### Penitential Rite
- You, Lord, saw Mary's humility: *Lord, have mercy.*
- You, Lord, are like us in everything, except sin: *Christ, have mercy.*
- You, Lord, dwell within us: *Lord, have mercy.*

### Gloria

### Prayer
God, bountiful Father, you found in Mary a faithful response to your plan of salvation; following the example of her responsiveness to your call, may we be able to fulfil, in ourselves, what you envisaged for each one of us, in your plan of redemption. Through Christ…

## 3. LITURGY OF THE WORD

### Introduction to the Readings
God is completely dedicated to the work of human salvation. In Mary, this was totally possible. Thanks to the obedience of her faith and her collaboration, we have all been blessed. Mary was gracious, but at the cost of great sacrifice.

## Readings

Gen. 3:9-15. 20. *Psalm.* Eph. 1:3-6. 11-12. *Acclamation.* Lk. 1:26-38. *Brief silence.*

## Reflection

The figure of Mary has been greatly idealised. There is a multitude of examples in art, in literature, in popular customs and in many people's consciousness. Our image of Mary is based on what we read in scripture. Today, we picture her open to the Spirit and full of grace. God has not found a better manner, readiness and state of being than he found in Mary. That is why he brought about, in her, the miracle of being a virgin and a mother.

We conjure up the image of Mary as a believer, meditating upon God's plans in her heart, knowing how to walk in the obscurity of faith, but always trusting in her religious experience. And we picture her as immaculate, contemplating, in her, a way of life that is wholesome to the very core, gracious and worthy from its conception. Mary is an inspiration for us to go more deeply into our conversion. We believe that the Spirit cleanses us from all sin and is capable of making our lives fruitful, in the way that Mary's life bore fruit.

In celebrating Mary, immaculate and full of thanksgiving, we feel inside us a great desire for a life of purity and genuine commitment. (*Silence for internal reflection.*)

## Creed

## Prayer of the Faithful

- Let us pray for the world, that God's message of salvation may reach to every corner.
- Let us pray for the Church, that it may spread abundant redemption effectively.
- Let us pray for married couples, that they may make of their homes a little Church, sensitive to God's calls.
- Let us pray for our community, that it may flourish in a pure and exemplary way.
- Let us keep a tender remembrance for all mothers, that they may collaborate, like Mary, in the worthy upbringing of their children.
- For these and for all our resolutions, *let us pray to the Lord.*

## Offerings

- *White flower or flowers:* Lord, accept our desire to lead an honest, faithful life, without sin.
- *Mirror:* Lord, Mary is a mirror for us, an example of values and virtues.

## 4. RITE OF COMMUNION

## Introduction

Mary was praised by Jesus, because she listened to the Word of God and fulfilled it. She is, for the Church, a presence full of meaning and a special witness. Let us learn from Mary the knowledge of how to be in communion with Jesus.

## Hymn

## Prayer

We bless you, God of history,
because you have made a simple woman great.
Mary is the highest example
for believers of all times
who want to live in obedience to your Word.
Her life, full of grace, draws our admiration.
God of all goodness, we celebrate Mary,
who is present in our community,
Mother of the Church,
a fruitful, free, immaculate and
co-redeeming Christian.
With her, we proclaim your greatness.
Today, also, you can work wonders
if, like her, we say to you with sincerity:
"here is the servant of the Lord…"
O Lord, our God, we are proud of Mary,

as Jesus was.
In her person can be found
all the happiness of the Kingdom
because she listened to the Word
and brought it into life.
In communion with her and with Jesus,
we say to you with trust: Our Father…

## Sign of Peace

## Distribution of Communion: Hymn

## Act of Thanksgiving (Magnificat)
My soul magnifies the Lord,
and my spirit rejoices in God, my Saviour;
because he has regarded the low estate of his servant.
From henceforth, all generations shall call me blessed
because he that is mighty has done great things for
me:
holy is his name,
and his mercy reaches the faithful
from generation to generation.
He has shown strength with his arm:
he scatters the proud in heart,
he puts down the mighty from their seats
and exalts the humble,
he fills the hungry with good things
and the rich he sends empty away.
Glory be to the Father, to the Son, and to the Holy Spirit,
as it was in the beginning, is now and ever shall be,
world without end. Amen.

## 5. CONCLUDING RITE

## Resolution
To be open to the Spirit and to allow him to intervene:
"He that is mighty has done great things for me".

## Blessing

## Conclusion
We have celebrated Mary, great in spirit and
wholesome to her very core. May the veneration,
which we feel towards her, go to strengthen our
holiness of life, avoiding all sin. Let us continue in
the pure and honest example that she has left us.
God loves us as free beings, living a dignified life.

## Final Hymn and Dismissal

# Index